THE NATURE AND
OF PRECE

Neil Duxbury examines how precedents constrain legal decision-makers and how legal decision-makers relax and avoid those constraints. There is no single principle or theory which explains the authority of precedent but rather a number of arguments which raise rebuttable presumptions in favour of precedent-following. This book examines the force and the limitations of these arguments and shows that although the principal requirement of the doctrine of precedent is that courts respect earlier judicial decisions on materially identical facts, the doctrine also requires courts to depart from such decisions when following them would perpetuate legal error or injustice. Not only do judicial precedents not 'bind' judges in the classical-positivist sense, but, were they to do so, they would be ill suited to common-law decision-making. Combining historical inquiry and philosophical analysis, this book will assist anyone seeking to understand how precedent operates as a common-law doctrine.

NEIL DUXBURY is Professor of Law at the London School of Economics.

THE NATURE AND AUTHORITY OF PRECEDENT

NEIL DUXBURY

CAMBRIDGE UNIVERSITY PRESS
Cambridge, New York, Melbourne, Madrid, Cape Town, Singapore, São Paulo, Delhi

Cambridge University Press
The Edinburgh Building, Cambridge CB2 8RU, UK

Published in the United States of America by Cambridge University Press, New York

www.cambridge.org
Information on this title: www.cambridge.org/9780521713368

© Neil Duxbury 2008

This publication is in copyright. Subject to statutory exception
and to the provisions of relevant collective licensing agreements,
no reproduction of any part may take place without
the written permission of Cambridge University Press.

First published 2008

Printed in the United Kingdom at the University Press, Cambridge

A catalogue record for this publication is available from the British Library

ISBN 978-0-521-88579-9 hardback
ISBN 978-0-521-71336-8 paperback

Cambridge University Press has no responsibility for the persistence or
accuracy of URLs for external or third-party internet websites referred to
in this book, and does not guarantee that any content on such
websites is, or will remain, accurate or appropriate.

To
M. E. D.

CONTENTS

Preface   *page* ix
Table of cases   xii

1   Introduction: the usable past   1
    1. Precedent   1
    2. Positivism and precedent   14
    3. A theory of precedent?   22

2   Why does English law have a doctrine of precedent?   31
    1. The formation of a doctrine of precedent   31
       a. The ambiguous role of classical legal positivism   37
       b. Precedent and reason   48

3   Precedents as reasons   58
    1. Looking for a certain *ratio*   67
       a. The complexity of case-law   68
       b. Definitions and tests   76
       c. The point of the search   90
    2. Shortcuts to reason   92
    3. Pre-emptive precedent?   99
    4. Conclusion   108

4   Distinguishing, overruling and the problem of self-reference   111
    1. Distinguishing   113
    2. Overruling   116
    3. The power to overrule oneself   122
    4. The authority of the Practice Statement   129
       a. Constitutional impropriety   131
       b. 'Believe me, I always lie'   139

5 Why follow precedent? 150
   1. Consequentialist justifications   153
   2. Deontological arguments   167
   3. Conclusion   182

Index   184

PREFACE

I wrote this book while serving as the deputy head of the law school and the director for all the undergraduate law admissions programmes at the University of Manchester. In both roles I, like many of those around me, would often try to invest an argument with more authority by saying – if not always quite showing – that it was backed by a precedent. While sitting in committee rooms and carrying out administrative chores I found myself increasingly trying to make sense of such behaviour. Sometimes, pointing to a precedent was clearly a way of trying to be fair. But at other times I was sure it was the coward's way out or an excuse for inertia. The study which follows is mainly about judicial precedent. But there are plenty of instances where, in trying to illuminate a problem, I draw upon more general instances of decision-making by precedent, many of which, I confess, came to mind in administrative contexts when I am sure I should have been concentrating on other matters.

In so far as this book is concerned specifically with judicial precedents, it is not supposed to present the law relating to precedent in any particular jurisdiction. Rather, it is an exercise in understanding precedent as a jurisprudential concept. In undertaking this exercise I have relied mainly on English law illustrations and problems, though quite often I have used examples from other systems, particularly American law, when those examples point to difficulties and insights which are not immediately apparent from the English sources. The book is not a textbook; none the less, I attempt that difficult balance between achieving a level of depth and technicality that will make the project valuable to professional legal thinkers and writing in a manner that will engage, intrigue and enlighten law students or indeed any non-specialist who is serious about understanding the intricacies of precedent. While the intricacies on which I focus are generally best described as theoretical rather than doctrinal, the point of the book is most definitely not to articulate a distinctive theory of precedent. Indeed, one of the claims of the book is that no one theory can offer a plausible comprehensive or systematic explanation of why precedents constrain. The purpose of this book, rather, is to examine the various possible explanations for such constraint, and to advance a number of arguments which might facilitate a better understanding of the nature and authority of precedent.

There is no harm in stating immediately, if very briefly, what those arguments are. First, the development of classical positivist jurisprudence was to a large degree an exercise in trying to explain the authority of precedent, and misgivings about the concept of binding precedent probably have less to do with the fact that earlier judicial decisions cannot literally bind as with the fact that such decisions cannot bind in the classical positivist sense. Secondly, even if a decision-maker feels no obligation to follow a precedent, the precedent might lead him to decide differently from how he would have decided if the precedent did not exist. Thirdly, precedents really are precedents, to adapt Bishop Butler's famous insight, and not another thing, and so any effort to equate precedent and precedent-following with some other legal concept or practice — the concept of a rule, for example, or the practice of reasoning by analogy — will fail to capture the *distinctive* nature and authority of precedent. Fourthly, reason — a concept which, in this context as in many others, needs disaggregating — played a special role in the formation of a common-law doctrine of precedent. Fifthly, respecting the principle that like cases be treated alike does not necessitate a doctrine of precedent. Indeed, one of the objectives of this book is to determine just what might generate the emergence of *stare decisis*, given that the principle of formal justice certainly cannot achieve this on its own. Finally, the doctrine of precedent, properly conceived, must allow the possibility of a court of last resort overruling as well as following its earlier decisions, for the doctrine requires that the court not only keep the law on track, but put it back on track when previously it has made mistakes. The value of the doctrine of precedent to the common law, we might say, is not simply that it ensures respect for past decisions but also that it ensures that bad decisions do not have to be repeated.

Those with no interest in quirky interludes about maverick jurists making fallacious arguments might resolve to skip section (4)(b) of chapter 4, though I expect that this advice will lead some readers to head there first. My principal reason for retaining that section is that the point to which it builds — that it matters little, if at all, if precedential authority does not satisfy the tests of logic — seems worth making. For recollections of Roy Stone, the jurist at the centre of the section, I am grateful to George Christie, Dave Fleming, Tom Hadden, Clifford Hall, John and Cherry Hopkins, Brian Simpson and John Tiley.

An amalgamation of early versions of chapters 2 and 4 was presented at the law faculties of McGill University, Montreal, and the University of Toronto in October 2005, and at the University of Minnesota Law School in April 2006. An early draft of chapter 3 was presented at the Institute of Advanced Legal Studies, London, in February 2006 and a late version of chapter 2 at the School of Law at the University of Virginia in April 2007. For detailed comments on chapter 3 I owe thanks to Brian Bix. I owe the same to Lillian BeVier, Ted White and Ian Williams for some very helpful observations on chapter 2, and for feedback on an entire first draft of the book I am immensely grateful to John Bell, Sean Coyle, Andrew Griffiths, Matt Kramer, Mark McGaw, William Lucy, Manolis Melissaris, Richard Posner, Mike Redmayne, Mark Reiff, Mike Wilkinson and the anonymous readers who acted for the Cambridge University Press. I am also indebted to Barry Cushman, Angela Fernandez, John Harrison, Caleb Nelson and Stephen Waddams for help and advice when my understanding of precedent as a common-law doctrine outside England proved deficient.

May 2007

TABLE OF CASES

Achen v. Pepsi-Cola Bottling Co. of Los Angeles, 105 Cal. App. 113; 233 P 2d 74 (1951)   84
Algama v. Minister for Immigration and Multicultural Affairs (2001) 115 FCR 253   118
Al-Mehdawi v. Secretary of State for the Home Dept [1990] 1 AC 876   83
Anastasoff v. United States, 223 F.3d 898, 899–900 (8th Cir. 2000)   6
Ashwander v. Tennessee Valley Authority, 297 U.S. 288 (1936)   118
Att. Gen. for Jersey v. Holley [2005] UKPC 23   137
Att. Gen. of St. Christopher, Nevis and Anguilla v. Reynolds [1980] AC 63   162
Att. Gen. v. Dean of Windsor (1860) HL Cas 369   42, 126
Att. Gen. v. De Keyser's Royal Hotel [1920] AC 508   44
Att. Gen. v. Ryan's Car Hire Ltd [1965] IR 642   127
Bayer v. Agropharm [2004] EWHC 1661   3
Bayliss v. Bishop of London [1913] 1 Ch. 127   45
Beamish v. Beamish (1861) 9 HL Cas 273   42, 120, 126
Behrens v. Bertram Mills Circus Ltd [1957] 2 QB 1   69
Bishop of Oxford v. Eades (1667) Vaugh. 18   34
Blumenthal [1983] 1 AC 854   161
Bole v. Horton (1673) Vaugh. 360   34, 67
Bright v. Hutton (1852) 3 HL Cas 341   42, 126
Brown v. Annandale (1842) 8 Cl. & Fin. 437   42
Brown v. Board of Education, 347 U.S. 483 (1954)   178
Brunner v. Greenslade [1971] Ch. 993   68
Caledonian Railway Co. v. Walker's Trustees (1882) LR 7 App. Cas. 259   126
Candler v. Crane, Christmas & Co. [1951] 2 KB 164   31, 71
Carroll v. Carroll's Lessee, 57 U.S. 275 (1853)   76
Cassell & Co. Ltd v. Broome [1972] AC 1027   58, 62–3
Central Asbestos Co. Ltd v. Dodd [1973] AC 518   71–2
Chevron U.S.A. v. Natural Resources Defense Council, 467 U.S. 837 (1984)   121
Connelly v. DPP [1964] AC 1254   74
D v. NSPCC [1977] 1 All ER 589   181–2
Da Costa en Schaake NV v. Nederlandse Belastingadministratie (Cases 28, 29 and 30/62) [1963] ECR 31   117
Davis v. Johnson (1979) AC 264; [1978] 2 WLR 182   103, 132, 147, 161

Donoghue v. Stevenson [1932] AC 562 86, 104
Earl of Oxford's Case (1615) 1 Rep. Ch. 1 53
Fitzleet Estates Ltd v. Cherry (Inspector of Taxes) [1977] 1 WLR 1345; 3 All ER 996 96, 118
Florida Department of Health v. Florida Nursing Home Association, 450 U.S. 147 (1981) 96
Flower v. Ebbw Vale Steel, Iron & Coal Co. Ltd [1934] 2 KB 132 68
Fortescue v. Vestry of St. Matthew, Bethnal Green [1891] 2 QB 170 124, 125
Furman v. Georgia, 408 U.S. 238 (1972) 79
Gallie v. Lee [1969] 2 Ch 17 158
Guinness v. Saunders [1990] 2 AC 663 3
Hamdan v. Rumsfeld, 126 S.Ct. 2749 (2006) 10
Hamdi v. Rumsfeld, 542 U.S. 1 (2004) 79
Hanslap v. Cater (1673) 1 Vent. 243 34
Harnett v. Fisher [1927] 1 KB 402 45
Harris v. Colliton (1658) Hard. 120 34
Heap v. Ind Coope and Allsopp Ltd [1940] 2 KB 476 150
Hedley Byrne & Co. v. Heller & Partners, Ltd [1962] 1 QB 396 70–1
Horton v. Sadler [2006] UKHL 27 127, 158
Hubbard v. United States, 514 U.S. 695 (1995) 117
Indermaur v. James (1886) LR 1 CP 274 60
Indyka v. Indyka [1969] 1 AC 33 119
In re De Keyser's Royal Hotel Ltd [1919] 2 Ch. 197 44
In re Hallet's Estate (1879) 13 Ch.D. 696 46
In re Harper and Great Eastern Ry Co. (1875) LR 20 Eq. 39 46
In re Harper and others v. National Coal Board (Intended Action) [1974] QB 614 71–2
In re Rayner [1948] NZLR 455 124
In re Spectrum Plus Ltd [2005] UKHL 41 163
Jacobs v. London County Council [1950] AC 361 72–3
James and Karimi [2006] EWCA Crim 14 137
Jones v. DPP [1962] 2 WLR 575 3
Jones v. Randall (1774) 1 Cowp. 37 9
Jones v. Secretary of State for Social Services [1972] AC 944 117, 122
Khawaja [1984] AC 74 119
Kirkbright v. Curwin (1676) 3 Keb. 311 34
Knuller v. DPP [1973] AC 435 24, 117
Kruse v. Johnson [1898] 2 QB 91 124
Lochner v. New York, 198 U.S. 45 (1905) 62
London, Chatham & Dover Ry Co. v. South Easter Ry Co. [1892] 1 Ch. 120 44
London Jewellers Ltd v. Attenborough [1934] 2 KB 206 73
London Street Tramways v. London County Council [1894] AC 489 125
London Tramways v. London County Council [1898] AC 375 42, 103, 125–6, 129–30, 132, 133, 134–7, 143, 145–8

Louisville, Cincinnati, and Charleston RR *v*. Letson, 43 U.S. 497 (1844) 123–4
MacPherson *v*. Buick Motor Co. 217 N.Y. 382; 111 N.E. 1050 (N.Y. 1916) 63
M'Cowan *v*. Wright (1852) 15 D. 229 64–5
M'Culloch *v*. Maryland, 17 U.S. (4 Wheat) 316 (1819) 152
Midland Silicones Ltd *v*. Scruttons Ltd [1962] AC 446 136
Miliangos *v*. George Frank (Textiles) Ltd [1976] AC 443 127, 158
Mirage Studios *v*. Counter-feat Clothing [1991] FSR 145 3
Mirehouse *v*. Rennell (1833) 1 Cl. & Fin. 527 18
Moragne *v*. States Marine, Inc., 398 U.S. 375 (1970) 29
Moses [2006] EWCA Crim 1721 137
The Mostyn [1928] AC 57 90
Myers *v*. DPP [1965] AC 1001 119
Nash *v*. Tamplin & Sons Brewery Brighton Ltd [1952] AC 231 91
Nordenfelt *v*. Maxim Nordenfelt Guns & Ammunition Co. Ltd [1894] AC 535 63
O'Brien *v*. Robinson [1973] AC 912 118
Ognel *v*. Paston (1587) 2 Leon. 84 51
Osborn *v*. Bank of the United States, 22 US 738 (1824) 152
Osborne to Rowlett (1880) 13 Ch.D. 774 41, 46
Panama and South Pacific Telegraph Co. *v*. India Rubber, Gutta Percha & Telegraph Works Co. (1875) LR 10 Ch. App. 515 150
Perry *v*. Whitehead (1801) 6 Ves. Jun. 544 42
Pfizer *v*. Eurofood [2001] FSR 17 3
Pillans and Rose *v*. Van Mierop and Hopkins (1765) 3 Burr. 1663 8
Planned Parenthood of S.E. Pennsylvania *v*. Casey, 505 U.S. 833 (1992) 93, 117
Plessy *v*. Ferguson, 163 U.S. 537 (1896) 160
Police Authority for Huddersfield *v*. Watson [1947] KB 842 125
President of India *v*. La Pintada [1985] AC 104 118
Pretoria City Council *v*. Levinson 1949 (3) SALR 305 84
Quill Corp. *v*. North Dakota, 504 U.S. 298 (1992) 162
R *v*. A (No. 2) [2002] 1 AC 45 128
R *v*. Albany [1915] 3 KB 716 44
R *v*. Beedie [1998] QB 356 74
R *v*. Caldwell [1982] AC 341 127
R *v*. Clarence (1889) LR 22 QBD 23 137
R *v*. G [2004] 1 AC 1034 127
R *v*. Greater Manchester Coroner, ex p. Tal [1985] QB 67 125
R *v*. Home Secretary, ex p. Hargreaves [1997] 1 WLR 906 164
R *v*. Knuller (Publishing etc.) Ltd [1973] AC 435 136
R *v*. Miller [1954] 2 QB 282 137
R *v*. Millis (1844) 10 Cl. & Fin. 534 42, 120, 126
R *v*. R [1991] All ER 481 137
R *v*. Robinson [1996] 1 SCR 683 117

R v. Salituro [1991] 3 SCR 654 124
R (On the Application of Al-Skeini and others) v. Secretary of State for Defence [2006] HRLR 7; [2005] EWCA Civ. 1609 10
R v. Smith (Morgan) [2001] 1 AC 146 137
R v. Taylor [1950] 2 KB 368 137–8
R v. Wilkes (1770) 4 Burr. 2527 121
Ras Behari Lal v. King Emperor [1933] All ER Rep. 723 98
Regents of University of California v. Bakke, 438 U.S. 265 (1978) 79
Richard West & Partners (Inverness) Ltd v. Dick [1969] 2 Ch. 424 68
Riggs v. Palmer, 115 N.Y. 506; 22 N.E. 188 (1889) 164
Robinson v. Bland (1760) 2 Burr. 1077 8
Ross Smith v. Ross Smith [1963] AC 280 119
Runyon v. McCrary, 427 U.S. 160 (1976) 162
Rust v. Cooper (1774) Cowp. 629 51
Rylands v. Fletcher (1868) LR 3 HL 330 127
Salford Corporation v. Lancashire County Council (1890) LR 25 QBD 384 70
Scruttons v. Midland Silicones Ltd [1962] AC 446 45
Sheddon v. Goodrich (1803) 8 Ves. Jun. 481 96
Smith v. Allwright, 321 U.S. 649 (1944) 95, 118
Smith v. Harris [1939] 3 All ER 960 148–9
Southern Pac. Co. v. Jensen, 244 U.S. 205 (1917) 112
Street v. Mountford [1985] AC 809 62
Stuart v. Bank of Montreal (1909) 41 SCR 516 124
SZEEU v. Minister for Immigration and Multicultural and Indigenous Affairs [2006] FCAFC 2 84
Tees Conservancy Commissioners v. James [1935] Ch. 544; (1935) 51 TLR 219 70
United States v. Crawley, 837 F.2d 291 (7th Cir. 1988) 68
United States v. Johnson, 256 F.3d 895 (9th Cir. 2001) 77
United States v. South Eastern Underwriters' Association, 322 U.S. 533 (1944) 118
United Steelworkers of America v. Board of Education, 209 Cal. Rptr. 16 (Ct. App. 1984) 83–4
The Vera Cruz (No. 2) (1880) 9 PD 96 13
Victorian Railways v. Coultas (1888) 13 App. Cas. 222 63
Viro v. R (1978) 141 CLR 88 124
Walkley v. Precision Forgings Ltd [1979] 1 WLR 606 127
W. B. Anderson & Sons Ltd v. Rhodes (Liverpool) Ltd [1967] 2 All ER 850 71
White v. Chief Constable of South Yorkshire Police [1999] 2 AC 455 63
Young v. Bristol Aeroplane Co. [1944] KB 718 103
Younghusband v. Luftig [1949] 2 JB 354 125

1

Introduction: the usable past

So often in life we are looking for ways to make decisions with which we will be content. The appropriate options will be determined by the circumstances of the decision, and so it would be impossible, in the abstract, to set out an exhaustive list of ways to decide. But some of those ways are obvious. We might act on our instinct, or deliberate on the reasons supporting different possible decisions, or treat some rule, formal or otherwise, as a reason which pre-empts all others. We might try to devise a strategy, as Solomon did, to make others reveal information that would make deciding easier. Or we might even, though only exceptionally, decide not to decide and entrust an outcome to chance. This book is concerned with one specific decision-making option: deciding on the basis of what was done when the same matter had to be resolved in the past. When we decide in this way, we decide according to precedent.

1. Precedent

A precedent is a past event – in law the event is nearly always a decision – which serves as a guide for present action. Not all past events are precedents. Much of what we did in the past quickly fades into insignificance (or is best forgotten) and does not guide future action at all. Understanding precedent therefore requires an explanation of how past events and present actions come to be seen as connected. We often see a connection between past events and present actions, and regard the former as providing guidance for the latter, when they are alike: if, in doing Y, we are repeating our performance of X, we may as well look back to X for guidance when doing Y. However, our recognition that the act we are about to perform is one we have undertaken before does not always lead us to treat the past event as a guide for present action. We might now see that our performance of X was wrong: the experience of X has taught us that when crossing the road, it makes sense first to look both ways. Or it may just be that our tastes have changed: our notion of what makes for clever behaviour or a good cup of coffee might alter over time, so that past attempts at impressing others and coffee-making now strike us not as wrong but as unsophisticated. Often, we repeat actions without feeling any commitment to performing them in the same way as we did before. A past event, in other words, may be just that, no matter that our present action replicates it.

To follow a precedent is to draw an analogy between one instance and another; indeed, legal reasoning is often described – by common lawyers at least – as analogical or case-by-case reasoning.[1] Not all instances of analogy-drawing, however, are instances of precedent-following. When I say of an athlete with exceptional stamina and strength that 'the guy is like a machine', I draw an analogy but I do not invoke a precedent. Similarly, although following a precedent entails looking for guidance to an established standard, to set a standard is not necessarily to set a precedent. The most studious pupil in the class is setting a standard – one by which other classmates might be judged and to which some of them might even try to conform. But that standard does not have to set a precedent: the standard might have been met or even exceeded by pupils in other classes, and even if the standard has never been achieved before it will not necessarily operate as a precedent (indeed, although setting a precedent means doing something new – unprecedented – not everything that is done for the first time is a precedent).

Experience often guides present action, but reasoning from precedent is not identical to reasoning from experience. When my youngest daughter made her case for my buying her a mobile phone on her eleventh birthday, she reasoned from precedent: her elder sister received a mobile phone for her eleventh birthday. When I refused to buy my youngest daughter a mobile phone on her eleventh birthday, I reasoned from the experience of her sister's inability to be a responsible mobile-phone owner at the age of eleven. When we make a decision on the basis of experience, we are valuing experience for what it teaches us. When we make a decision on the basis of precedent, we consider significant the fact that our current predicament has been addressed before, but we will not necessarily value the precedent for what it

---

[1] See Edward H. Levi, *An Introduction to Legal Reasoning* (Chicago: University of Chicago Press, 1949), 1–8.

teaches us.[2] Sometimes, we might even follow precedents of which we do not approve.[3]

Note that the decision on the basis of precedent emphasizes the *fact* of prior dealing with the current predicament. When we decide on the ground of precedent we appear to believe that part of the reason the precedent is authoritative is that it is not an imagined event.[4] Common-law courts, for example, recognize that hypothetical instances can be instructive and compelling and yet, as a general rule, they will accord more weight to previously decided cases.[5] Even when it is reasonable to speculate that a precedent is not merely hypothetical – when it is reasonable, that is, to think that it will exist somewhere – there is still

---

[2] See Frederick Schauer, 'Precedent' (1987) 39 *Stanford L. Rev.* 571–605 at 575.

[3] As, indeed, judges sometimes do: see *Jones* v. *DPP* [1962] 2 WLR 575, 633, CCA, *per* Lord Devlin ('[T]he principle of *stare decisis* . . . does not apply only to good decisions; if it did, it would have neither value nor meaning'); Jon O. Newman, 'Between Legal Realism and Neutral Principles: The Legitimacy of Institutional Values' (1984) 72 *California L. Rev.* 200–16 at 204 ('The ordinary business of judges is to apply the law as they understand it to reach results with which they do not necessarily agree').

[4] The authority of a precedent might be weakened, furthermore, because for one reason or another the prior court, in deciding the case, proceeded without a full determination of the facts: recent examples in English law would be *Bayer* v. *Agropharm* [2004] EWHC 1661 (summary judgment without full hearing); *Pfizer* v. *Eurofood* [2001] FSR 17 (defendant's side not being argued owing to his failure to appear during proceedings); *Mirage Studios* v. *Counter-feat Clothing* [1991] FSR 145 (claimant awarded interim injunction, bringing litigation to end before full hearing); and *Guinness* v. *Saunders* [1990] 2 AC 663, HL (claimant's case so unanswerable that it did not require a full trial).

[5] See S. L. Hurley, 'Coherence, Hypothetical Cases, and Precedent' (1990) 10 *Oxf. Jnl Leg. Studs* 221–51 especially at 246–7. There is no doubt that common-law courts generally do not treat hypothetical instances as precedents. The main reason for this is probably that to treat such instances thus risks diminishing doctrinal clarity, 'at least to the extent that abstract or tangential hypotheticals obscure what a judge was actually required to resolve in the immediate case.' Michael Abramowicz and Maxwell Stearns, 'Defining Dicta' (2005) 57 *Stanford L. Rev.* 953–1094 at 1037. But there is no reason in principle that a precedent cannot be established by a conclusion based on a fact which has not been determined by a court. An historical example of such a precedent would be the case decided on demurrer, whereby a court would take the opportunity to pronounce upon the rights of parties on the assumption that the facts are as the claimant alleged. Not all legal precedents, furthermore, are judicial decisions. There are instances, for example, where one jurisdiction will adopt the judicial precedents of another system in a codified form so that the courts of that jurisdiction can, instead of creating their own precedents or having to keep referring back to the precedents of the other system, find governing legal principles in consolidating legislation. Perhaps some of the best-known illustrations of precedents in legislative form are those created by Sir James Fitzjames Stephen and the other Victorian reformers who codified various English principles for use in Indian law. See generally, Eric Stokes, *The English Utilitarians and India* (Oxford: Clarendon Press, 1959).

an expectation that those arguing before decision-makers discover and present the precedent if it is to be taken into consideration.

Precedent-following is very obviously a backward-looking activity: when we decide on the basis of precedent, we treat as significant the fact that essentially the same decision has been made before. Perhaps less obvious is the fact that creating precedents, and even following precedents, can be a forward-looking activity. Today's decision-makers are tomorrow's precedent-setters, Karl Llewellyn appreciated, and so they have a 'responsibility for the precedents which their present decisions may make'.[6] Our decision today to do something new, or to affirm something old, may guide or influence decision-makers in the future. So it is that precedent, according to Frederick Schauer, 'involves the special responsibility accompanying the power to commit to the future before we get there'.[7] A significant constraint on decision-making activity might well be the decision-maker's imagination – his capacity, that is, to envisage just what the implications of a particular decision could be for future cases. Even when there is no precedent to guide a decision, the notion of precedent – awareness, that is, that what we do now may become a precedent – might still influence the decision-making process.

The point that precedents have a consequential as well as an historical dimension, while a good one, can be overemphasized. Since 'the conscientious decisionmaker must recognize that future conscientious decisionmakers will treat her decision as precedent', Schauer argues, 'today's conscientious decisionmakers are obliged to decide not only today's case, but tomorrow's as well'.[8] Certainly, there are times when there is little or no need to deliberate an issue because our predecessors were so scrupulous in dealing with it. But did they have to be so scrupulous?

---

[6] K. N. Llewellyn, 'Case Law', in *Encyclopaedia of the Social Sciences*, ed. E. R. A. Seligman (London: Macmillan, 1930), III, 249–51 at 251. In a similar vein, see Gerald J. Postema, 'Melody and Law's Mindfulness of Time' (2004) 17 *Ratio Juris* 203–26 at 214–15.

[7] Schauer, 'Precedent', 573. The same point has been made on many occasions by Neil MacCormick. See, e.g., Neil MacCormick, 'Why Cases Have Rationes and What These Are', in *Precedent in Law*, ed. L. Goldstein (Oxford: Clarendon Press, 1987), 155–82 at 160–1; 'Formal Justice and the Form of Legal Arguments' (1976) 6 *Études de logique juridique* 103–18.

[8] Schauer, 'Precedent', 589; see also Jan G. Deutsch, 'Precedent and Adjudication' (1974) 83 *Yale L. J.* 1553–84; MacCormick, 'Formal Justice and the Form of Legal Arguments', 110 ('[A]t any point in time, a court which is called upon to give a decision on any matter in litigation ought only to decide the case conformably to such reasons as it considers will be acceptable for the disposition of any similar case which may come up for decision by it at any later time').

Sometimes we will create precedents, even good precedents, unintentionally; it might even be the case that only in retrospect is a particular action seen to have set a precedent. It is hardly possible to be responsible about setting a precedent without the awareness that one is setting a precedent. Even with this awareness, furthermore, it is not clear why conscientious decision-makers 'are obliged', as opposed to likely or minded, to decide with an eye to the future. A decision-maker's priorities might legitimately be in the present; and even when there exists a strong feeling that the decision-maker has thought too little about the future, this is insufficient in itself to establish that there has been a breach of obligation. We might, but we do not have to, make decisions with the future in mind; and thoughts about the future might, but do not have to, constrain what we decide to do.

It is sometimes assumed to be in the nature of a precedent that it must be knowable to those who might be constrained by it.[9] But it is possible that a precedent might apply to our situation even though it is inconceivable that we would have discovered its existence before it was revealed to us. 'It is a firmly-established rule of interpretation', C. K. Allen wrote in 1925, 'that the Court may take its precedents from any intelligible source whatever – newspapers, manuscripts, historical documents, and sometimes simply the recollection of judges of cases which they have heard or heard of.'[10] If we must have judge-made law, Bentham argued, it ought at least to be systematically reported, for, without such reporting, the common law cannot be easily identified and it may be difficult if not impossible to tell if a court is relying on precedent or creating a new offence.[11] Yet, even once systematic

---

[9] See, e.g., Barbara Baum Levenbook, 'The Meaning of a Precedent' (2000) 6 *Legal Theory* 185–240.

[10] Carleton Kemp Allen, 'Precedent and Logic' (1925) 41 *LQR* 329–45 at 341.

[11] 'It is the Judges... that make the common law:– Do you know how they make it? Just as a man makes laws for his dog. When your dog does any thing you want to break him of, you wait till he does it, and then beat him for it ... What way then has any man of coming at this dog-law? Only by watching [Judges'] proceedings: by observing in what *cases* they have hanged a man, in what *cases* they have sent him to jail, in what *cases* they have seized his goods, and so forth.' Jeremy Bentham, *Truth* versus *Ashhurst; or Law as it is, contrasted with what it is said to be* (London: Moses, 1823 [1792]), 11–12. Dr Johnson had already expressed much the same sentiment in the Scottish Court of Session. See Johnson to Boswell, 1 July 1772, in James Boswell, *The Life of Samuel Johnson*, ed. R. W. Chapman (Oxford: Oxford University Press, 1998 [1791]), 496–7 ('To permit a law to be modified at discretion, is to leave the community without law ... It is to suffer the rash and ignorant to act at discretion, and then to depend for the legality of that action on the sentence of the Judge. He that is thus governed, lives not by law, but by

reporting had become established in English law, the danger of surprise precedents – 'unexploded land mines, ready to do damage'[12] – persisted. Such precedents are a danger not so much to judges (though a court might be embarrassed to have to find its way around a precedent it had never known existed) as to barristers, who could be put at a considerable disadvantage in the courtroom because opposing counsel successfully cites as authority a decision which he has located in the form of a verbatim transcript available only by special permission from a court's private library.[13] The availability of electronic transcripts from legal databases has lessened this danger considerably;[14] nevertheless, the phenomenon of the surprise precedent remains significant for our purposes because it provides a reason for doubting the claim that 'a

---

opinion ... He lives by a law (if law it be,) which he can never know before he has offended it'). On Bentham's case for an authoritative system of law reporting, see Michael Lobban, *The Common Law and English Jurisprudence 1760–1850* (Oxford: Clarendon Press, 1991), 122–3.

[12] John P. Dawson, *The Oracles of the Law* (Buffalo, NY: Hein, 1986 [1968]), 84.

[13] For a general discussion of the position in English law, see O. M. Stone, 'Knowing the Law' (1961) 24 *MLR* 475–80; R. J. C. Munday, 'New Dimensions of Precedent' (1978) n.s. 14 *JSPTL* 201–17 at 207–13. In the United States, decisions of federal district courts are not binding precedents, be they published or unpublished. With regard to federal circuit courts, the panel deciding a case can designate its opinion as being either 'for publication' or 'not for publication'. Published circuit-court opinions are, subject to a few exceptions, considered to bind district courts within the relevant circuit and subsequent panels of that circuit (though the full circuit can overrule them when sitting *en banc*). Opinions designated 'not for publication', even though available on Lexis and Westlaw, are not binding precedents or even persuasive authority. In 2000, the Eighth Circuit suggested that denying such opinions the status of binding precedent may be contrary to Article III of the US Constitution. See *Anastasoff* v. *United States*, 223 F.3d 898, 899–900 (8th Cir. 2000). Few judges appear to have been receptive to this suggestion, though some law professors have been sympathetic to it: see, e.g., Lauren Robel, 'The Practice of Precedent: *Anastasoff*, Noncitation Rules, and the Meaning of Precedent in an Interpretive Community' (2002) 35 *Indiana L. Rev.* 399–421.

[14] Of course, the very fact that many precedents which would once have been 'unpublished' are now available electronically creates its own problems, not least because it is likely to be especially difficult to determine what is authoritative precedent when databases enable lawyers easily to present opposing sets of more or less equally convincing prior decisions on nearly any legal issue. See, generally, Susan W. Brenner, *Precedent Inflation* (New Brunswick, NJ: Transaction, 1992), 175–312. In English law, the Court of Appeal has in recent years sought to discourage unnecessary reliance on unreported cases: see *Practice Direction (Court of Appeal (Civil Division))* [1999] 1 WLR 1027, 1059 ('Permission to cite unreported cases will not usually be granted unless advocates are able to assure the court that the transcript in question contains a relevant statement of legal principle not found in reported authority and that the authority is not cited because of the phraseology used or as an illustration of the application of an established legal principle').

precedential decision's meaning in law is inherently public' – that the decision 'must be publicly accessible'.[15] Any such decision is likely to be publicly accessible, but it does not have to be.

Precedents are inherently public, Levenbook argues, because they are exemplary.[16] 'Rather than think of precedent as laying down a rule, it is more helpful to think of it as setting an example.'[17] Levenbook is certainly right to resist equating precedents, even judicial precedents, with rules. There is certainly evidence throughout the history of the common law, furthermore, of courts regarding individual precedents as illustrating general legal principles.[18] But this does not mean that precedents can be accurately characterized as exemplary. In establishing a precedent we will usually, but not always, set an example as well. When I raised my elder son's pocket money my younger son correctly spied a precedent – one upon which he would try to rely in due course – but he would have been mistaken if he had interpreted my action to be somehow illustrative or exemplary (which is not to deny that I could have made the raise serve as an example had I wished to do so). Likewise, when a court modifies an established legal principle a new precedent is created but not necessarily a new example. Even when a precedent does set an example, the exemplary nature of the precedent will not be the source of its authority. '[P]recedent guides best', according to Levenbook, 'when the example it sets is taken as an example of what is to be done, or is to be avoided'.[19] The fact that a particular precedent provides a good example, however, is not sufficient to explain why that precedent is treated as authoritative, for we often admire an example that has been set – and may even recognize it as the epitome of decency, good manners, healthy living or whatever – without feeling compelled to follow it. Certainly, in this study, we will have reason now and again to refer to the exemplary nature of precedents. But precedents, though they often serve as examples, are not merely examples. They have more of a claim on our attention than examples do.

---

[15] Levenbook, 'The Meaning of a Precedent', 186, 219. Possibly, Levenbook is assuming that what we have noted to be the position in American law is the position everywhere.
[16] See *ibid.*, 226–7.   [17] *Ibid.*, 186.
[18] See J. H. Baker, 'Records, Reports and the Origins of Case-Law in England', in *Judicial Records, Law Reports, and the Growth of Case Law*, ed. J. H. Baker (Berlin: Duncker and Humblot, 1989), 15–46 at 38; Gerald J. Postema, 'Some Roots of our Notion of Precedent', in *Precedent in Law*, 9–33 at 23.
[19] Levenbook, 'The Meaning of a Precedent', 199.

Would it make more sense to characterize precedents as customary rather than exemplary? The characterization is misleading, because precedents and customs are not only distinct from but may even counter one another: in admitting female members, for instance, an institution might set a precedent which breaks from its custom. In relation to the common law, the characterization might at first seem more appropriate. Both precedents and custom are, after all, common-law sources of received wisdom: the judge who decides on the basis of either finds authority in past practice. For at least five reasons, however, judicial precedent cannot be equated with custom. First, precedent and custom can oppose one another in law as they can elsewhere. The claim that precedents can only establish law when they are consistent with 'the custom and course in a court' dates back at least to the mid fifteenth century.[20] More than three centuries later, the sentiment was memorably articulated by Blackstone: 'it is an established rule to abide by former precedents, where the same points come up again in litigation', he wrote, '[y]et this rule admits of exception ... For if it be found that the former decision is manifestly absurd or unjust, it is declared, not that such a sentence was *bad law*, but that it was *not law*; that is, that it is not the established custom of the realm.'[21] Secondly, whereas judges who follow precedents are relying on the work of earlier courts, the customs to which judges look for authority need not have been legally recognized. When, in 1765, Lord Mansfield contended that consideration was not necessary for the creation of binding contracts between commercial parties, he relied not on precedent but on what he understood to be prevailing mercantile custom.[22] Thirdly, custom differs from precedent in that it may be immemorial: to decide by reference to precedent is to

---

[20] Two legal historians cite as authority for this proposition a report of cases from the fifth year of Edward IV (1466), the *Long Quinto*: see J. W. Tubbs, *The Common Law Mind: Medieval and Early Modern Conceptions* (Baltimore: Johns Hopkins University Press, 2000), 45; and T. Ellis Lewis, 'The History of Judicial Precedent' (pt. III) (1931) 47 *LQR* 411–27 at 412–13. (The other published parts of Lewis's incomplete study are at (1930) 46 *LQR* 207–24, 341–60; (1932) 48 *LQR* 230–47.)

[21] William Blackstone, *Commentaries on the Laws of England*, 4 vols. (Chicago: University of Chicago Press, 1979 [1765–9]), I, 69–70.

[22] See *Pillans and Rose* v. *Van Mierop and Hopkins* (1765) 3 Burr. 1663. For a short while, the argument was accepted as good law, though its time had certainly passed by the end of the 1770s: see A. W. B. Simpson, *A History of the Common Law of Contract: The Rise of the Action of Assumpsit* (Oxford: Clarendon Press, 1975), 617–19. It is worth noting also that Mansfield was by no means opposed in principle to the doctrine of precedent. Sometimes he found precedents that served his objectives, and in such instances was not averse to following them: see, e.g., *Robinson* v. *Bland* (1760) 2 Burr. 1077. See also

compare the present case with an identifiable earlier event, whereas decisions on the basis of custom often justify an outcome by observing that nobody remembers a time when the question in hand was resolved in any other way.[23] Fourthly, common-law judges do not follow precedents simply because they exist; they follow – or, for that matter, distinguish or overrule – precedents because those precedents support particular lines of reasoning. A custom, on the other hand, will be considered relevant or irrelevant by a court not because of the reasons it embodies but because it has been generally accepted by a particular community in the past.[24] Finally, perhaps the most decisive evidence that precedent and custom are different forms of legal authority is the common law itself, for, as will become clear in the next chapter, the common law existed as a form of customary law long before there was a doctrine of precedent.

Judged in the abstract, the activity of adhering to precedents cannot be shown to be a good or a bad thing; the fact is that it can be either. A precedent might liberate or constrain: knowing that the action I am about to take has been taken before might embolden me ('my predecessor did this, so why shouldn't I?') or it might inhibit me ('how could I ever match up to the standard set by my predecessor?').[25] Our reliance on precedent will often help us to win an argument or persuade others, or lead others to believe that we are being fair or at least consistent

---

Michael Lobban, *A History of the Philosophy of Law in the Common Law World, 1600–1900* (Dordrecht: Springer, 2007), 106 who observes that although, in *Jones* v. *Randall* (1774) 1 Cowp. 37, Mansfield emphasized common-law principle over precedent, he was nevertheless setting out his argument 'in a case of first impression. To argue thus was not to go against the common law as a system of precedent, but only to say that in cases of first impression, judges decided on the basis of natural reason.'

[23] For this classic common-law philosophy, see, e.g., Sir Matthew Hale, *The History of the Common Law of England*, 6th edn (London: Butterworth, 1820; 1st edn 1713), 21 ('the law *leges non scriptae* ... have acquired their binding power and force of laws, by a long and immemorial usage'); Blackstone, *Commentaries*, I, 67 ('in our law the goodness of a custom depends upon its having been used time out of mind; or, in the solemnity of our legal phrase, time whereof the memory of man runneth not to the contrary').

[24] See Stephen R. Perry, 'Judicial Obligation, Precedent and the Common Law' (1987) 7 *Oxf. J. Leg. Studs* 215–57 at 253–4.

[25] Sometimes, we might make a point of describing a past action as a precedent when doing so serves to justify our current behaviour: when employees in an organization take a lunch break, for example, they normally have no need to convince anyone that their having done the same in the past indicates that their behaviour is acceptable in the current instance; but if, today, a group of employees takes a very long lunch break, they might try to convince others of the acceptability of their behaviour by pointing out that, within the organization, the taking of long lunch-breaks by similarly-situated employees is not unprecedented.

because we are treating the present instance in the same way as we treated a materially similar past instance. On other occasions, our appeals to precedent may be a sign of weakness rather than strength. Sometimes, we may adhere to a precedent because we are simply too lazy, unimaginative or (a different kind of weakness) pressed for time to think about a problem afresh. Sometimes, we might abide by a precedent because we are not sufficiently bold to take action which would most likely establish a new precedent for which future generations might hold us responsible. 'Every public action which is not customary', F. M. Cornford archly wrote, 'either is wrong, or, if it is right, is a dangerous precedent. It follows that nothing should ever be done for the first time.'[26] Behind the satire lies a serious point: in establishing a new precedent we might commit ourselves or our successors to a course of action the full implications of which are either not yet apparent to us or are apparent but unacceptable to us. Our unwillingness to abandon an established precedent in such instances could indicate timidity, but could equally be a sign of prudence; for it is sometimes sensible to be wary of a slippery slope, just as it may be sensible to worry about establishing new precedents in the immediate aftermath of extreme events or when emotions run high. Adherence to a precedent does not have to be a conservative strategy: one might be deciding to keep faith with the radical reasoning of one's immediate forebears, for example, rather than deciding to support a less progressive approach to a problem. More often than not, however, following a precedent serves the cause of restraint rather than creativity.

In areas of life where creativity is the norm, precedents are likely to have less value, one might suspect, than in those areas where more emphasis is placed on maintaining stability. But matters are not quite so simple. First, precedent-setting can be creative in that it can fill a void. In a particular case, a court might be unsure of its jurisdiction – about whether, for example, it has the power to try a foreign detainee[27] – and so might establish a precedent whereby it creates authority for itself (and for future courts for which its precedents hold good), at least until the legislature or a higher court determines that the law should be otherwise.

---

[26] F. M. Cornford, *Microcosmographia Academica: Being a Guide for the Young Academic Politician*, 6th edn (London: Bowes & Bowes, 1964; 1st edn published 1908), 23.

[27] See, e.g., *Hamdan* v. *Rumsfeld*, 126 S.Ct. 2749 (2006); *R (On the Application of Al-Skeini and others)* v. *Secretary of State for Defence* [2006] HRLR 7; [2005] EWCA Civ. 1609, CA (Civ Div).

In such an instance, a court may be an effective law-making body owing to the tacit consent of a legislature which (perhaps conspicuously) fails to cancel out the precedent.[28] Secondly, scope for creativity may depend on the number and diversity of applicable precedents: a decision-maker might proceed with broad discretion where there are no precedents, with narrow discretion where there is a clear precedent or line of precedent, but again with broad discretion if there is a range of precedents pointing to different conclusions.[29] Thirdly, creative activity may be activity with an eye to precedent. Although those engaged in essentially creative endeavours, such as artists or improvisational musicians, are unlikely to be considered especially talented if they simply strive to replicate the work of their predecessors, they can nevertheless be genuinely original by working within and contributing to a tradition – neither following nor overruling but distinguishing, to use common lawyers' language. It is sometimes argued similarly that philosophizing is an activity antithetical to precedent-following. To hold a particular philosophical viewpoint because it has been held by others in the past is – no matter that those others might be the most eminent philosophers – not to philosophize.[30] To try to justify that viewpoint on no basis other than that it has been held by others would strike nearly all philosophers as unsound.[31] But again, even though philosophizing is not precedent-following, philosophers will invariably, and understandably, take account of the accomplishments and the mistakes of their philosophical

---

[28] On the idea that a court's capacity to make law might be inferred from the fact that some of its precedents have been implicitly consented to by the legislature, see Morton J. Horwitz, *The Tranformation of American Law, 1780–1860* (Cambridge, Mass.: Harvard University Press, 1977), 23.

[29] See Stefanie A. Lindquist and Frank B. Cross, 'Empirically Testing Dworkin's Chain Novel: Studying the Path of Precedent' (2005) 80 *New York Univ. L. Rev.* 1156–1206 at 1204 ('In the initial period [of a common law system], attitudes clearly impact judicial decisionmaking because judges must create legal doctrine almost from whole cloth ... Following the development of some clear precedents, however, the influence of attitudes may be moderated as judges feel bound by those clear and controlling decisions. As more time passes and more precedents are decided, however, the proliferation of available prior decisions in turn expands judges' discretion to decide cases in accordance with their attitudes simply because they have more precedents from which to choose. The influence of precedent could thus be conceptualized as quadratic or curvilinear over time').

[30] See Anthony T. Kronman, 'Precedent and Tradition' (1990) 99 *Yale L.J.* 1029–68 at 1031–6.

[31] See Frederick Schauer, *Profiles, Probabilities, and Stereotypes* (Cambridge, Mass.: Belknap Press, 2003), 273 ('Philosophers treat an argument from precedent as essentially a fallacy ...').

predecessors. Precedents can provide valuable examples of which it makes sense to be mindful even when precedent-following is, for good reasons, considered bad practice.

The extent to which a precedent is valued may have less to do with the question of whether one is expected to be creative or discover truth and more to do with that of whether one is required to make decisions. Not all decision-makers value precedents equally, however. Political decisions are often made with the specific objective of discrediting the initiatives of previous governments: indeed, it is usually taken for granted that political parties will at least purport to treat similar instances differently, because policy-differentiation is part and parcel of political power struggle. Politics is also a domain in which emphasis tends to be placed as much on the performance of the precedent-setters as on the precedents that they set. Such emphasis can sometimes make political precedents constrain in perverse ways. It is conceivable, for example, that the attitude of the leaders of I^2 towards the state of I^3 might worry some other governments considerably, but that those governments are hesitant to act against I^2 because of the severe international criticism to which they were subjected after intervening in the similarly worrying affairs of I^1. Yet the behaviour of I^2 might be more worrying than was that of I^1, and those governments minded to take military action against I^2 may have a very strong case. But their action against I^1 might loom in the background as an inhibiting precedent, even though that action rested on a weaker case and so in all reality ought not to be treated as a precedent.

If there is a basic point to be emphasized, it is that precedents can make all sorts of demands on our attention. Much of this book is concerned with the classic common law argument that precedents set by courts do not merely claim the attention of, but actually *bind*, other courts. This is the doctrine of *stare decisis* – i.e., earlier judicial decisions must be followed when the same points arise again in litigation.[32] Although it would be a mistake to think that courts in civil-law jurisdictions never follow precedents,[33] it is fair to say that *stare decisis* is very

---

[32] The full Latin expression is *stare decisis et non quieta movere* (abide by earlier decisions and do not disturb settled points).
[33] See John Henry Merryman, *The Civil Law Tradition: An Introduction to the Legal Systems of Western Europe and Latin America*, 2nd edn (Stanford, Ca.: Stanford University Press, 1985), 46–7; Jerzy Wróblewski, 'The Concept and the Function of Precedent in Statute-Law Systems' (1974) 7 *Archivum Juridicum Cracoviense* 7–20 at 8; Albert Mayrand, 'L'autorité du précédent au Québec' (1994) 28 *Revue Juridique Thémis* 771–97 at 793–4

much a common-law – and indeed, we will see, a modern common-law – doctrine and that continental lawyers tend to think of precedent as persuasive argument rather than as legal authority. The thrust of the discussion so far has been that decision-makers often *feel* bound to follow precedents. *Stare decisis*, however, has it not that common-law judges feel bound, but that they are bound, to follow precedents. Do past decisions really ever bind future courts?

'The "binding force" of precedents has', according to Allen, 'through constant and often unthinking repetition, become a kind of sacramental phrase which contains a large element of fiction.'[34] A judge is trained to believe 'that the most conclusive logic is the analogy of antecedent cases, especially if they have been decided by Courts of higher jurisdiction than his own. By these we say he is "bound." But he is only bound intellectually ... It is he himself who must decide whether the precedent is authoritative or not.'[35] The notion that judges are 'intellectually' bound looks to amount to the unhelpful claim that 'precedents ought always to be followed except when they should not'.[36] Indeed Allen's argument, one commentator insists, 'becomes more mystifying on every reading'.[37] The assertion 'that courts are not *really* bound by earlier decisions' only holds good so long as we are intent on 'giving the word "bound" a too literal meaning, and imagining that being bound by case law involves some sort of psychological compulsion which removes the need for decision or the possibility of choice, in the way in which being bound by cords involves a physical compulsion'.[38] But Allen's argument does not require that we be quite so literal. His argument is perfectly

('In theory, the attitude of the common law provinces [of Canada] regarding the authority of precedent remains different from that of Quebec. But in fact, these attitudes are now very similar, owing to the relaxation of the doctrine of *stare decisis* and, even in civil law countries, the considerable growth of the role of case-law'); and generally *Interpreting Precedents: A Comparative Study*, ed. D. N. MacCormick and R. S. Summers (Aldershot: Ashgate, 1997).

[34] Allen, 'Precedent and Logic', 334.
[35] *Ibid.*, 333–4. See also *The Vera Cruz (No. 2)* (1880) 9 PD 96, 98, *per* Brett M. R. ('But there is no statute or common law rule by which one court is bound to abide by the decision of another of equal rank, it does so simply from what may be called the comity among judges. In the same way there is no common law or statutory rule to oblige a Court to bow to its own decisions, it does so again on the grounds of judicial comity').
[36] Richard A. Wasserstrom, *The Judicial Decision: Toward a Theory of Legal Justification* (Stanford, Ca.: Stanford University Press, 1961), 46.
[37] A. W. B. Simpson, 'The *Ratio Decidendi* of a Case and the Doctrine of Binding Precedent', in *Oxford Essays in Jurisprudence*, ed. A. G. Guest (Oxford: Oxford University Press, 1961), 148–75 at 149.
[38] *Ibid.*, 173–4.

understandable, rather, as an effort to highlight the inability of classical positivist jurisprudence to account for the notion of binding precedent: precedents lack genuine capacity to bind not because they do not literally fetter judges in the process of decision-making, but because they are not equivalent to legal rules which are followed for fear of the likely consequences in the event of non-compliance. Common-law judges are not sanctioned for declining to follow precedent, and so precedents do not constrain judges in the classical positivist sense. But this does not mean that positivist jurisprudence is unenlightening on the subject of precedent. For anyone wishing to understand the authority of precedent, in fact, classical legal positivism is a particularly good position from which to start.

2. Positivism and precedent

The proposition that laws bind, while unlikely to startle anybody, is one which legal philosophers rightly accord serious attention. The binding force of legal rules or norms, the classical legal positivist claims, consists in the fact that they are backed by sanctions emanating from a habitually-obeyed authoritative source. Hans Kelsen repeatedly emphasized in the process of developing his so-called Pure Theory of Law that these rules or norms are not moral norms: morality merely condones conduct conforming to, and disapproves of conduct contravening, its norms, whereas law is a coercive order which seeks to attach sanctions to behaviour which opposes its norms.[39] In this respect, he noted, 'the Pure Theory of Law continues in the tradition of nineteenth-century positivist legal theory'[40] – the theory according to which, in the words of John Austin, '[t]he binding virtue of a law lies in the sanction annexed to it'.[41]

It is well known that this theory of law as coercive orders was dismantled by H. L. A. Hart in *The Concept of Law*. Yet, before the theory

---

[39] See, e.g., Hans Kelsen, *General Theory of Norms*, trans. M. Hartney (Oxford: Oxford University Press, 1991; orig. German publ. 1979), 97–8; *Pure Theory of Law*, 2nd edn, trans. M. Knight (Berkeley: University of California Press, 1967; orig. German publ. 1960), 62; 'Law and Morality' (1960), in Hans Kelsen, *Essays in Legal and Moral Philosophy*, ed. O. Weinberger, trans. P. Heath (Dordrecht: Reidel, 1973), 83–94 at 86.

[40] Hans Kelsen, *Introduction to the Problems of Legal Theory*, trans. B. L. and S. L. Paulson (Oxford: Oxford University Press, 1992; orig. German publ. 1934), 26.

[41] John Austin, *The Province of Jurisprudence Determined*, ed. W. E. Rumble (Cambridge: Cambridge University Press, 1995 [1832]), 151.

had come under Hart's scrutiny, at least one of its shortcomings was starkly highlighted by the doctrine of *stare decisis*. The doctrine brings with it numerous difficulties – not least that of determining which cases are materially alike. But the difficulty which *stare decisis* posed for classical legal positivism was very specific. Though a decision of a court must (unless successfully appealed) be accepted by the litigants, and though it may establish a precedent which is more generally binding on the citizenry, it is not immediately clear what it means to say – even though we often do say – that the decision binds future courts. Cross and Harris, in *Precedent in English Law*, observe that '[t]he peculiar feature of the English doctrine of precedent is its strongly coercive nature'.[42] English judges, unlike their counterparts in many other jurisdictions, '*must* have regard to' the previous decisions of higher courts, and 'are sometimes obliged to follow a previous case although they have what would otherwise be good reasons for not doing so'.[43] As a piece of doctrinal description, this statement is unremarkable. But from the perspective of classical legal positivism, it poses a serious difficulty. For what does it mean to say that precedents bind? The answer seems to be that precedents bind because judges consider themselves to be bound by them, or at least bound to take account of them.[44] Yet if

---

[42] Rupert Cross and J. W. Harris, *Precedent in English Law*, 4th edn (Oxford: Clarendon Press, 1991), 3.

[43] *Ibid.*

[44] 'We say that [the judge] is bound by the decisions of higher Courts; and so he undoubtedly is. But the superior Court does not impose fetters upon him; he places the fetters in his own hands ... The humblest judicial officer has to decide for himself whether he is or is not bound'. Carleton Kemp Allen, *Law in the Making*, 3rd edn (Oxford: Clarendon Press, 1939), 247–8. For reiterations and elaborations of the point, see Allen, 'Precedent and Logic', 333–4; N. E. Simmonds, *Central Issues in Jurisprudence: Justice, Law and Rights*, 2nd edn (London: Sweet & Maxwell, 2002), 146; and Joseph Jaconelli, 'Do Constitutional Conventions Bind?' (2005) 64 *Cambridge L.J.* 149–76 at 176. For the notion that a court might not consider itself bound to follow precedent but still consider itself bound to take account of precedent when making decisions, see James Hardisty, 'Reflections on *Stare Decisis*' (1979) 55 *Indiana L.J.* 41–69 at 48. One might think that in the absence of a rule or a recognized judicial declaration to the effect that this is required practice, such a convention will never be regarded by judges as a duty. But common-law judges sometimes do treat such conventions thus: examples would be where there are informal but well-recognized judicial norms against treating, say, foreign precedents or the works of living treatise writers as legal authority. The important point for the purposes of the discussion here, nevertheless, is that judges could, according to the classical positivist account of legal authority, no more be said to be bound to take account of precedents than they could be said to be bound to follow them.

precedents bind, must there not be an identifiable sanction applicable to a judge who refuses to respect *stare decisis*? 'If a judge persistently and vociferously declined to follow cases by which he was bound', Cross and Harris reply,

> it is possible that steps would be taken to remove him from his office, but it would be a mistake to think in terms of such drastic sanctions for the judge's obligation to act according to the rules of precedent. Those rules are rules of practice, and, if it is thought to be desirable to speak of a sanction for the obligation to comply with them, it is sufficient to say that non-compliance might excite adverse comment from other judges. Needless to say, there are not many examples of such comment in the law reports because the obligation to follow a practice derives its force from the fact that the practice is followed with a high degree of uniformity.[45]

The idea of the doctrine of precedent creating an occasion for judicial lawbreaking is treated by Cross and Harris with near bewilderment. The question of what ought to be done about a judge who flagrantly abuses the doctrine does not tax them for the simple reason that judges do not behave thus. Although a formal sanction could be applied to a judge for eschewing precedent, the likelihood of this occurring is remote because concerns about matters such as reputation and fear of informal criticism motivate judges to treat precedents as binding upon them. Judges, to put the matter bluntly, are likely to consider it prudential to set limits on their own behaviour by according precedents authority. There is nothing naive about Cross and Harris's assessment. Where judges do not wish to follow a precedent it is commonly assumed that they will either distinguish the precedent from the present case or overrule the precedent on the basis of an especially compelling reason or set of reasons. Neither judges nor jurists pay much attention to the question of what should happen to the judge who is regularly and manifestly disrespectful towards and neglectful of precedent, probably because that judge rarely if ever exists outside fictional literature.

For the classical legal positivist, however, the idea that precedents bind future decision makers is intelligible only if there is a stipulated doctrine or sanction which will be *prima facie* applicable to those decision-makers when they ignore precedents. Without such a doctrine or sanction, it is unclear how one decision can be said to require another.

---

[45] Cross and Harris, *Precedent in English Law*, 99.

Bentham was forthright on this point: although we speak of a judge creating a rule when pronouncing a decision, this decision can be 'nothing more than a *particular* rule, bearing upon the individual person and things in question.'[46] '*Rules*? yes,' he asserted, '*Rules of law*? No', for the binding force of the decision does not extend beyond the particular instance.[47] Austin similarly, though he stopped short of identifying 'judiciary law' as law improperly so-called, could not bring himself to say 'that any judiciary rule is good or valid law'.[48] The 'direct and proper purpose' of adjudication 'is not the establishment of the rule, but the decision of the specific case to which the judge applies' that rule.[49] Precedents, therefore, are best described not as law but as evidence of how judges have interpreted the law.[50] Hobbes appreciated that precedents may be treated as authoritative, but did not consider that they must be: judicial reason, he claimed, is neither the artificial perfection of reason extolled by Coke nor the 'right reason' of the sovereign, but merely the natural reason of any competent person; judges are as prone to error as anyone else, and so while a judge today might well follow an example set by his forebears because he finds it satisfactory, he should not consider it binding – even 'though sworn to follow it' – if he considers it mistaken.[51]

It may seem odd that the classical legal positivists should have been dismissive (as regards Bentham, the better word would be contemptuous)[52] of the notion of binding precedent. Why did they not regard *stare decisis* as something to be properly explained rather than disparaged? Although it is difficult to say precisely when the English courts began to consider themselves bound by rules of precedent, there is little doubt that the change had not fully taken place by the end of the period during which the classical positivists wrote. By the late eighteenth century, there

---

[46] Jeremy Bentham, 'To the Citizens of the Several American United States' (1817), in *The Works of Jeremy Bentham*, 11 vols., ed. J. Bowring (Edinburgh: Tait, 1843), IV, 478–507 at 485.
[47] *Ibid.*, 484.
[48] John Austin, *Lectures on Jurisprudence or the Philosophy of Positive Law*, 2 vols., 5th edn, ed. R. Campbell (London: Murray, 1885), II, 655.
[49] *Ibid.*, 621.
[50] See *ibid.*, 531 (on 'precedent ... considered as evidence of the previous state of the law').
[51] Hobbes, *Leviathan*, II. 26. 24.
[52] Bentham's best quotations on the subject are put together, and his attitude is well captured, by Shirley Robin Letwin, *On the History of the Idea of Law*, ed. N. B. Reynolds (Cambridge: Cambridge University Press, 2005), 155–7.

certainly existed among the English judiciary a practice of following precedents, but the fact that there was as yet no clear and unchallengeable court hierarchy made it difficult and often impossible to say that one decision was binding on another because of the source from which it emanated.[53] By the middle of the nineteenth century, indeed by the time Austin had completed his *Lectures on Jurisprudence*, the doctrine of binding precedent was clearly in the making. Parke J. observed in 1833 that 'for the sake of attaining uniformity, consistency and certainty', rules derived from precedents must, unless they are 'plainly unreasonable and inconvenient', be applied 'to all cases which arise'.[54] The following year, James Ram wrote in *The Science of Legal Judgment* of how a precedent binds 'under many circumstances', though he identified only two: 'if in the mind of the Court [the precedent] is wholly unimpeachable ... or, if impeachable, the objection to which it is so exposed, is not, in the consideration of the Court, sufficient to exclude its title to be authority'.[55] Although *stare decisis* was in the making, however, not until the later decades of the nineteenth century did the rules of precedent begin to solidify.[56] It is therefore not surprising that classical legal positivists did not consider the idea of binding precedent to pose a serious jurisprudential problem.[57]

---

[53] See Allen, *Law in the Making*, 210. Allen developed his argument in response to William Holdsworth, who maintained that the doctrine of precedent had become established in England by the latter half of the eighteenth century: see W. S. Holdsworth, 'Case Law' (1934) 50 *LQR* 180–95; A. L. Goodhart, 'Case Law – A Short Replication' (1934) 50 *LQR* 196–200; Carleton Kemp Allen, 'Case Law: An Unwarrantable Intervention' (1935) 51 *LQR* 333–46; and W. S. Holdsworth, 'Precedents in the Eighteenth Century' (1935) 51 *LQR* 441–2.

[54] *Mirehouse* v. *Rennell* (1833) 1 Cl. & Fin. 527, 546. In the year after this decision, James Parke was transferred from the King's Bench to the Court of Exchequer, whereupon he acquired his best-remembered title of Baron Parke.

[55] James Ram, *The Science of Legal Judgment* (Philadelphia: Littell, 1835; orig. English edn 1834), 66, 67. Cf. his observation only two years earlier, in his *A Practical Treatise of Assets*, that the 'weight' of authority behind a case can depend on a variety of factors, such as whether 'it was determined by a "strong" Court', or one 'composed of judges of great reputation', or by 'a single judge distinguished for his learning'. James Ram, *A Practical Treatise of Assets, Debts and Incumbrances* (Philadelphia: Littell, 1835; orig. English edn 1832), pp. iii–iv.

[56] See Jim Evans, 'Change in the Doctrine of Precedent during the Nineteenth Century', in *Precedent in Law*, 35–72 at 57–63.

[57] Cf. Richard Nobles and David Schiff, *A Sociology of Jurisprudence* (Oxford: Hart, 2006), 72–86, who similarly observe that classical positivism cannot satisfactorily account for *stare decisis* but who use modern systems theory to explain the failure.

It would be silly, however, to think that the problem which *stare decisis* poses for classical legal positivism is unimportant because the doctrine did not properly come into being until the heyday of classical positivist writing had passed. The proposition that judges are bound by precedents does raise a serious jurisprudential question: how are they so bound, if not by threat of legal sanction? Hobbes and his immediate heirs did not answer this question (as we have observed, not surprisingly) and so they left later philosophers of legal authority with a great deal of work to do. But what is surprising is the jurisprudence produced by the immediate heirs of Austin. These jurists did not have the excuse that the doctrine of precedent had not yet found its feet. They had every reason to discuss the doctrine, and indeed most of them did discuss it. Their focus, however, was invariably on specific technical difficulties – the questions of how to determine the *ratio decidendi* of a case and whether a court of last resort should be able to review its own former decisions were perennial favourites – rather than on the general problem of how legal positivism might explain the authority of judicial precedents.[58] English jurisprudence in the wake of Austin, as Hart appreciated, was more often than not an exercise in explaining the common law rather than in developing legal philosophy.[59]

It was Hart who turned the tide. *The Concept of Law* was first published in 1961, the same year that marked the appearance of the first edition of Rupert Cross's *Precedent in English Law*.[60] Jurisprudential analyses of precedent often draw upon a passage in *The Concept of Law* in which the notion of precedent does not explicitly feature – the passage in which Hart discusses the principle of treating like cases alike.[61] Since precedent-following entails the idea of comparing like cases it is not

---

[58] See, e.g., A. L. Goodhart, *Essays in Jurisprudence and the Common Law* (Cambridge: Cambridge University Press, 1931), 1–26; Frederick Pollock, *A First Book of Jurisprudence for Students of the Common Law* (London: Macmillan, 1896), 309–25.

[59] See H. L. A. Hart, 'Philosophy of Law and Jurisprudence in Britain (1945–1952)' (1953) 2 *Am. J. Compar. L.* 355–64 at 357–8.

[60] Each of these two authors, in the preface to his book, thanks the other for reading and commenting on the typescript. Both books were published in the Clarendon Law Series, which Hart edited at that time. For Hart on Cross's views on precedent, and for his account of their jointly-conducted seminars on criminal responsibility in the 1960s, see H. L. A. Hart, 'Arthur Rupert Neale Cross, 1912–1980' (1984) 70 *Proc. Brit. Acad.* 405–37 at 428–33.

[61] H. L. A. Hart, *The Concept of Law*, 2nd edn (Oxford: Clarendon Press, 1994), 159–60. Hereafter *CL*. For a representative jurisprudential analysis, see Kenneth I. Winston, 'On Treating Like Cases Alike' (1974) 62 *California L. Rev.* 1–39.

surprising that Hart's discussion of this principle should be fairly prominent in the relevant jurisprudential literature. Only from a more general reading of *The Concept of Law*, however, does it become clear how the idea of judges being constrained by precedent, even though not subject to specific sanctions for ignoring precedent, is not incompatible with legal positivism.

The basic elements of Hart's legal philosophy are well known, and so they can be presented with the minimal detail necessary to show how he upgraded the positivist conception of precedent. Social rules differ from habits, Hart observed, because they provide reasons to act in particular ways. Nevertheless, 'to use in connection with rules of this kind the words "obligation" or "duty" would be misleading'.[62] Social rules exist wherever there applies to a group a standard of behaviour deviation from which is likely to lead to criticism and pressure for conformity. Though members of the group may 'feel bound' to behave appropriately because of the anticipated consequences of deviation, 'such feelings are neither necessary nor sufficient for the existence of "binding" rules'.[63] The distinguishing feature of rules which create an obligation, rather than merely make one feel obliged, has often been attributed to the fact that the sanctions for their breach tend to be 'definite and officially organized'[64] and therefore knowable in advance. But Hart exposed the inadequacies of this predictive theory. Although an observer might anticipate that a judge will apply a particular legal rule to punish an offender, thereby looking to the rule to predict the outcome, the judge himself will 'not look upon the rule as a statement that he and others are likely to punish deviations'.[65] Rather, the judge 'takes the rule as his *guide* and the breach of the rule as his *reason* and *justification* for punishing the offender'.[66] The rule functions as a legal rule because the judge recognizes its validity from what Hart called the internal point of view; that is, 'the rule satisfies the tests for identifying what is to count as law in his court'.[67]

One of the reasons that the internal point of view represents such a crucial development in the philosophy of legal positivism is that it illustrates why certain types of practice, such as the conventions of precedent-following or of statutory interpretation, can still be understood as authoritative even though they might not be backed by

---

[62] *CL*, 86. [63] *CL*, 57. [64] *CL*, 10. [65] *CL*, 11. [66] *Ibid*.
[67] *CL*, 105. In much the same vein, see G. J. Warnock, *The Object of Morality* (London: Methuen, 1971), 54, 62–3.

penalties for non-compliance.[68] Hart famously explains the internal point of view as the adoption of 'a critical reflective attitude'[69] to patterns of behaviour which are shared by people engaged in a common enterprise such as a game or, indeed, adjudication. To say that judges adopt an internal point of view towards the activity of judging is to say that they accept the rules which apply to that activity as standards for the appraisal of their own behaviour and the behaviour of other judges.[70] 'Individual courts of the system though they may, on occasion, deviate from these rules must, in general, be critically concerned with such deviations as lapses from standards'.[71] That system is intelligible as a system of legal authority because judges generally identify certain patterns of behaviour, such as precedent-following, as composing 'a public, common standard of correct judicial decision'.[72] When judges follow precedents they do so not because they fear the imposition of a sanction, but because precedent-following is regarded among them as correct practice, as a norm, deviation from which is likely to be viewed negatively.

Although Hart's explanation of the internal point of view has often been understood to mean the adoption of a critical reflective attitude towards rules, and although his regular emphasis in *The Concept of Law* on the 'internal aspect of rules' almost forces this interpretation, it is important to note that his more general argument is that the internal point of view is adopted not primarily towards rules but towards 'certain patterns of behaviour'.[73] His occasional remarks on precedent illustrate the point. Though a system of precedent may 'produce ... a body of rules',[74] he observes, a precedent itself might best be described not as a

---

[68] Although Hart's explication of the internal point of view highlights the inadequacy of sanction-centred theories of law, it would be a complete mistake to think that Hart was therefore of the view that law need not contain sanctions. ' "Sanctions" are ... required' in all apart from the smallest, most closely-knit societies, he argued, 'not as the normal motive for obedience, but as a *guarantee* that those who would voluntarily obey shall not be sacrificed to those who would not. To obey, without this, would be to risk going to the wall.' *CL*, 198.

[69] *CL*, 57.

[70] *CL*, 98. See, generally, Scott J. Shapiro, 'What is the Internal Point of View?' (2006) 75 *Fordham L. Rev.* 1157–70.

[71] *CL*, 116.   [72] *Ibid*.

[73] *CL*, 57. For salutary warnings against interpreting the critical reflective attitude as directed towards rules and nothing else, see Matthew H. Kramer, *In Defense of Legal Positivism: Law without Trimmings* (Oxford: Oxford University Press, 1999), 251–3; Jules L. Coleman, *The Practice of Principle: In Defence of a Pragmatist Approach to Legal Theory* (Oxford: Oxford University Press, 2001), 82–3.

[74] *CL*, 135.

legal rule but as an instance of 'communication by authoritative example'.[75] Like legal rules, these examples are 'open-textured',[76] and 'there is no authoritative or uniquely correct formulation of any rule to be extracted from cases'.[77] The extraction of a rule from a case might lead a court to narrow or widen the range of instances to which the case applies[78]; and so it might be claimed that judges, by virtue of the doctrine of precedent, are able to engage in 'legislative activity', to 'perform a rule-producing function' which is 'very like the exercise of delegated-rule making powers by an administrative body'.[79]

The argument that judges can make law is not, however, the one which Hart wanted to emphasize. It is certainly important to concede that a common-law system of precedent gives rise to indeterminacy – that case-law may yield not 'one uniquely correct answer' to a problem but only answers which are 'a reasonable compromise between many conflicting interests' – and that in cases of indeterminacy judges exercise discretion.[80] But it is a 'salient fact', he stresses, that 'the life of the law consists to a very large extent in the guidance both of officials and private individuals by determinate rules which, unlike the applications of variable standards, do *not* require from them a fresh judgment from case to case.'[81] The rule-sceptic's 'contention that ... there is nothing to circumscribe the area of open-texture' ignores the fact that the law embodies 'legal standards of behaviour' which are accepted, by judges and others, from the internal point of view.[82]

3. A theory of precedent?

Hart's notion of the internal point of view enables us to see that the language of classical legal positivism does not serve us well for the purpose of understanding the authority of judicial precedent. Indeed, his reflections help us to see why one nineteenth-century civilian writer should have believed (incorrectly) that precedential authority has to be understood 'less as a command and more as advice, compliance with which cannot reasonably be withheld',[83] and why one modern-day

---

[75] CL, 126–7.   [76] CL, 128.   [77] CL, 134.   [78] See CL, 134–5.
[79] CL, 135.   [80] CL, 131–2.   [81] CL, 135.   [82] CL, 137–8.
[83] Theodor Mommsen, *Römisches Staatsrecht*, 3 vols., 3rd edn (Graz: Akademische Druck- und Verlagsanstalt, 1953; 3rd edn, orig. publ. 1887–8), III², 1034 ('... mehr als ein Ratschlag und weniger als ein Befehl, ein Ratschlag, dessen Befolgung man sich nicht füglich entziehen kann'). The belief is incorrect because (as Hart appreciated) one will often have good reasons for not following a precedent.

English judge should have likened precedents to Jewish mothers.[84] Specific decisions can be especially weighty – because of the eminence of the judge, say, or the composition of and consensus among the decision-making panel. Sometimes, furthermore, the authority of precedent will rest not in a specific decision but in a series of decisions which sediment to form something which lawyers and judges will commonly refer to as a 'rule', even though this rule might not have been expressly formulated in the case law.[85] Jurists will often do much of the work in constructing or amplifying the rule – indeed, it is in legal treatises and textbooks that we most commonly find case-law cast in the form of concise, rule-like statements.[86] Judges are under no obligation to pay attention to jurists; nevertheless, treatise and textbook writers' accounts of rules and principles will often become established in professional usage, and so their explanations and summaries of what particular decisions or lines of decision stand for may well have an impact in chamber and in the courtroom as well as in the classroom.

Perhaps it is because case-law is often treated and presented as if it were itself a body of legal rules that it is sometimes assumed that precedents have binding force rather as statutory rules have binding force. But the reality is that precedents, unlike statutes, do not bind judges in an all-or-nothing fashion, that the binding force of a precedent is best explained not in terms of its validity (this being a non-scalar concept) but in terms of its authority (of which there can be degrees).[87] Indeed, not for nothing is this study concerned with the nature and *authority* of precedent. If judges were bound by precedents much as they are bound by statutes, the opportunities for judge-made law to evolve would be considerably limited; but if precedents had absolutely no capacity to constrain, there would be no point to the doctrine of *stare decisis*. The idea of precedents having authority is meant to capture the fact that the truth lies somewhere between these two extremes, that the

---

[84] Stephen Sedley, *On Never Doing Anything for the First Time* (Reform Club, London. Atkin Lecture, 2001), 6 ('Precedent is a Jewish mother. You don't have to do what it tells you, but it makes you feel terrible about not doing it').

[85] See N. E. Simmonds, *The Decline of Juridical Reason: Doctrine and Theory in the Legal Order* (Manchester: Manchester University Press, 1984), 115–16.

[86] See Roscoe Pound, 'What of *Stare Decisis*?' (1941) 10 *Fordham L. Rev.* 1–13 at 7, 13; Max Radin, 'The Method of Law' [1950] *Washington Univ. L. Q.* 471–97 at 472–3; Ronald Dworkin, *Taking Rights Seriously*, rev. edn (London: Duckworth, 1977), 110–11.

[87] See Perry, 'Judicial Obligation, Precedent and the Common Law', 243; Schauer, 'Precedent', 591–2; and, more generally, Richard Bronaugh, 'Persuasive Precedent', in *Precedent in Law*, 217–47.

law that courts create is the law they often feel obligated and are obligated to follow.[88]

It might be objected that this simply returns us to the unhelpful proposition that precedents can only bind judges intellectually. It would be useful to know why judges should sometimes feel obliged to follow precedents, and why sometimes they should not. One response might be that a court feels an obligation to follow a precedent because the precedent provides the correct answer to the problem at hand. But this response is unenlightening. The correct answer is simply the judgment of an earlier court, and the fact that the present court is favourably disposed to that answer does not mean that the present court is required to follow it. All the response tells us, in fact, is that we might expect the present court to choose to follow the precedent because it likes the answer which the precedent generates. The authority of the precedent is independent of the court's view as to its correctness or incorrectness; indeed, common-law judges occasionally observe that the fact that they consider an earlier decision to be incorrect is unlikely to be a sufficient reason for their departing from it.[89] But how, then, are we to explain precedent following? Judicial precedents clearly do have *some* authority – indeed, their capacity to constrain decision-makers can be considerable – but from where does this authority derive?

It is important not only to think of judicial precedents as authoritative rather than as having the qualities of binding legal rules, but also to appreciate that the authority of precedent resists satisfactory explanation by reference to some overarching theory. Precedents have authority for a variety of reasons. Perhaps the most commonly cited reason is that to accept precedents as authoritative is to facilitate consistency and fairness in decision-making: when decision-makers treat precedents as

---

[88] Cf. Roger A. Shiner, 'Precedent, Discretion and Fairness', in *Law, Morality and Rights*, ed. M. A. Stewart (Dordrecht: Reidel, 1983), 93–136 at 102 ('it will not do either to try to represent the "must" of binding precedent as the "must" of logical necessity, or to move from the reasons for rejecting that thought to eschewing talk of courts' being "bound" altogether').

[89] See, e.g., *Knuller* v. *DPP* [1973] AC 435, 455, *per* Lord Reid. For the argument that the authority of a precedent depends on whether or not it offers an objectively just solution to the problem at hand, see Rudolph Laun, 'Stare Decisis' (1938) 25 *Virginia L. Rev.* 12–25 at 21–2. Laun, who was clearly a civilian jurist, appears to be strongly influenced by the primarily nineteenth-century Germanic argument that the authority of the positive law depends upon its capacity to reflect and promote popular feelings of right (*Rechtsgefühl*) – or, as Laun puts it, 'the given sense of justice of the people' (*ibid.*, 21).

constraints they increase the likelihood that like cases will be treated alike. The implications of this proposition are considered in detail in chapter 5, though the commonest objection to it – that the notion of treating like cases alike is an empty one until supplemented by some explanation of what is to count as material likeness[90] – is easily anticipated. The main point of chapter 2 is to show that this reason cannot explain the emergence of a doctrine of precedent in English law, for the idea that like cases ought to be treated alike not only long predates *stare decisis* – it can be found in classical Greek philosophy – but was accepted by common lawyers before they began to treat individual decisions as legal authorities.

The English doctrine of *stare decisis* did not begin to take shape until the eighteenth century. Why should *stare decisis* have come into being at this particular point in history? Some jurists have seen more than just coincidence in the fact that classical legal positivism and the doctrine of binding precedent emerge in roughly the same period, and various arguments have been advanced to the effect that the first development is the main cause of the second. It is claimed in chapter 2 that none of these arguments is convincing. The principal reason for the emergence of *stare decisis*, I shall argue, is the change in the structure of the trial during the sixteenth century: parties began to settle pleadings in advance of the hearing, thus leaving arguments concerning the sufficiency of those pleadings to be addressed post-verdict. A consequence of this development was that judges began more regularly to produce reasoned decisions rather than merely steer parties towards agreement on what should be pleaded. As judges began more regularly to produce reasoned decisions, case-law began increasingly to take the form of what we nowadays recognize to be judicial precedent. This process was aided, in due course, by the establishment of reliable, professionally-operated law reports, the development of shorthand and its utilization by reporters and, in the 1870s, the introduction of the hierarchical appellate court system. But these developments consolidated rather than produced the doctrine of *stare decisis*. The first and crucial stage in the development of *stare decisis* was that judgments came to be supported by reasons.

Part of the explanation for the authority of judicial precedents, then, is that they provide reasons for a decision. But anybody who has read any case law knows that the reasons supporting a decision can be many and varied. Which reasons count? Assuming this question can be

---

[90] See Hart, *CL*, 159.

answered, furthermore, how do the reasons which count have authority? Why, that is, should later decision-makers look to them and conclude that they are not only reasons but reasons which it makes sense to follow? In determining which reasons count, common lawyers traditionally speak of a distinction between the reason for deciding, or *ratio decidendi*, and the tangential observations, or *obiter dicta*, normally provided by judges in the process of reaching the decision. Speaking of the distinction is often much easier than making it: the reason for a decision and the tangential observations are often not easily extricated from one another, some cases appear not to yield a *ratio* and many yield more than one. In chapter 3 we consider these and other difficulties that jurists have identified with the notion of a *ratio decidendi*, along with their principal efforts to render that notion determinable. None of these efforts is entirely successful, and it is not at all surprising that some jurists have concluded that the quest to determine a sure-fire method of determining the *ratio decidendi* of a case is bound to fail. Nor is it surprising, however, that the quest should have been undertaken. Academic lawyers want to guide students in the art of extracting important information from case law, and quite often consider advising the judiciary to be part of their scholarly function, and so it would have been odd indeed if jurists were completely unmoved by the challenge of devising a method by which anyone from the legal novice to the most senior judge could reliably and without too much difficulty determine the authoritative part of a precedent.

If the *ratio* guiding yesterday's decision persuades decision-makers today, they may as well reapply it when required to decide on materially identical facts. A precedent, in other words, might be followed because it is a ready-made answer to a problem that has already been litigated. The reason for following the precedent in this instance is instrumental: the precedent is a shortcut which saves today's court the cost of considering the problem afresh. Using precedents as shortcuts has its hazards. A court might settle on an applicable precedent too readily, failing to see that the case in hand is significantly different from the earlier one or involves deeper issues of principle (the more we rely on precedents, Dr Johnson is supposed to have remarked, the less often we will take principles seriously),[91] so raising the likelihood of later courts having

---

[91] See Samuel Johnson to Sir Alexander Macdonald, 27 March 1772, cited in Boswell, *The Life of Samuel Johnson*, 468 ('the more precedents there are, the less occasion is there for law; that is to say, the less occasion is there for investigating principles').

to revisit the problem. No doubt part of the explanation for the authority of judicial precedents, none the less, is that judges value them as ready-made reasons which can often cut the costs of decision-making. A somewhat less obvious explanation of precedent-following is that the judge who decides cases according to the doctrine of *stare decisis* recognizes precedents to be authoritative directives which cut off any latitude for him to reach a decision on the basis of his own independent judgment. As an explanation of the authority of precedents in particular, this 'exclusionary' account ought to be treated with caution: although the occasional, unequivocally-worded precedent might well operate in an exclusionary fashion, most allow judges considerable scope to use their own independent judgment to modify and extend legal principles without necessarily disturbing the precedent itself.

The doctrine of precedent entails both constraint and creativity. If precedents bound absolutely, we have noted already, judges would have very little capacity and opportunity to develop the common law; but if judges could ignore precedents completely, the doctrine would not exist in any meaningful sense. The purpose of chapter 4 is to consider the principal ways in which the doctrine of precedent enables judges to contribute to the growth of the common law. When judges distinguish cases they sometimes exercise a modest and constrained law-making function by amending the identified *ratio* of a precedent so that it henceforth applies only when there arises both the material facts to be found in the precedent case plus some further fact or set of facts. Overruling, like distinguishing, changes a common law ruling established by a precedent. By comparison, however, it is a bolder and more explicit act of law-making: whereas distinguishing a precedent means modifying its *ratio*, overruling means repealing it. It is not surprising, therefore, that common law courts of last resort have overruled their own precedents only when there are special reasons for so doing; indeed, for much of the twentieth century the House of Lords went so far as to accept the principle that it was virtually always bound to follow its own decisions. No doubt one of the reasons that courts overrule only exceptionally is that the court which overruled frequently would risk making a mockery of *stare decisis*. One of the objectives of chapter 4, nevertheless, is to show that overruling is not merely compatible with but peculiarly supportive of *stare decisis*; for if it is accepted that a purpose of the doctrine is to curb the arbitrary exercise of judicial discretion, courts ought to be able to overrule precedents, their own precedents included, in order to correct earlier precedents which misrepresent the range of legitimate judicial discretion on particular points of law.

Controversy surrounding the House of Lords' power to overrule its own precedents has less to do with the power itself than with the manner in which it was acquired. The binding force of judicial precedent is often explained in terms of hierarchy: generally, that is, a court is said to be bound to follow precedents established by a superior court. But precedent can work horizontally as well as vertically – that is, judges might be bound by the precedents of a court of co-ordinate jurisdiction, or by precedents of their own court's making. The statement that a court is bound by its own precedents usually refers to the fact that a court of last resort has resolved to treat its own prior decisions as always correct. Nowadays, the supreme courts of the major common law jurisdictions do not consider themselves bound to follow their own precedents – even though, as already noted, they do not overrule those precedents lightly. Generally, within common law jurisdictions, the fact that courts of final appeal have determined for themselves how they will treat their own precedents has caused little or no controversy. England, however, is something of an exception. We will see in chapter 4 that when, in 1966, the House of Lords declared that it would henceforth be free to depart from its own precedents, many academic lawyers cried foul.

Why should anybody have objected to the House of Lords' initiative? By 1966, nobody appeared to be of the view that it was desirable for the House to be committed to following its own precedents. Indeed, some of those precedents made for such questionable or unwelcome law that it seemed wrong not to overrule them. So, why cry foul? One objection was that it was for Parliament, rather than the House of Lords, to change the status of the House of Lords' precedents. Various jurisprudential arguments are rehearsed in chapter 4 in an effort to show why the House of Lords' initiative could be accepted as legitimate even though constitutionally questionable. A second objection was that the House of Lords' manoeuvre was self-referential and illogical – an effort to establish a binding precedent to the effect that its precedents do not bind. It is argued in chapter 4 not only that this objection cannot be sustained but that, even if the objection could be sustained, evidence of the illogicality of the manoeuvre would hardly be tantamount to demonstrating its invalidity. Indeed if there is an erroneous assumption from which this second objection derives, it is that law must meet the tests of logic.

'Very weighty considerations underlie the principle that courts should not lightly overrule past decisions', the second Justice Harlan observed. 'Among these are the desirability that the law furnish a clear guide for the conduct of individuals, to enable them to plan their affairs with assurance against untoward surprise; the importance of furthering fair and expeditious adjudication by eliminating the need to relitigate every relevant proposition in every case; and the necessity of maintaining public faith in the judiciary as a source of impersonal and reasoned judgments. The reasons for rejecting any established rule must always be weighed against these factors.'[92] The final chapter of this book examines these and other considerations for following precedents. Most justifications of precedent seek to support the activity by reference to its consequences. The persuasiveness of any consequentialist justification of precedent-following will depend upon what we think of the consequences; indeed, what one person discerns to be a laudable objective for following a precedent might be interpreted by another person as a lamentable objective. By following a precedent, one observer might argue, a judge has commendably avoided spending time and energy doing the reasoning which has already been done, or done in large measure, by an earlier court. But another observer might consider this judge unduly expedient or even lazy, relying on a precedent too readily when the case at hand in fact requires fresh deliberation. The primary deontological argument for precedent-following, that there is inherent value in treating like cases alike, demands not only an explanation of what it means for two cases to be alike – cases, like snowflakes, are never identical – but also demonstration that treating cases thus really is intrinsically good. There are many reasons to be suspicious, we will see, of the basic claim that like cases should be treated alike. Ensuring consistency of treatment among similarly-situated parties requires criteria for determining what it means to be similarly-situated. Predicting one's chances of success in court will be difficult if not impossible if one cannot be sure that the court will treat as a precedent the case which one considers to be like one's own. When a court struggles to choose between conflicting precedents, or where the meaning of an earlier judgment is ambiguous, it might well be that the decision-making process is more protracted than would have been the case had the matter been resolved without any consideration of existing case-law.

That there are limitations to arguments for precedent-following on grounds of consistency, predictability, efficiency and so on does not mean that such arguments are unsupportable. Rather, the central claim

[92] *Moragne v. States Marine, Inc.*, 398 U.S. 375, 403 (1970).

of this final chapter is that any account of precedential authority is necessarily contingent and incomplete. The claim is not intended as a criticism, for the necessarily limited nature of any justification of precedent-following has no significant bearing on the suitability of the practice to common-law decision-making. Just as judges are not bound by precedents in the classical positivist sense, so too arguments which support following judicial precedent are never water-tight. The reasons for following precedents, we might say, are, like precedents themselves, always defeasible. Perhaps common lawyers would be less attracted to deciding by precedent were this not the case.

2

Why does English law have a doctrine of precedent?

Showing that there is a precedent to support a decision is often a good way of ensuring that the decision is taken. But pointing to a precedent will not always be sufficient to make one's actions authoritative. Children sometimes argue rigidly and remorselessly from the premise of like treatment, yet their citations of precedent, rather than bolstering their cases, will often show that they have grasped neither the bigger picture, nor the range of experiences and concepts on which a more mature decision-maker would rely. Not that the danger of over-dependence on precedent is confined to children. Constant recourse to precedent might indicate that a decision-maker has few or no other solutions at his disposal; indeed, the domain of precedent can sometimes be that proverbial box outside which the unimaginative fail to think. Confidence in the decision-maker who constantly follows previous decisions could diminish over time, furthermore, because unswerving adherence to precedent might betray a fondness for the easy option or an unwillingness to think seriously about what is at stake. So it is that great jurists and judges have appreciated that adjudication calls for valour as well as caution, and that occasionally the decision which is likely to command our attention and respect in the future is the one which rejects what we did in the past.[1]

1. The formation of a doctrine of precedent

There exists a considerable amount of rigorous historical research charting the development of the doctrine of precedent between

---

[1] See Frederick Pollock, 'Judicial Caution and Valour' (1929) 45 *LQR* 293–306; also *Candler* v. *Crane, Christmas & Co.* [1951] 2 KB 164, 178, CA, *per* Denning L.J. ('the timorous souls ... were fearful of allowing a new cause of action. On the other side there were the bold spirits who were ready to allow it if justice so required. It was fortunate for the common law that the progressive view prevailed').

medieval and modern times. One of the main insights of this research is that common-law judges have not always resorted to earlier judicial decisions as sources of authority. This is not to say that medieval common lawyers never took account of precedent. Maitland showed that as early as the thirteenth century, precedents could be entered on a plea roll as the source of a plea, and that litigants and advocates would very occasionally search the rolls for precedents which might help their cause.[2] But the notion of precedent which existed in the medieval courts was very different from that which was to emerge later. The medieval judicial precedent was, strictly speaking, nothing more than the judgment entered on the plea roll; the reasons informing the judgment and the guiding authorities, if there were any, formed no part of the record, and, since legal discussion normally preceded the trial, one could be sure neither of what had been argued nor that there had been argument at all.[3] While courts would occasionally follow and even distinguish precedents,[4] nobody yet believed that a court could be bound by a previous decision. Far more important was the common erudition of the legal profession, as kept alive primarily by the oral traditions of the Inns of Court and Chancery.[5] Medieval law reporters did sometimes write down the observations of judges, but in doing so they were not necessarily reporting authoritative proclamations of common erudition; indeed, it may well have been that some of these observations were considered worthy of note because they were decidedly unorthodox.[6] Certainly, a precedent could make an impression on lawyers because it was evidence of common learning, but no single precedent would be accepted as authority in preference to such

---

[2] Frederick Pollock and Frederic William Maitland, *The History of English Law Before the Time of Edward I*, 2nd edn, 2 vols. (Cambridge: Cambridge University Press, 1968 [1898]), I, 184 nn 1–2. The plea rolls, which commenced in 1194, are the records of the steps taken in litigation in the central common-law courts.

[3] J. H. Baker, *The Law's Two Bodies: Some Evidential Problems in English Legal History* (Oxford: Oxford University Press, 2001), 30–1.

[4] See Pollock and Maitland, *The History of English Law*, I, 183–4; J.W. Tubbs, *The Common Law Mind: Medieval and Early Modern Conceptions* (Baltimore: Johns Hopkins University Press, 2000), 43–4. Proper citation of a precedent required voucher of the record of judgment: J. H. Baker, *An Introduction to English Legal History*, 4th edn (London: Butterworths, 2002), 197.

[5] See J. H. Baker, *The Third University of England: The Inns of Court and the Common-law Tradition* (London: Selden Society, 1990), 12–22; 'Introduction' (1977) 94 *Selden Society* 23–396 at 123–4, 161.

[6] See Baker, 'Introduction', 160–1; *Law's Two Bodies*, 19–20.

learning.⁷ Indeed although, in the medieval courts, precedents were sometimes treated as evidence of what the law was commonly held to be, the occasional judge or serjeant would pointedly remark that precedents must not be mistaken for law.⁸

The status of judicial precedents began to change in the early Tudor period. During the second half of the sixteenth century the idea of common learning was still evident in the case-law.⁹ However the revival of the special verdict, and an increasing inclination on the part of judges to determine the law by decisions on demurrer and motions after trial, meant that courts were more likely to treat earlier decisions as supportive (though not determinative) of a particular result, at least where those decisions were accompanied by reasons.¹⁰ The sixteenth-century lawyer's tendency to rely ever more on abridgements, and the emergence during this period of compilations of cases illustrating points of law settled by the central courts, probably also contributed to the increased

---

⁷ See J. H. Baker, 'Records, Reports and the Origins of Case-Law in England', in *Judicial Records, Law Reports, and the Growth of Case Law*, ed. J. H. Baker (Berlin: Duncker & Humblot, 1989), 15–46 at 38; *Law's Two Bodies*, 68–70; 'Introduction', 163 ('There is implicit in all the discussions a reverence, not for the single decision, but for the current of authority or the most reasonable opinion: that, presumably, is what "common erudition" was'). Even if the medieval courts had been inclined to treat particular cases as authority, the manner in which the Year Book manuscripts were compiled militated against the practice. 'There was no standard means of referencing a case, no standard pagination or foliation in the manuscripts; there would not always even have been a standard text. A particularly famous case might be known by its name, but for the most part references were vague or, increasingly through the fifteenth century, to "our books" rather than to any instance within them.' David J. Ibbetson, 'Case Law and Judicial Precedents in Mediaeval and Early-Modern England', in *Auctoritates. Xenia R. C. van Caenegem Oblata*, ed. S. Dauchy, J. Monballyu and A. Wijffels (Brussels: Wetenschappelijk Comité voor Rechtsdeschiedenis, 1997), 55–68 at 67. The problem of referencing was eased once the Year Books had been printed and, in the process, supplemented with a standard citation form; but the task of printing them all was not completed until 1558.

⁸ See the opinions cited by Tubbs, *The Common Law Mind*, 45; and Baker, *Law's Two Bodies*, 30–1, 99–100. The attitude seems to have been that '[t]here is all the difference in the world between the argument that we should do something now because we did it once before, and the argument that we should do something now because that is what we do.' Ibbetson, 'Case Law and Judicial Precedents', 68.

⁹ See Baker, *Law's Two Bodies*, 81.

¹⁰ Baker, *Introduction to English Legal History*, 198–9; also Ibbetson, 'Case Law and Judicial Precedents', 61 ('By 1600 we find judges giving explicit recognition to previous cases as reasons for their decision in a later case. There was a sense that a prior judicial decision itself was an authority which pointed in the direction of some particular result in a later case, even if it did not absolutely determine it').

emphasis on case-law as a source of authority.[11] This subtle shift in emphasis was certainly evident to Coke in his *Commentary upon Littleton*: 'our book cases are the best proofs what the Law is', he wrote, and 'are principally to be cited for the deciding of cases in question, and not any private opinion', for an argument drawn from authority is the strongest in law ('Argumentum ab authoritate est fortissimum in Lege').[12]

But although, by the seventeenth century, the courts were paying more attention to precedents than they ever had before, it would be a mistake to think that judges now considered individual decisions to be binding. Hale C.J. professed to abide by the principle of *stare decisis* in the 1670s, but he did not conceive of courts being bound to follow precedents.[13] Other judges of the period, including Hale's colleague, Vaughan C.J., emphasized their obligation to abide by statutes, and in declining to follow precedents would cite the Roman maxim *judicandum est legibus non exemplis* (adjudication is to be according to declared law, not precedent).[14] Vaughan also echoed Hobbes, observing that if a judge considers the judgment of another court to be erroneous, then 'he ... in his own conscience ought not to give the like judgment, for that were to wrong every man having a like cause, because another was wronged before'.[15] Precedents were valued and could be significant, but the doctrine of *stare decisis* as modern common lawyers understand it would not emerge for some time yet.

The last three paragraphs point to a straightforward conclusion: the common law does not need the doctrine of precedent in order to function. 'In the period around 1600', Gray has observed, '*stare decisis*

---

[11] See John P. Dawson, *The Oracles of the Law* (Buffalo: Hein, 1986 [1968]), 64–5; J. H. Baker, 'English Law and the Renaissance' (1985) 44 *Cambridge L.J.* 46–61 at 57, 59–60; *An Introduction to English Legal History*, 188.

[12] Sir Edward Coke, *The First Part of the Institutes of the Laws of England. Or, a Commentary upon Littleton*, 10th edn (London: printed by Harper & Walthoe, 1703; 1st edn pub. 1628), 254a. See also Baker, *The Law's Two Bodies*, 81–2.

[13] See *Hanslap* v. *Cater* (1673) 1 Vent. 243 ('he said it was his rule, *stare decisis*'); *Kirkbright* v. *Curwin* (1676) 3 Keb. 311.

[14] See, e.g., *Bishop of Oxford* v. *Eades* (1667) Vaugh. 18, 27; *Harris* v. *Colliton* (1658) Hard. 120, 122.

[15] *Bole* v. *Horton* (1673) Vaugh. 360, 383. Cf. Hobbes, *Leviathan*, II. 26. 24 ('[A]ll the sentences of precedent judges that have ever been, cannot altogether make a law contrary to natural equity ... [T]here is no place in the world, where [a manifest condemnation of the innocent] can be an interpretation of a law of nature, or be made a law by the sentences of precedent judges, that had done the same. For he that judged first, judged unjustly; and no injustice can be a pattern of judgment to succeeding judges').

was not the governing rule ... [J]udges ... argued ... about whether such and such is a rule of law, without feeling compelled in the more modern manner to prove it by decided cases.'[16] 'To a historian at least', Simpson elaborates:

> any identification between the common law system and the doctrine of precedent, any attempt to explain the nature of the common law in terms of *stare decisis*, is bound to seem unsatisfactory, for the elaboration of rules and principles governing the use of precedents and their status as authorities is relatively modern, and the idea that there could be binding precedents more recent still. The common law had been in existence for centuries before anybody was very excited about these matters, and yet it functioned as a system of law without such props as the concept of the *ratio decidendi*, and functioned well enough.[17]

Not until the eighteenth century does the modern doctrine of *stare decisis* begin to take shape;[18] indeed, as was observed in the previous chapter, we are some decades into the next century before it becomes what we would now consider fully formed. Acknowledging as much raises the important question of timing: why should precedent have moved from the periphery to the nub of the common law system just when it did?

Answering this question by pointing to the virtues associated with *stare decisis* does not get us very far. The argument that precedent-following became accepted judicial practice because lawyers and litigants value the benefits that it brings – benefits such as consistency of

---

[16] Charles M. Gray, 'Parliament, Liberty, and the Law', in *Parliament and Liberty from the Reign of Elizabeth to the English Civil War*, ed. J. H. Hexter (Stanford: Stanford University Press, 1992), 155–200 at 158–9.

[17] A. W. B. Simpson, 'The Common Law and Legal Theory', in *Oxford Essays in Jurisprudence*, 2nd ser., ed. A. W. B. Simpson (Oxford: Clarendon Press, 1973), 77–99 at 77. The concept of the *ratio decidendi* or 'reason for deciding' is examined in the next chapter.

[18] See Gerald J. Postema, 'Philosophy of the Common Law', in *The Oxford Handbook of Jurisprudence and Philosophy of Law*, ed. J. Coleman and S. Shapiro (Oxford: Oxford University Press, 2002), 588–622 at 589. In the United States, the doctrine starts to take shape in the early decades of the nineteenth century (see Frederick G. Kempin, Jr., 'Precedent and *Stare Decisis*: The Critical Years, 1800 to 1850' (1959) 3 *Am. J. Leg. Hist.* 28–54) although, as in England, the notion of precedents as evidence of the law clearly existed before that period: see Charles J. Reid, Jr., 'Judicial Precedent in the Late Eighteenth and Early Nineteenth Centuries: A Commentary on Chancellor Kent's Commentaries' (2006) *Univ. of St. Thomas Legal Studies Research Paper* no. 06–28; also William E. Nelson, *The Americanization of the Common Law: The Impact of Legal Change on Massachusetts Society, 1760–1830* (Cambridge, Mass.: Harvard University Press, 1975), 18–20, 154–6.

treatment, legal certainty and efficiency in decision-making – raises yet more troublesome questions. First of all, why not invert the argument? Lawyers and litigants, after all, may place a similar value on not following precedent: when a court follows a decision and thereby rules in one party's favour, the losing party will probably wish the court had not followed that decision. Secondly, and more importantly for our purposes, why, if we value benefits such as consistency, certainty and efficiency in decision-making, has *stare decisis* not always been a feature of the common law? One possible answer is that these benefits can only be properly appreciated once precedent-following has become a convention and the rewards of the activity are being reaped: perhaps the reason the doctrine of precedent evolved very gradually, in other words, is that common lawyers were not quick to recognize its virtues. But it is not clear why common lawyers should not always have valued the benefits associated with precedent-following much as they do today. It is certainly possible that modern expectations of legal systems, rather like modern expectations of medicine, are higher than they were in the past – that, as compared with earlier generations, we are less resigned to, say, inconsistency or uncertainty or inefficiency in legal decision-making. But conceding this possibility does not explain why the doctrine of precedent did not develop at an earlier stage in the history of the common law, because what we expect the law to achieve is likely to be something different from what we would like it to achieve. Consider, for example, consistency of treatment as one of the benefits to be derived from precedent-following. Even if medieval lawyers and litigants believed that courts were unlikely to be adept at, say, ensuring that like cases are treated alike, this would not have stopped them from *wanting* like cases to be treated alike. Aristotle considered the impulse to dispense such treatment a basic element of justice.[19] There is certainly some evidence that this impulse informed common-law thinking long before the emergence of *stare decisis*. The author of Bracton explicitly acknowledged the principle that like cases should be adjudged alike, and in the Year books we find not only the same but also judges occasionally taking the trouble to say why particular cases were *not* alike.[20] The crucial and

---

[19] *Nicomachean Ethics*, V. 2. 1131^a–1131^b.

[20] See J. H. Baker, 'Records, Reports and the Origins of Case-Law in England', in *Judicial Records, Law Reports, and the Growth of Case Law*, ed. J. H. Baker (Berlin: Duncker & Humblot, 1989), 15–46 at 37; *An Introduction to English Legal History*, 197; Tubbs, *The Common Law Mind*, 44.

intriguing point for our purposes is that the common law could accommodate this impulse without a strong doctrine of precedent. There is a difficulty, in other words, in arguing that the doctrine emerged because it upholds particular virtues; for if those virtues were appreciated before the doctrine existed, the question remains as to why the doctrine should have emerged when it did.

a. The ambiguous role of classical legal positivism

This means, then, that the doctrine of precedent must have emerged because something happened. But what did happen? Some jurists argue that it is with the advent of classical positivist jurisprudence that *stare decisis* becomes established within the common law tradition. One of the arguments of the previous chapter was that classical positivism lacked the conceptual apparatus to explain how a precedent might be considered binding on future decision-makers. If this argument is correct, it would be odd to uphold positivism as the reason for the emergence of the doctrine of binding precedent.

Odd, but not necessarily implausible: for a philosophy does not have to accommodate a particular way of thinking in order to contribute to its development. But even if we heed this proviso, the question remains whether there genuinely is a link between the growth of precedent and the onset of classical positivism. There are at least four arguments in the affirmative. The first and most straightforward of these has it that the analytical approach developed by Bentham and Austin helped lawyers to 'identify the materials to be seen as rules'.[21] This is not specifically an argument connecting positivism to the rise of the doctrine of precedent, but rather a more general claim that the emergence of positivism affected judicial thinking. 'The type of analytical jurisprudence developed by Bentham and Austin', Lobban explains, 'could elaborate concepts and definitions to show the lawyer and the judge what he should be looking for, and thereby enable judges to look beyond the narrow boundaries of forms of action'.[22] Lobban himself, having made this observation, proceeds to consider how the impulse to conceptualize made its way into nineteenth-century contract law. Commenting on

---

[21] Michael Lobban, *The Common Law and English Jurisprudence 1760–1850* (Oxford: Clarendon Press, 1991), 288.
[22] Ibid., 258.

the great English contracts treatises of that period, he observes that 'it was largely after the publication of Austin's *Lectures* that a more philosophic view of concepts was put forward'.[23] The argument is thus developed with reference to how a particular category of jurists, rather than judges and lawyers, came to identify what counted as legal rules. Whether classical legal positivism had much of an impact even on this process is debatable. The most insightful and influential of the nineteenth-century contracts writers, Pollock and Anson, drew inspiration from Savigny and Pothier rather than Austin (for whose jurisprudence Pollock in particular had very little time).[24] Of the major contracts jurists of the period, only Leake made visible use of Austin.[25] However, the greater problem with this first argument – and we will see that it applies equally to the other arguments linking positivism and *stare decisis* – is that it is difficult to know what impact the jurisprudence had on the judges. For even if analytical jurisprudence did provide lawyers and judges – leave aside jurists – with guidance enabling them to conceptualize, say, contract law more carefully, it is not at all obvious that the guidance was accepted.

What we can say for certain is that the classical legal positivists, though they had little enthusiasm for judge-made law, did not assume that the judge is merely 'the mouth that pronounces the words of the law'.[26] Austin, as we saw in the last chapter, could find no test or criterion which might be used to demonstrate that such law is valid law. This conclusion did not lead him to follow Bentham, however, and declare that judiciary law must therefore not deserve the title of law. While '[i]t seems to be denied by Bentham, that judiciary law is properly law ... [i]t appears to me that judiciary law ... quadrates with Bentham's own definition of a genuine but tacit command'.[27] In fact, the more Austin deliberated over judicial decision-making, the less inhibited he seemed to become about treating it as a valid source of

---

[23] *Ibid.*, 260.
[24] See P.S. Atiyah, *The Rise and Fall of Freedom of Contract* (Oxford: Clarendon Press, 1979), 682–3. For Pollock on Austin, see e.g., Frederick Pollock, 'Law and Command' (1872) n.s. 1 *Law Magazine & Rev.* 189–205.
[25] Leake followed Austin in arguing that the two principal classes of legal rights are rights to things and rights against persons. See Stephen Martin Leake, *The Elements of the Law of Contracts* (London: Stevens & Sons, 1867), 1–6.
[26] Charles Louis Montesquieu, *The Spirit of the Laws*, trans. T. Nugent (New York: Hafner, 1949 [1748]), 159.
[27] Austin, *Lectures*, 642.

law.[28] What troubled him about judiciary law was not, primarily, the problem of showing that it is law properly so-called, but the question of whether such law is something to be welcomed or lamented. Certainly, like Bentham, he saw reason to lament: 'every system of judiciary law has all the evils of a system which is really vague and inconsistent ... [A] system of judiciary law (as every candid man will readily admit) is nearly unknown to the bulk of the community, although they are bound to adjust their conduct to the rules or principles of which it consists.'[29] Unlike Bentham, however, he considered that judge-made law is a phenomenon about which it is possible to be too negative. '[T]here is more of stability and coherency in judiciary law', Austin argued, 'than might, at the first blush, be imagined'.[30] The 'well-made statute', he asserted, 'is incomparably superior to a rule of judiciary law'.[31] Yet he also observed that judiciary law, 'when made on appeal, after solemn argument and deliberation, ... may be made with as much care and foresight, perhaps, as any statute law'.[32]

Austin, it will have been noticed, struggled to be unequivocal. But he was in no doubt that common-law judges make law. The notion that they are merely mouthpieces declaring the law he memorably dismissed as a 'childish fiction', promoted mainly by judges themselves.[33] This refusal to countenance the declaratory theory of the common law is at the heart of the second argument linking the emergence of *stare decisis* with the rise of legal positivism. 'Bentham and Austin exposed the nonsense of the declaratory theory of precedent', MacCormick remarks; once their 'theories had become part of the intellectual bag-and-baggage of the law, it was clear that judges could no longer hide behind the declaratory theory if they wished to dissent from previous authorities'.[34] If judges have a duty to find and declare the law themselves, they can only be bound to follow the ruling of another court where that ruling is itself a correct declaration of the law. If the earlier court made a mistake, judges deciding the case in hand must declare the law by doing something other than following the precedent. But what else could they do? Austin's point, according to MacCormick, was that they had to legislate, and that since this was a matter of necessity they should 'legislate

---

[28] See, e.g., *ibid.*, 664 ('The truth ... is ... that the general grounds or principles of judicial decisions are as completely Law as statute law itself').
[29] *Ibid.*, 652.   [30] *Ibid.*   [31] *Ibid.*, 661.   [32] *Ibid.*, 651.   [33] *Ibid.*, 634.
[34] D. N. MacCormick, 'Can *Stare Decisis* be Abolished?' [1966] *Juridical Rev.* 197–213 at 204–5.

openly'.³⁵ However, MacCormick adds, 'Austin's invitation was not accepted'.³⁶ Though many nineteenth-century English judges came to recognize the shortcomings of the declaratory theory, conceding that they performed a law-making function was something 'they would not do'.³⁷

The basic difficulty can be seen clearly in a paper read by Walker Marshall to the Juridical Society in November 1860.³⁸ Marshall disapproved of the principle that a final court of appeal should be bound by its own decisions – not a principle to which the House of Lords was committed in 1860, but one which Marshall rightly suspected it was edging towards.³⁹ 'Tribunals of final jurisdiction are not infallible',⁴⁰ he noted, and even when such tribunals reach decisions which are widely regarded to be correct, there is no guarantee that they will be regarded thus forever.⁴¹ His main objection to the claim that the House of Lords should be bound by its own precedents, however, was that those precedents would thereby become unalterable other than by legislation, thus attributing to the judicial decisions of the House a legal status much the same as that accorded to statutes.⁴² Inferior tribunals ought to follow the precedents of appeal courts, even when those precedents are erroneous, for were the tribunal not to do this 'the suitor against whom judgment was given would certainly take the case to the Court of Error and have the judgment reversed'.⁴³ But *stare decisis*, Marshall insisted, has 'no such moral force in the case of a decision of a court of co-ordinate jurisdiction'⁴⁴ – including when a court of last resort asks whether it should be bound by a decision which the same court reached in the past. 'In that case, the court is at liberty to say – "This decision is in our opinion mistaken; it is an erroneous exposition of the law; it is not

---

³⁵ *Ibid.*, 205. ³⁶ *Ibid.* ³⁷ *Ibid.*

³⁸ Walker Marshall, 'Is a Judicial Tribunal, either of the Last Resort or Otherwise, Bound by the Principles Laid Down by Itself on Previous Occasions?' (1860) 2 *Juridical Society Papers* 331–50.

³⁹ On the House of Lords' gradual move during the nineteenth century towards considering itself bound by its own decisions, see Jacob E. Landau, 'Precedents in the House of Lords' (1951) 63 *Juridical Rev.* 222–33 at 222–6.

⁴⁰ Marshall, 'Judicial Tribunal', 341.

⁴¹ 'If the rule that a court of ultimate appeal is absolutely bound by its own decisions were adopted, no allowance would be made for that change of morals, manners, and sentiments which the revolution of a few generations often effects in a people, and which insensibly operates upon and modifies the spirit in which the law is administered.' *Ibid.*, 348.

⁴² *Ibid.*, 345. ⁴³ *Ibid.*, 334. ⁴⁴ *Ibid.*

law, according as we understand law to be, drawing our inspiration from its own sources – from general or special custom, from the imperishable logic of sound reason, or the language of the legislature.'"[45] If a final court of appeal is denied this liberty, if it is bound to decide an issue today as it decided it in the past, we commit ourselves to the 'fallacy ... that in so deciding the court laid down *the law*'.[46] But '[t]he decisions of our courts are not themselves law, they are valuable as expositions of the law'.[47]

Marshall seemed unsure of his ground. Lower-court judges should recognize a precedent to be valuable as an exposition of the law, and should declare the law as according with that precedent even when they consider the precedent wrong; but a court of final appeal, or a court considering the decision of another with coordinate jurisdiction, should not hesitate to declare its own or its coordinate's precedent to be an erroneous exposition of the law if that is what it appears to be. The declaratory theory, in other words, holds good normally but not always, for it need not, indeed should not, be rigidly adhered to by courts of last resort. Marshall insisted, however, that judges do not make law. So, when courts of final appeal find error in and thereby decline to follow their own precedents, what are they doing? They are not necessarily creating law, for they might determine, for example, that the relevant precedent has been abrogated by statute. Even if a court looks not to a statute in refusing to follow a precedent but instead to, say, immemorial custom and common usage, it might still be contended that the declaratory theory is valid, for judges are declaring the law to be something other than what the precedent suggests. '[I]t is not sufficient that the case should have been decided on a principle if that principle is not itself a right principle, or one not applicable to the case', Sir George Jessel remarked in 1880, 'and it is for a subsequent Judge to say whether or not it is a right principle, and, if not, he may himself lay down the true principle'.[48] But to say that the judge, in laying down the true principle, is simply declaring the law according to custom and usage is to leave unexplained how courts deal with new points of principle and how, more generally, common-law doctrine evolves. The point is not that judges must address these matters by creating new laws out of nothing – custom might well provide guidance, as might public policy, considerations of natural justice and juristic opinion, among other things. The

---

[45] *Ibid.* [46] *Ibid.*, 337. [47] *Ibid.*, 334. Emphasis omitted.
[48] *Osborne to Rowlett* (1880) 13 Ch.D. 774, 785.

point, rather, is that when judges decline to follow a precedent for some reason other than the requirements of legislation, it is unrealistic to think that they never create law but only bring it to light.[49]

MacCormick appears to think that the rise of classical legal positivism led the House of Lords to grapple as uncertainly with the concept of precedent as had Marshall.[50] There is no doubt that, throughout the nineteenth century, the House of Lords did struggle. In 1801, Lord Eldon suggested that the House was not bound by its own decisions.[51] In 1898, in *London Tramways* v. *London County Council*, it established that it was.[52] And for the best part of the century it dithered.[53] For MacCormick, the positivists' demolition of the declaratory theory explains why the House of Lords struggled as it did.

> The real reason for the modern development of *stare decisis* was the destruction of the foundation on which the old attitude to precedent rested. When judges could no longer argue that in rejecting previous decisions they were merely restating the 'true' common law, they chose not to grasp the nettle and concede that their function was to improve the law by remaking it.[54]

If classical legal positivism had become part of the intellectual bag-and-baggage of the law, one would expect the nettle to have been grasped. Neither Bentham nor Austin denied that judge-made law was a fact of life, and Austin grudgingly conceded that such law, for all its drawbacks, was not without some virtue. Why should positivism have led judges to realize that the declaratory theory cannot adequately

---

[49] On the many weaknesses of the declaratory theory, see generally Jim Harris, 'Retrospective Overruling and the Declaratory Theory in the United Kingdom – Three Recent Decisions' (2002) 26 *Revue de droit de l'Université libre de Bruxelles* 153–81; though cf. J. M. Finnis, 'The Fairy Tale's Moral' (1999) 115 *LQR* 170–5 at 172–3 ('The "declaratory theory of law" ... if ... taken as a "historical", descriptive assertion, ... is of course falsified by the fact that the common law's rules have changed over the centuries. But it is better taken as a way of stating an important element in judicial duty ... : the duty of judges to differentiate their authority and responsibility ... from that of legislatures').

[50] See MacCormick, 'Can *Stare Decisis* be Abolished?', 204–6.

[51] 'A rule laid down by the House of Lords cannot be reversed by the Chancellor ... The rule must remain, till altered by the House of Lords.' *Perry* v. *Whitehead* (1801) 6 Ves. Jun. 544, 547–8 (emphasis omitted).

[52] *London Tramways* v. *London County Council* [1898] AC 375.

[53] See, e.g., *Brown* v. *Annandale* (1842) 8 Cl. & Fin. 437, 453; *R* v. *Millis* (1844) 10 Cl. & Fin. 534; *Bright* v. *Hutton* (1852) 3 HL Cas 341; *Att. Gen.* v. *Dean of Windsor* (1860) HL Cas 369, 381, 391–3; *Beamish* v. *Beamish* (1861) 9 HL Cas 273, 338.

[54] MacCormick, 'Can *Stare Decisis* be Abolished?', 206.

explain what they do when they reject earlier decisions, yet not have led them to face up to the fact that they sometimes make law?

Perhaps the answer is that the lessons of classical legal positivism made little impact on the courts. It is impossible to say with certainty that this answer is correct. Although Bentham had formulated his own version of legal positivism by 1782, the major details of it were not published until 1945.[55] His arguments for the reform of the court system and his castigation of judge-made law would have been fairly well known: the court-reform initiative was taken up by Henry Brougham in the 1820s,[56] and the case for the establishment of the Law Reports was partly based on Bentham's argument, noted in chapter 1, that if we must have judge-made law then we should at least have systematically arranged and reported precedents.[57] The possibility of many

---

[55] Jeremy Bentham, *Of Laws in General*, ed. H. L. A. Hart (London: Athlone Press, 1970). This book lay unearthed among Bentham's papers until its discovery in 1945 by Professor Charles Everett of Columbia University. According to Hart, 'in broad outline the theory of law which this book presents is the same as that to be found in Austin's *Province of Jurisprudence Determined* and his *Lectures on Jurisprudence or the Philosophy of Positive Law*. For like Austin's theory, Bentham's is an imperative theory of law in which the central concepts are those of sovereign and command, and the definitions of both sovereign and command are at first sight very similar in the two authors. But Bentham expounds these ideas with far greater subtlety and flexibility than Austin and illuminates aspects of law largely neglected by him.' H. L. A. Hart, *Essays on Bentham: Studies in Jurisprudence and Political Theory* (Oxford: Clarendon Press, 1982), 108.

[56] See Chester W. New, *Life of Henry Brougham to 1830* (Oxford: Clarendon Press, 1961), 391 ('in law reform he was the disciple of Bentham'); Robert Stewart, *Henry Brougham 1778–1868: His Public Career* (London: Bodley Head, 1986), 234–5; also *Speeches of Henry Lord Brougham*, 4 vols. (Edinburgh: Black, 1838), II, 287 ('The age of Law Reform and the age of Jeremy Bentham are one and the same. He is the father of the most important of all branches of Reform, the leading and ruling department of human improvement. No one before him had ever seriously thought of exposing the defects in our English system of Jurisprudence').

[57] See, e.g., the article from the *Daily Telegraph*, 30 November 1864, repr. in W. T. S. Daniel, *The History and Origin of the Law Reports* (London: Clowes, 1884), 237–40 at 238–9 ('Instead of everybody knowing the law, nobody knows it ... How is this? The answer is, that law has developed and propagated itself with such amazing fecundity that the most assiduous industry cannot trace all its ramifications ... First, there is the statute-book – the net result of the public labours of Parliament year after year ... [B]ut ... this mass is insignificant in comparison with the "judge-made law", the code of juridical decisions. We have six Chancery courts, three Common Law Courts, and several Courts of Appeal, besides other tribunals sitting day by day during a great part of the year; and all these seats of justice contribute to swell the mighty flood of English jurisprudence. Every one of their decisions constitutes a precedent which, so long as it is not overruled, binds Courts of co-ordinate jurisdiction in analogous cases. Of course, many of the judgments contain no

nineteenth-century judges knowing anything about Bentham's conception of legal positivism, however, seems remote.[58] With Austin, the picture is even more unclear. That nineteenth century judges cannot be found referring either to him or to his work tells us little if anything, for jurists of this era were only occasionally cited in court, and almost never during their lifetime (Austin died in 1859).[59] In 1865, four years after the reissue of Austin's *The Province of Jurisprudence Determined*, his widow wrote of how she was 'assured by barristers that there is a perfect enthusiasm about it among *young* lawyers – men among whom it was unknown till since [sic] I published the second edition'.[60] Even if the assurance was sincere – one cannot help wondering if barristers were telling Mrs Austin what they suspected she wanted to hear – it does not amount to evidence that there was enthusiasm for Austinian positivism among judges. Indeed real evidence, rather than speculation, that classical legal positivism influenced judicial thinking about precedent is thin on the ground. By the end of the nineteenth century the House of Lords, in *London Tramways*, concluded that the law should be declared to be as its own precedent stipulates where a previous decision of the House materially resembles the case at hand and no statutory authority compels a different result. If judges really had become wise to the shortcomings of the declaratory theory owing to the impact of legal

---

new principles, and are therefore omitted from the published legal reports. But, notwithstanding these omissions, the multitude of reported cases is far too great').

[58] Cf. Mortimer N. S. Sellers, 'The Doctrine of Precedent in the United States of America' (2006) 54 *Am. J. Comparative Law* 67–88, who discerns a nineteenth-century 'road of extreme *stare decisis*' (*ibid*., at 86), on which the 'British common law became increasingly rigid and formalistic, under the influence of Jeremy Bentham and his disciples' (*ibid*., 72). When judges did demonstrate any knowledge of Bentham, it was Bentham the legal reformer who tended to capture their imagination: see, e.g., *London, Chatham & Dover Ry Co.* v. *South Easter Ry Co.* [1892] 1 Ch. 120, 140, CA, per Lindley L. J. (referring to Bentham's attack on the usury laws, as expounded in his *Defence of Usury* [London: Payne, 1787]).

[59] Albert Venn Dicey (d.1922), who was largely sympathetic to Austin's jurisprudential premises but none the less critical of his account of parliamentary sovereignty, was one of the few nineteenth-century jurists to be cited by the courts during his own lifetime: see, e.g., *R* v. *Albany* [1915] 3 KB 716, 726, per Darling J; *In re De Keyser's Royal Hotel Ltd* [1919] 2 Ch. 197, 205, CA (*arguendo*); *Att. Gen.* v. *De Keyser's Royal Hotel* [1920] AC 508, 526, HL, per Lord Dunedin; and, for Dicey on Austin's account of sovereignty, A. V. Dicey, *Introduction to the Law of the Constitution*, 8th edn (London: Macmillan, 1927), 68–74. The other obvious example of such a jurist was Frederick Pollock, who, as noted already, was no Austinian.

[60] Mrs Austin to M. Guizot, 2 March 1863, in Janet Ross, *Three Generations of Englishwomen: Memoirs and Correspondence of Mrs John Taylor, Mrs Sarah Austin, and Lady Duff Gordon*, 2 vols. (London: Murray, 1888), II, 138.

positivism, it seems odd that this conclusion should have been reached – let alone that a significant number of senior judges would continue to speak up for the declaratory theory well into the twentieth century.[61]

MacCormick's argument, in essence, is that *stare decisis* was a comforting doctrine for an earlier generation of judges who, owing to the impact of positivism, recognized the limitations of the declaratory theory but could not candidly acknowledge their law-making capacity. According to this account, although the doctrine of precedent does not require judges simply to declare the law, their creative role is more or less confined to the activity of distinguishing – to narrowing existing rules rather than creating entirely new ones. Neither this argument nor the first one which we considered – that classical positivism helped lawyers and judges to identify just what could count as a legal rule – does anything more than suggest why judges, armed with positivist insights, might have been attracted to a doctrine of binding precedent. The third argument to be considered makes a more robust connection between legal philosophy and legal doctrine. The argument proceeds from the classical positivist idea that the sovereign tacitly commands subjects to avoid behaviour to which courts have in the past attached a punishment. Although, as we have seen, classical positivists struggled with, and in

---

[61] See, e.g., *Bayliss* v. *Bishop of London* [1913] 1 Ch. 127, 137, *per* Farwell L.J.; *Harnett* v. *Fisher* [1927] 1 KB 402, 424, *per* Scrutton L.J.; *Scruttons* v. *Midland Silicones Ltd* [1962] AC 446, 467–9, *per* Lord Simons; also P. B. Mignault, 'The Authority of Decided Cases' (1925) 3 *Can. Bar Rev.* 1–24 at 23–4; H. K. Lücke, 'The Common Law: Judicial Impartiality and Judge-Made Law' (1982) 98 *LQR* 29–93 at 45–50; Rupert Cross and J. W. Harris, *Precedent in English Law*, 4th edn (Oxford: Clarendon Press, 1991), 30. For Cross and Harris, one of the reasons that the declaratory theory persisted is that it is not quite as blunt an instrument as it might at first seem. The theory has obvious normative value for anyone who argues that 'anything in the nature of judicial legislation' (*ibid.*) is contrary to the rule of law: judges ought to do no more than declare the law, a proponent of this argument would have it, even though judicial legislation may be a reality. Anyone who subscribes to this argument might also value the declaratory theory for its capacity to conceal the retrospective nature of judicial legislation. 'A way of disguising the retrospective character of such a judgment would be to maintain the doctrine that the court was doing no more than state a rule which anyone could have deduced from well-known principles or common usage' (*ibid.*). Whether the declaratory theory really does perform this disguising function seems open to doubt, for the theory is that judges do not legislate, not that they do not legislate retrospectively. Cross and Harris seem to assume the declaratory theory presents judicial legislation as non-retrospective legislation, because what looks to be legislation is simply the court finding and declaring common law principles that already existed. But the declaratory theory simply does not present judicial decision-making as legislation, retrospective or otherwise. For a proponent of the theory, the claim that it conceals the retrospective character of judicial legislation concedes too much.

Bentham's case even scorned, the notion that judicial precedents are laws, they nevertheless accepted that 'judge-made laws' embody commands. Once lawyers began to think of case-law as commands of this sort, it has been argued, it became natural for the legal profession to want to know just when and where these commands existed and whom they bound.[62] Austin was puzzled as to how the question of their existence might be answered. 'Is it the *number* of decisions in which a rule has been followed, that makes it law binding on future judges? or is it the *elegentia* of the rule ... or its consistency and harmony with the bulk of the legal system? Or is it the *reputation* of the judge or judges by whom the case or cases introducing the rule were decided?'[63] He omitted to mention what is probably the most obvious answer: that the capacity of a precedent to constrain – i.e., to serve as a command – depends on the level of the court which creates it. This answer leaves unresolved the problem of determining the authority of conflicting decisions of courts of coordinate jurisdiction – a problem which vexed Marshall and other nineteenth-century lawyers.[64] If judicial decisions are commands, and if courts of equal rank and jurisdiction provide different solutions to what is essentially the same problem, which command prevails? Classical positivism, so the argument goes, encouraged lawyers and judges to

[62] See Jim Evans, 'Change in the Doctrine of Precedent during the Nineteenth Century', in *Precedent in Law*, ed. L. Goldstein (Oxford: Clarendon Press, 1987), 35–72 at 69–70 ('Bentham believed that the sovereign tacitly commanded subjects to avoid that behaviour to which courts were in fact prone to attach a "punishment" as a consequence of past cases ... Austin believed that the sovereign must be understood as tacitly commanding that the grounds of judicial decisions be observed in the future as rules of conduct ... It was this view of law ... which influenced the approach to precedent. For once lawyers began to think of case-law as just a set of rules of this sort, established by the rulings in cases, it became natural to want to define just when these rules existed and whom they bound').

[63] Austin, *Province*, II, 655.

[64] Marshall took the view that 'where several courts have a co-ordinate jurisdiction, ... each exercises an independent judgment upon any case which is presented to it, uncontrolled by any decision to which any other Court of co-ordinate jurisdiction may have arrived upon the same point'. Marshall, 'Judicial Tribunal', 336–7. This was the position eventually taken by the great nineteenth-century Master of the Rolls, Sir George Jessel. Cf. *In re Hallet's Estate* (1879) 13 Ch.D. 696, 712 with *In re Harper and Great Eastern Ry Co.* (1875) LR 20 Eq. 39, 43; and see also *Osborne to Rowlett* (1880) 13 Ch.D. 774, 779 ('I used to think myself bound by any decision of a Vice-Chancellor that was twenty years old; but the Court of Appeal held in one instance that I was not so bound. I then reconsidered my position, and thought I was not bound by any decision of a Court of co-ordinate authority: accordingly I have since frequently declined to follow such authority'); and Sir Frederick Pollock, *A First Book of Jurisprudence for Students of the Common Law* (London: Macmillan, 1896), 304–5.

consider which courts' commands should prevail when the commands can be seen to conflict.

Even if we accept that positivism did exert such an influence, it is not clear that this third argument takes us especially far in understanding the formation of the doctrine of precedent. For the argument is really an effort to show that, through legal positivism, lawyers and judges came to recognize that precedents can bind vertically and horizontally – it explains the classification of precedents once it had become common to treat individual judicial decisions as legal authority, in other words, but does not explain why such decisions should have acquired this status in the first place. The fourth argument linking the emergence of classical legal positivism with the development of the doctrine of precedent offers a clue as to what this last explanation might be. We saw in the last chapter that Hobbes was as wary of the notion of binding precedent as were Bentham and Austin. But his perspective differs somewhat from theirs. Judicial decisions, he agreed, can be understood as tacit commands of the sovereign. '[C]ommand is directed to a man's own benefit; and counsel to the benefit of another man', and while 'a man may be obliged to do what he is commanded ... he cannot be obliged to do as he is counseled'.[65] '[L]aw in general, is not counsel, but command' – not a command 'of any man to any man', but addressed only to those, such as judges, who occupy a position of obligation to the sovereign.[66] So it is that judges exercise delegated authority. But to describe the judicial role thus does not adequately capture Hobbes's account of it. Judges, he argued, are entrusted to exercise 'natural reason' in a manner compatible with how the sovereign would have employed such reason.

> The interpretation of the law of nature, is the sentence of the judge constituted by the sovereign authority, to hear and determine such controversies, as depend thereon; and consisteth in the application of the law to the present case. For in the act of judicature, the judge doth no more but consider, whether the demand of the party be consonant to natural reason, and equity; and the sentence he giveth, is therefore the interpretation of the law of nature ...[67]

For Hobbes, therefore, precedents embody not just what the sovereign would have commanded, but also what he would have reasoned, were he deciding the case. '[T]he judge is to take notice, that his sentence

---

[65] Hobbes, *Leviathan*, II. 25. 4. [66] Ibid., II. 26. 2. [67] Ibid., II. 26. 23.

ought to be according to the reason of his sovereign'.⁶⁸ Reliance on precedent is, Hobbes insisted, often indicative of a childlike inability to discern for oneself the right course of action.⁶⁹ Yet, despite his rather low opinion of precedent-following, he was able, as Postema has observed, to set out a positivist argument connecting precedent and reason.⁷⁰

b. Precedent and reason

Of all the classical positivist efforts to explain why the doctrine of precedent materialized, this last argument – Hobbes's argument – seems to be the most promising. This is not because there is anything especially plausible about the assumption that judges endeavour to replicate the reasoning of the sovereign, but because Hobbes recognized that the use of reason was integral to judicial-decision making in the seventeenth century. By this point in history, as we have noted, English judges were increasingly paying attention to precedents even though *stare decisis* was not yet an established doctrine. The clue to the explanation for this increased attention is there in Hobbes: the authority delegated to judges was not merely authority to issue commands but also authority to provide reasons. The reasons that judges provide for the decisions that they reach, whether or not they represent the will of the sovereign, have directive force. 'There has been no plan in the development of the common law,' Milsom observes, but this does not mean that there has been nothing to guide its evolution: '[t]he reasoning adopted yesterday may not have caused today's result; but it governs the terms in which today's dispute is put to a court, or is not put because the lawyers cannot now make a case of it.'⁷¹ For Coke and Hale, Postema observes, reason implied consistency:

> In 17th century common law parlance, for a . . . judgment to be 'against reason' (or often 'inconvenient') was for it to be inconsistent with the law as a whole, to fail to fit coherently into the common law. To understand law as rational (*summa ratio*, as Coke liked to say) was not to regard it as derivable from universal first principles, but rather to approach it on the

---

⁶⁸ *Ibid.*, II. 26. 14. ⁶⁹ See *ibid.*, I. 11. 21.
⁷⁰ See Gerald J. Postema, 'Some Roots of our Notion of Precedent', in *Precedent in Law*, 9–33 at 11–13; and, more generally, Postema, *Bentham and the Common Law Tradition* (Oxford: Clarendon Press, 1986), 46–60.
⁷¹ S. F. C. Milsom, 'Reason in the Development of the Common Law' (1965) 81 *LQR* 496–517 at 497–8.

assumption that it exists as a coherent whole. 'Rational' meant 'rationally coherent'. The 'reason' and 'certainty' of the law, Hale argued, depended on judges 'keep[ing] a constancy and consistency of the law to itself'.[72]

It is worth pointing out immediately that this is not to claim that reason demanded like cases be treated alike.[73] The requirement was that judgments be consistent with the law as a whole, not with specific earlier decisions. Ensuring the former might also ensure the latter, but not necessarily. As Blackstone remarked, *'the law,* and the *opinion of the judge'* – which, in context, can be interpreted to mean precedent – 'are not ... one and the same thing; since it may sometimes happen that the judge may *mistake* the law'.[74] The limited capacity of reason to encourage precedent-following is, however, a minor concern in this context. Far more important is the question of what was meant by reason, for there is no doubt that Coke and Hale accorded this term legal significance very different from that ascribed to it by Hobbes. Coke and Hale were of the view that judicial reason was not the natural reason of any competent person but the cultivated or 'artificial' reason that comes from study and experience of the law over a long period of time.[75] The

---

[72] Gerald J. Postema, 'Classical Common Law Jurisprudence (Part I)' (2003) 2 *Oxf. Univ. Commonwealth L.J.* 155–80 at 178. The quotation in the last sentence of the passage is adapted from Matthew Hale, 'Reflections by the Lrd. Chiefe Justice Hale on Mr Hobbes His Dialogue of the Lawe' (c. 1675), in Sir William Holdsworth, *A History of English Law*, 3rd edn, 9 vols. (London: Methuen, 1922–6), V, 500–13 at 506.

[73] Coke, it ought to be noted, sometimes did appear to claim as much: see, e.g., his Preface to the *Book of Entries* (orig. Latin folio 1614), repr. in English in *The Selected Writings of Sir Edward Coke*, 3 vols., ed. S. Sheppard (Indianapolis: Liberty Fund, 2003), II, 558–62 at 561 ('The learned Sages of the law doe found their judgement upon legall reason and judiciall President; the one they find in our bookes of yeres and termes, the other out of records formerly examined and allowed: These two, Reason and President are *clarissima mundi lumina* [the clearest lights of the world].... [I]t is safe for the Client and the Councellor also (if he respect his conscience) to follow Presidents formerly approved and allowed'). But he also emphasized consistency with law and reason over precedent: cf. Slade's Case (1602), repr. in *ibid.*, I, 116–24 at 120 ('in divers Cases precedents do not make a Law ... [H]e who would have advantage of precedents ought to search for them at his peril, ... for if none, or no usual precedents are not shewn, the Court ought to adjudge according to Law and reason'); also Preface to Part Three of the *Reports* (1602), repr. in *ibid.*, I, 59–78 at 60.

[74] William Blackstone, *Commentaries on the Laws of England*, 4 vols. (Chicago: University of Chicago Press, 1979 [1765–9]), I, 71. Blackstone is here elaborating the proposition 'that precedents and rules must be followed, unless flatly absurd or unjust' (*ibid.*, 70).

[75] See, e.g., Sir Edward Coke, *Twelfth Reports, Prohibitions del Roy* (1607) 12 Co. Rep. 63, 64; Hale, 'Reflections by the Lrd. Chiefe Justice Hale on Mr Hobbes His Dialogue of the Lawe', in Holdsworth, *A History of English Law*, V, 500–13; and, generally, Donald R. Kelley, *The*

duty of the Hobbesian judge is not to reach decisions which cohere with the law as a whole, but to reach decisions which represent the natural reason of the sovereign – endeavouring to fulfil this duty might, but it does not have to, generate legal consistency. The demands of artificial reason, by contrast, encourage decision-making with an eye to consistency, for such reason requires that lawyers and judges argue and decide in accordance with that in which they have immersed themselves: the reports and digests which record, however imperfectly, the arguments and decisions of their forebears.[76] Pocock, writing about Hale, notes how:

> He regarded the records of the law as very nearly all the evidence existing concerning the history of the law, and these records, as he knew, did not often rehearse the circumstances in which they had been made and were in essence little more than a series of declarations of what the immemorial law was, through which nevertheless ran a thread of almost imperceptible change ... To him the law was in flux, constantly being restated by people, parliament and judges in response to their immediate practical needs, and what was of importance was that they had chosen to do this rather by restating old decisions than by creating new out of their rational estimate of each situation as it arose.[77]

If anything, this passage overemphasizes the place of precedent – the restating of old decisions – in seventeenth-century common-law thought. Hale himself, indeed, was prepared to say of judicial decisions what John Austin could never quite bring himself to say: that although they bind 'as a Law between the Parties thereto ... they do not make a Law properly so called, (for that only the King and Parliament can do)'.[78] Nevertheless, Hale continued, although individual judicial rulings do not have the authority of law, 'they have a great Weight and Authority in Expounding, Declaring, and Publishing what the Law of this Kingdom is'.[79] Coke similarly emphasized that 'in our law, examples

---

Human Measure: Social Thought in the Western Legal Tradition (Cambridge, Mass.: Harvard University Press, 1990), 180–3.

[76] See J. G. A. Pocock, 'Burke and the Ancient Constitution – A Problem in the History of Ideas' (1960) 1 *Historical Jnl* 125–43 at 132–3; Gerald J. Postema, 'Classical Common Law Jurisprudence (Part II)' (2003) 3 *Oxf. Univ. Commonwealth L.J.* 1–28 at 8.

[77] Pocock, 'Burke and the Ancient Constitution', 137.

[78] Sir Matthew Hale, *The History of the Common Law of England*, ed. C. M. Gray (Chicago: University of Chicago Press, 1971 [1713]), 45.

[79] Ibid.

are good arguments',[80] and that '[t]he reporting of particular cases or examples is the most perspicuous course of teaching the right rule and reason of the law'.[81] The point for emphasis – one which Gerald Postema has been developing for the past two decades – is that although, by the seventeenth century, precedents were not legal authorities, they were nevertheless important because lawyers and judges would often consider them to exemplify proper legal reasoning.[82] This does not mean that it was taken for granted that precedents illustrate what the common law requires. In the eighteenth century, Lord Mansfield cautioned against elevating 'particular cases' above the 'general principles [that] run through cases and govern the decision of them',[83] and even in the seventeenth century the prevailing argument was not that precedents can be assumed to illustrate the right rule and reason of the law, but that they must be 'tried' to see whether they do serve that function and whether they might profitably be reformulated or refined.[84] A connection between precedents and reason had, nevertheless, been established: though 'reason' lacked a fixed meaning, seventeenth-century lawyers tended to agree with Coke that reason is the life of the law,[85] and generally appreciated that anyone who sought to understand this life, and any judge who wished to build upon common-law wisdom, would do well to pay attention to the past decisions of the courts. Precedents had not quite become everything;[86] but they had certainly moved towards centre stage.

Precedents, then, became the dominant form of authority used in legal argument because they came to be seen as offering reasons for

---

[80] *Ognel* v. *Paston* (1587) 2 Leon. 84, 86. Coke's point in this particular instance was that precedents ('examples') may sometimes illustrate not the general rule but an exception to it: see Baker, *Law's Two Bodies*, 20–1.

[81] Coke, *The Reports of Sir Edward Coke*, vol. III (Dublin: Moore, 1793 [1607]), p. ix (preface). Though Coke's reference to 'examples' in *Ognel* v. *Paston*, it is worth mentioning, was a reference not to reported law but to the record of the court. In Ognel's case, furthermore, the record was not of a decision but of the fact that the relevant writs had been issued.

[82] See, e.g., Postema, 'Some Roots of our Notion of Precedent', 22–3; 'Classical Common Law Jurisprudence (Part II)', 17.

[83] *Rust* v. *Cooper* (1774) Cowp. 629, 632.

[84] See Thomas Hedley, speech to the House of Commons, 28 June 1610, in *Proceedings in Parliament 1610. Vol. II: House of Commons*, ed. E. R. Foster (New Haven: Yale University Press, 1966), 170–97 at 176–9; also Postema, 'Classical Common Law Jurisprudence (Part II)', 13–14.

[85] See Sir Edward Coke, *Institutes of the Laws of England* (1628), I, 97^b.

[86] Cf. Baker, *Law's Two Bodies*, 85.

particular rules and doctrines. By the sixteenth century, reported decisions were ever more often reasoned decisions.[87] But why should this have happened? In the middle ages, first of all, the formulary system, which required that pleadings preceded the trial and were conducted within a framework defined by the writs, had militated against visible judicial deliberation and the reporting of reasoned opinions. It was not only the arrangement of trial proceedings that made reasoned judgments unlikely; there was also the generally risk-averse manner in which litigation was conducted. Pleadings were advanced orally and often tentatively: a plea would most likely be withdrawn if counsel sensed from the reaction of a court or opposing party that continuing with it would meet with no success. 'Litigation', Baker observes, 'was not conceived of as a means of refining the law. Nor were counsel concerned with the improvement of jurisprudence'.[88] By the beginning of the sixteenth century, however, parties were quite regularly settling their pleadings in advance of trial, thus leaving disputes as to the merits of those pleadings to be dealt with after a verdict had been given. Earlier judges had tended to be advisers or mediators rather than decision-makers, steering parties towards agreement on the issue to be disputed in pleading rather than making a legal ruling.[89] But the shift towards post-verdict arguments gradually eliminated this advisory role, so that the judge's principal function became that of decision-maker.[90] As the focal point of the trial moved from the pleadings to the decision, lawyers, their clients and even law reporters increasingly expected judges to provide reasons for what they decided.[91] This expectation was often dashed; indeed, by the early seventeenth century, judges were still sometimes resistant to providing reasons for their decisions.[92] The altered form of the trial had changed the tide, nevertheless, so that by 1600 the idea of the single reasoned decision as a distinct source of law, though by no means yet fully accepted, was clearly emerging.[93]

---

[87] See *ibid.*, 81.
[88] Baker, 'Records, Reports and the Origins of Case-Law in England', 40.
[89] 'There was a tendency to evade a definite ruling on a point of law, and the pleaders were often requested "to ease the court" and not to bring forward difficult questions.' T. Ellis Lewis, 'The History of Judicial Precedent' (pt. I) (1930) 46 *LQR* 207–24 at 219.
[90] See Ibbetson, 'Case Law and Judicial Precedents', 66.
[91] See Baker, *Introduction to English Legal History*, 198–9.
[92] See Baker, *Law's Two Bodies*, 16–17.
[93] See Ibbetson, 'Case Law and Judicial Precedents', 68; Baker, *Introduction to English Legal History*, 199.

Although the shift to post-verdict arguments sowed the seeds of *stare decisis*, it would be at least another 200 years before the doctrine came into bloom. Why should the process have taken so long? The haphazard growth of law reporting could not have helped. The printing of the Year Books and the emergence of named reports in the sixteenth century might have led lawyers to pay more attention to individual cases as sources of law. But it would be very easy to overemphasize this point. The purpose of the Year Books had been to provide lawyers and law students not with precedents but with lessons in the intricacies of pleading. 'Most of what is reported in the Year Books consists of oral interchanges between judges and serjeants, and it is very hard – often impossible – to extract from these reports anything like a decision on any point at all.'[94] The nominate reports which succeeded the Year Books were often of such poor quality that judges forbade their citation in court; and as with the Year Books, the purpose of the reports was primarily to educate and instruct would-be lawyers rather than to set out usable precedents.[95] In any event, by the seventeenth century there were, outside Chancery,[96] too few reliable reported decisions to operate as

---

[94] Ibbetson, 'Case Law and Judicial Precedents', 66; in a similar vein, see John Hanna, 'The Role of Precedent in Judicial Decision' (1957) 2 *Villanova L. Rev.* 367–84 at 374–5.

[95] It is unclear whether the reports were intended primarily to instruct practitioners or to instruct students, but there is no doubt that they were intended to provide information rather than to be used in the course of legal practice. See David Ibbetson, 'Law Reporting in the 1590s', in *Law Reporting in Britain*, ed. C. Stebbings (London: Hambledon Press, 1995), 73–88.

[96] So far as the doctrine of precedent is concerned, equity reports show that the equity courts were somewhat ahead of the game. Equity judges appear by the early seventeenth century to have been quite regularly relying upon precedents as recorded in the Chancery Register's Books to guide their decisions in like cases, though in looking to prior decisions judges were usually looking for similar actions on similar facts and were not especially interested in what earlier judges had to say. See, generally, W. H. D. Winder, 'Precedent in Equity' (1941) 57 *LQR* 245–79; Michael Macnair, 'The Nature and Function of the Early Chancery Reports', in *Law Reporting in Britain*, 121–32; though cf. Henry Campbell Black, *Handbook on the Law of Judicial Precedents, or The Science of Case Law* (St. Paul, Minn.: West, 1912), 30–6 (claiming that principles of equity had their origins in common-law decisions). It is not particularly surprising that this should have happened given that, by the Tudor period, equity courts were more often than not concerned with teasing out the merits of individual cases rather than applying legal rules. For a summary of Chancery jurisprudence around this time, see *Earl of Oxford's Case* (1615) 1 Rep. Ch. 1, 6–7, *per* Lord Ellesmere C. ('The cause why there is a Chancery is that men's actions are so diverse and infinite that it is impossible to make any general law which may aptly meet with every particular act and not fail in some circumstances. The office of the Chancellor is to correct men's consciences for

constraints on courts when deciding analogous cases.[97] Although the printing of named reports (most of which was carried out in the mid seventeenth century) meant that lawyers no longer had to rely on manuscripts of cases, the process highlighted and indeed often compounded the inaccuracies of the more inferior collections.[98] Francis Bacon, eight months after having been elected as Lord Keeper of the Seal in March 1617, sought to appoint official law reporters to produce accurate reports of important cases. Just what Bacon wanted from these reporters, and what they ought to receive in return, he spelled out in Aphorisms 74 and 75 of his *Example of a Treatise on Universal Justice*:

> Let this be the method for taking down judgments and committing them to writing. Record the cases precisely, the judgments themselves word for word; add the reasons which the judges allege for their judgments; do not mix up the authority of cases brought forward as examples with the principal case; and omit the perorations of counsel, unless they contain something very remarkable.
>
> Let the reporters be taken from the most learned counsel, and receive a liberal salary from the state. But let not the judges themselves meddle with the reports; lest from being too fond of their own opinions, and relying on their own authority, they exceed the province of a reporter.[99]

Bacon's initiative failed, largely because it depended on the cooperation of lawyers who did not want it to succeed.[100] He had, nevertheless,

---

frauds, breach of trusts, wrongs and oppressions of what nature soever they be, and to soften and mollify the extremity of the law').

[97] This is not to claim that a case could only constrain later courts if it was reported. Sometimes, an earlier case would be treated as authority because the record of it was brought into court to corroborate counsel's memory of the case, or to verify the accuracy of a law report. It is perhaps worth observing more generally that the distinction which we draw today between manuscript and printed text was by no means as clear in the seventeenth century: in libraries, for example, manuscript and print were shelved side by side, and manuscripts for private circulation were quite often issued as supplements to printed works (particularly political works). See generally David McKitterick, *Print, Manuscript and the Search for Order 1450–1830* (Cambridge: Cambridge University Press, 2003), 22–52.

[98] See Baker, *Introduction to English Legal History*, 182–3.

[99] Francis Bacon, 'Example of a Treatise on Universal Justice or the Fountains of Equity, by Aphorisms: one Title of it', in *The Works of Francis Bacon*, ed. J. Spedding, R. L. Ellis and D. D. Heath, 14 vols. (London: Longmans, 1861–79), V, 88–110 at 104. See also Daniel R. Coquillette, *Francis Bacon* (Edinburgh: Edinburgh University Press, 1992), 110–11, 253.

[100] See Spedding's comment in *The Works of Francis Bacon*, XIII, 267–8 ('Its success depended upon the co-operation of those who did not wish it to succeed. The law

espied the law reports of the future.[101] Significant improvements in the quality of reporting would have to wait until the middle of the eighteenth century, when Lord Mansfield, as Lord Chief Justice of England, not only refused to entertain incomplete and inaccurate reports (whatever the reputation of the reporter) but also attracted first-rate reporters to the King's Bench.[102] Principal among these was Sir James Burrow. 'There had been a few good reporters before him', Wallace observes, '[b]ut presenting as he does ... the grounds or reasons of the judgment, he gives us reports which make the perfection of the art'.[103] Burrow was followed by Henry Cowper and Sylvester Douglas, both of whom produced reports of a quality and style similar to Burrow's own.[104] By the end of the eighteenth century, published law reports, produced by professional reporters, had been commissioned for all four superior courts.[105] Other accurate, professionally-administered reports succeeded or ran alongside these series during the nineteenth century until, in 1865, the Council of Law Reporting was established and began issuing the first numbers of the Law Reports.

The standard of law reporting improved in the nineteenth century, not only because the activity became steadily more professionalized, and eventually institutionalized, but also because the development of the Pitman shorthand system in the 1830s made it possible for reporters to reproduce judicial opinions more or less verbatim.[106] By the mid

> cannot be made simpler, cheaper, speedier, surer, and more generally intelligible, without the help and consent of the lawyers; and it is the interest of the lawyers that the law should be intricate, costly, slow, uncertain, and intelligible to none but themselves'); also Coquillette, *Francis Bacon*, 200, 214–15 n. 54.

[101] Holdsworth, *A History of English Law*, V, 374 ('Bacon, at the beginning of the seventeenth century, had already foreshadowed the shape which the reports will eventually assume').

[102] On Mansfield's view of inferior law reports, see James Oldham, *English Common Law in the Age of Mansfield* (Chapel Hill: University of North Carolina Press, 2004), 30–1; C. H. S. Fifoot, *Lord Mansfield* (Oxford: Clarendon Press, 1936), 14, 214–15.

[103] John William Wallace, *The Reporters*, 4th edn (Boston: Soule & Bugbee, 1882), 446, 448.

[104] See Wallace, *The Reporters*, 450. Wallace observes that the same can be said of the so-called *Term Reports*, produced by Sir Edward Hyde East and Charles Durnford between 1785 and 1800 (and by East alone from 1800 to 1814). *Ibid.*

[105] The *Term Reports* for King's Bench, *Henry Blackstone* for Common Pleas, *Vesey Junior* for the Chancery and *Anstruther* for the Exchequer.

[106] On the development of shorthand in the nineteenth century, see Sir Isaac Pitman, *A History of Shorthand*, 3rd edn (London: Pitman & Sons, 1891; 1st edn publ. 1852); and Matthias Levy, *The History of Short-hand Writing* (London: Trübner & Co., 1862). On earliest uses by law reporters (mainly criminal trial reporters), see James Fitzjames Stephen, *A History of the Criminal Law of England*, 3 vols. (London: Macmillan, 1883), I, 383; G. Glover Alexander, 'The Province of the Judge and of the Jury' (1905–6) 31

nineteenth century, law reporting had become accurate to the point that reporters would customarily send judges transcripts of their oral judgments for approval and correction.[107] The fact that reporters were generally replicating the *ipsissima verba* of the judges would most likely have contributed to the fortification of *stare decisis*; for a prior decision in an analogous case is likely to be less easy to ignore or even distinguish if the reasons informing that decision are presented clearly, in their entirety and with the approval of the judges who articulated them.[108] The introduction of the hierarchical system of appellate courts under the Judicature Acts 1873–75 further helped to consolidate the doctrine of precedent, for, once this system was established, judges looking to earlier analogous decisions for guidance could be constrained by the status of the precedent-setting court rather than by the quality of its reasoning alone. As was intimated earlier, however, this development merely added to a trend that had already been established. The doctrine of *stare decisis* did not come about because of the creation of a hierarchy of courts, even though the introduction of that hierarchy did much to consolidate it.[109] The doctrine evolved, rather,

---

Law Mag. & Rev. Quart. Rev. Juris. (5th ser.) 1–24, 184–204, 289–315, 451–65 at 5–6; John H. Langbein, 'The Criminal Trial before the Lawyers' (1978) 45 *U. Chicago L. Rev.* 263–316 at 265; 'Shaping the Eighteenth-Century Criminal Trial: A View from the Ryder Sources' (1983) 50 *U. Chicago L. Rev.* 1–136 at 12. As might be expected, in other jurisdictions, and in other areas of reporting, the introduction of shorthand had much the same impact: see, e.g., Thomas Hodgins, 'Origin of Short-hand Reporting in the Courts' (1908) 28 *Canadian Law Times & Rev.* 139–46; Oswald M. T. Ratteray, 'Verbatim Reporting Comes of Age' (1973) 56 *Judicature* 368–73; Elizabeth G. McPherson, 'Reporting the Debates of Congress' (1942) 28 *Quarterly Journal of Speech* 141–8 at 147.

[107] See Sir Frederick Pollock, *Essays in the Law* (London: Macmillan, 1922), 252, 255–6. In 1662, legislation was passed requiring that law reports only be printed with the consent of the Lord Chancellor, the Lord Keeper of the Seal, the Lord Chief Justice, or the Lord Chief Baron. The legislation expired after thirty years, and in any event had imposed upon the holders of these offices only an obligation to peruse the reports to judge their general quality and authenticity rather than carefully read them to check for errors. See Wallace, *The Reporters*, 34–7 n 3.

[108] See Baker, *Introduction to English Legal History*, 200; cf. also Patrick Devlin, *The Judge* (Oxford: Oxford University Press, 1981), 180 ('[I]n England case law is not something which is made by judges alone. Judges spin and others weave. Each time a judge gives a reasoned judgment he spins a thread. It is for the law reporters to decide in the first instance whether the thread can be woven into the law. They have a vital and underestimated part to play in the making of the law, for it is their reports which provide the material for the textbooks and in the lower courts it is the law in the textbooks that is usually applied').

[109] See David Pugsley, 'Two Systems of Precedent' (1981) 15 *Law Teacher* 7–17 at 10, who observes not only that the doctrine of precedent existed in English law before 1875 but

primarily because the shift to post-verdict arguments made reasoned judgments more visible and significant, and because gradual improvements in law reporting (including headnote writing)[110] ensured that, in general, such judgments were carefully documented and the key points of reasoning easily identifiable. For counsel, seeking a judicial precedent became a matter of searching for an analogous earlier decision, reached by an appropriate court, based on reasoning which, if considered persuasive by the court deciding the current case, would probably guarantee a ruling in their client's favour. The authority of precedent has much to do with the fact that precedents came to be understood, and valued, as sources of reason, not merely as rulings, in materially identical cases.

Once a link is made between precedent and reason, however, two important questions arise. Within any particular judicial decision, first of all, which reasons matter the most? Appellate decisions normally contain more than one argument: a panel of judges might produce a plurality of opinions; their opinions might lead to the same conclusion yet their arguments may differ; and even within a single opinion it might be possible to detect various lines of reasoning. Not everything within a judicial decision will be considered part of the precedent. For a while during the twentieth century, common-law legal philosophers seemed especially eager to find something akin to a method which would make it possible to separate the authoritative part of a decision from the remainder. The second question concerns not the idea that precedents embody reasons but the proposition that precedents *are* reasons. When we rely on a precedent as a reason for making a decision, does it operate as a particular type of reason? Perhaps the obvious answer to this question is that we use the precedent as something akin to shorthand reasoning – a way to avoid investing the same energy in the same problem twice. We will see, however, that this is not the only possible answer, and that, while the first question raised here is one which rarely captures the imagination of modern legal philosophers, the second still taxes them considerably. There are, in fact, analytical legal philosophers today who would argue that understanding the authority of precedents requires an appreciation of their capacity to function as a specific type of reason.

---

also that a legal system might have a court hierarchy without having a developed doctrine of *stare decisis*, as is the case in France.

[110] See Percy H. Winfield, *The Chief Sources of English Legal History* (Cambridge, Mass.: Harvard University Press, 1925), 192.

3

Precedents as reasons

Precedent, we have seen, is inadequately accounted for by classical legal positivists. Part of the reason for this is that classical positivists wanted to explain the validity of laws. Validity, being a non-variable concept, is poorly suited to analyses of precedential authority.[1] The idea of judges formulating decisions so that they might bind as a statute binds is not inconceivable. But it is simply not what common-law judges do. Lord Wright seemed to think differently when, writing during the era when the House of Lords considered itself bound by its own precedents, he observed that, if the House determines a principle on a particular set of facts then, should the materially same facts arise again, the earlier decision 'is to be treated as if part of an Act of Parliament'.[2] But according to Lord Reid, although judges will sometimes interpret earlier decisions of the House 'as if they were provisions in an Act of Parliament' – especially when the decision is composed of a single speech – such interpretations are never appropriate, for:

> it is not the function of noble and learned Lords or indeed of any judges to frame definitions or to lay down hard and fast rules. It is their function to enunciate principles and much that they say is intended to be illustrative or explanatory and not to be definitive.[3]

---

[1] See Stephen R. Perry, 'Judicial Obligation, Precedent and the Common Law' (1987) 7 *Oxf. Jnl. Leg. Studs* 215–57 at 243; and Frederick Schauer, 'Precedent' (1987) 39 *Stanford L. Rev.* 571–605 at 591–2.

[2] Lord Wright, 'Precedents' (1943) 8 *Cambridge L.J.* 118–45 at 126.

[3] *Cassell & Co. Ltd* v. *Broome* [1972] AC 1027, 1085, HL. The claim that such interpretations are never appropriate is an overstatement. If, for example, the House of Lords in an earlier case made an unequivocal ruling to compensate for the vagueness or obscurity of a particular statutory provision, subsequent courts might well treat the ruling as if it were itself a hard and fast rule. On occasions, furthermore, the House of Lords may be specifically entrusted with the task of clarifying the law, as is the case, for example, when an Attorney-General's reference is passed on to it by the Court of Appeal under the Criminal Justice Act 1972, s. 36(3).

Not only are courts not required to draft the rules on which they act but, even when judges do take especial care to formulate a principle precisely, it is unlikely that it will be interpreted in the same way that a section in a statute would be interpreted.[4] Case law is peculiarly revisable in a way that enacted law is not: the judge who carefully articulates a principle is not determining its formulation in future disputes over materially identical facts – the likelihood, rather, is that it will be moulded and remoulded in the hands of successive courts.[5] We might even question whether it is correct to speak of precedents being interpreted. Although judges interpret statutes – and will sometimes consider the entire meaning of a statute to depend on the interpretation of a single word within it – they customarily purport to follow or distinguish or overrule precedents. Since the recorded case is not a strict verbal formulation of a principle, only exceptionally will judges conceive their task to be one of interpreting specific words or phrases within a case rather as they might focus on the precise wording of a statute. Instead, they will consider if the case is factually similar to or different from the case to be decided.[6] Case-law, we might say, unlike statute law, tends to be analogized rather than interpreted.

It might be objected that there is some sleight of hand in the claim that, because precedents lack the binding qualities of statutes, it is wrong to characterize precedents as binding. Cannot precedents have binding qualities which are *sui generis*? They can, and indeed do. But the notion of 'binding precedent' does not capture any of these qualities – it offers no insight into how the capacity of earlier decisions to constrain today's judges is different from that of statute law to do the same. In some of his

---

[4] See A. W. B. Simpson, 'The *Ratio Decidendi* of a Case and the Doctrine of Binding Precedent', in *Oxford Essays in Jurisprudence*, ed. A. G. Guest (Oxford: Oxford University Press, 1961), 148–75 at 162. See also Rolf Sartorius, 'The Doctrine of Precedent and the Problem of Relevance' (1967) 53 *Archiv für Rechts- und Sozialphilosophie* 343–66 at 353 ('[W]hat would be surprising would be the existence of any such thing as *the rule* established by a particular judicial decision in the manner in which there is such a thing as *the statutory rule* which is established by a particular instance of proper legislative enactment').

[5] Joseph Raz, *The Authority of Law: Essays on Law and Morality* (Oxford: Clarendon Press, 1979), 195. Hereafter *AL*. See also Rupert Cross and J. W. Harris, *Precedent in English Law*, 4th edn (Oxford: Clarendon Press, 1991), 73; Frederick Schauer, 'Is the Common Law Law?' (1989) 77 *California L. Rev.* 455–71 at 464.

[6] See Simpson, 'The *Ratio Decidendi* of a Case', 157–8; Raz, *AL*, 188. Interpretation of specific words or phrases uttered by judges is probably more likely in lower courts – i.e., when lower court judges need, in order to follow precedent, to work out the implications of a particular statement in an appeal court judgment.

earlier work, Ronald Dworkin recognized this problem and formulated a distinction intended to capture the peculiar nature and scope of precedential constraint: the distinction between the enactment force and the gravitational force of a precedent.[7] Occasionally, judges will find in a precedent 'a canonical form of words' that they are content to treat as the settled formulation of a common-law rule, rather as if the formulation were akin to the wording of a statute.[8] In this sense, a precedent might have enactment force. But such force, even when a precedent exhibits it, will not, according to Dworkin, encompass the entire influence that the precedent might have on later decisions. A judge might consider a precedent persuasive, for example, even though it is distinguishable from the case being decided. When judges resort to precedents in the process of deciding, they are reasoning not from a particular rule – as in the case of statutory interpretation – but for a particular ruling: they are making a case for treating the precedent as having some bearing on the case in hand.[9] Judges deciding the same case will often disagree about the extent to which particular precedents have gravitational force over that case, but they will nevertheless recognize that gravitational force is a quality that precedents possess. The justifications they provide for their decisions will, to varying degrees and in different ways, exhibit the pull of precedent.

The gravitational force of a precedent cannot be explained, Dworkin argues, by reference to the language of the judgment. Rather, it 'rests on the idea that fairness requires the consistent enforcement of rights', which means 'treating like cases alike'.[10] To this argument it might be objected that particular rights could be enforced consistently but insensitively within a jurisdiction, so that like cases are resolved in the same unjust way. To object thus, however, is implicitly to assume that justice and fairness go hand in hand. Dworkin rightly rejects this assumption: justice entails fairness (what he came to term integrity), but fairness does not have to entail justice. 'A judge ... might think it unjust to require compensation for any emotional injury. But if he accepts integrity and knows that some victims of emotional injury have already been given a right to compensation, he will have a reason for deciding in favor of'

---

[7] See Ronald Dworkin, *Taking Rights Seriously* (London: Duckworth, 1978), 110–23.

[8] See *ibid.*, 110–11. An example of such a formulation would be the rule in *Indermaur* v. *James* (1886) LR 1 CP 274 concerning occupiers' liability: see Simpson, 'The *Ratio Decidendi* of a Case', 158.

[9] See Dworkin, *Taking Rights Seriously*, 112.   [10] *Ibid.*, 116, 113.

others who seek compensation for emotional injury.[11] For Dworkin, deciding in a manner consistent with earlier decisions means taking account 'of the arguments of principle necessary to justify those decisions';[12] and taking account of arguments of principle means acknowledging their place not only within particular precedents but also as part of a larger 'scheme of abstract and concrete principles that provides a coherent justification for all common law precedents and, so far as these are to be justified on principle, constitutional and statutory provisions as well'.[13] The objection that consistent treatment is not necessarily tantamount to fair treatment is met, in other words, with the response that like cases are not simply treated alike but ideally will be situated within a larger framework of justification; and it is the quality and acceptability of this larger framework – the fairness of the legal system itself – which explains why the judge who seeks to enforce rights consistently is likely to be acting fairly.[14]

It seems perfectly possible that a judge who enforces rights consistently while being attentive to the bigger picture – making decisions which not only take account of precedent but which also fit with a coherent set of principles justifying the entire body of constitutional, statutory and common-law provisions – could still be perpetuating the injustices of a wicked legal system.[15] The objective here, however, is not to develop a critique of Dworkin's account of precedent but to highlight its value; for by emphasizing the notion of gravitational force he

---

[11] Ronald Dworkin, *Law's Empire* (London: Fontana, 1986), 177.
[12] Dworkin, *Taking Rights Seriously*, 113.   [13] *Ibid.*, 116–17.
[14] See Ronald Dworkin, *Justice in Robes* (Cambridge, Mass.: Belknap Press, 2006), 79, 123–4, 250 ('... coherence, not simply with particular doctrines here and there, but, as best as it can be achieved, principled coherence with the whole structure of law'). A similar line of argument is developed by Scott Hershovitz, 'Integrity and *Stare Decisis*', in *Exploring Law's Empire: The Jurisprudence of Ronald Dworkin*, ed. S. Hershovitz (Oxford: Oxford University Press, 2006), 103–18 at 113–15. Dworkin's jurisprudence provides a good illustration of why it is a mistake to think that when judges reason analogically they must always be reasoning from precedent; for his argument is that adjudication, properly conceived, requires a judge to draw analogies not only with earlier decisions on materially identical facts but also with decisions in unrelated fields of law which none the less contain appurtenant reasoning. The judge, in other words, will think across a range of decisions rather than simply downwards along a particular line of them. See Ronald Dworkin, *Life's Dominion: An Argument about Abortion and Euthanasia* (London: HarperCollins, 1993), 146; and also, more generally, Frederick Schauer, 'Why Precedent in Law (and Elsewhere) is Not Totally (or Even Substantially) About Analogy' (August 2007) *Kennedy School of Government Research Working Paper* RWP07-036.
[15] See Matthew H. Kramer, *In Defense of Legal Positivism: Law without Trimmings* (Oxford: Oxford University Press, 1999), 176–7.

illustrates that it is a mistake to treat precedent-following as equivalent to the interpretation of binding legal rules.[16] Gravitational force is, like authority, variable: not only might judges disagree about the significance of a particular precedent, or about what principle it should be understood to have established, but they might even disagree as to whether it should be acknowledged to have established a principle at all.[17]

The argument that the authority of judicial precedents is variable prompts an obvious question: what determines the degree to which any particular precedent is authoritative? The weight of a precedent can depend on many factors. Generally speaking, the higher the court the stronger the precedent: common-law judges in higher courts may sometimes consider the precedents of lower courts persuasive, but they will not consider themselves constrained to follow them in the way that lower-court judges usually feel obliged to follow higher-court precedents.[18] A precedent which represents the unanimous view of a panel of judges will probably be more authoritative than one which represents a majority view, or one which represents the view of a judge deciding alone.[19] Decisions of highly-regarded judges may carry more weight than those of comparative lightweights.

---

[16] For a general critique, see David Pannick, 'A Note on Dworkin and Precedent' (1980) 43 *MLR* 36–43.

[17] See Dworkin, *Taking Rights Seriously*, 112.

[18] For the types of reasons that a lower court might use for not following the precedent of a higher court, see Rafael Gely, 'Of Sinking and Escalating: A (Somewhat) New Look at Stare Decisis' (1998) 60 *Univ. Pittsburgh L. Rev.* 89–147 at 116–17; Evan H. Caminker, 'Why Must Inferior Courts Obey Superior Court Precedents?' (1994) 46 *Stanford L. Rev.* 817–73 at 856–65. In the American context, Caminker claims, a lower court's refusal to follow a higher court's precedent will occasionally resemble civil disobedience – as, for example, when the Ninth Circuit flouted Supreme Court precedent on the death penalty (see *ibid.*, 818–19).

[19] But bear in mind three provisos. First, a panel of judges might in a particular case demonstrate unanimity as to what the result should be but the judges might disagree as to their reasoning. Later courts might consider the authority of the precedent to be diminished because the reasoning was not unanimous. Secondly, although the presence of dissenting opinions might make particular decisions less authoritative than they might otherwise have been, such opinions can sometimes take on a life of their own – even, sometimes, becoming more 'authoritative' than the precedent itself: an example would be Justice Holmes's dissent in *Lochner* v. *New York* 198 U.S. 45 (1905). Thirdly, single-opinion judgments, particularly in final courts of appeal, sometimes make powerful precedents (perhaps especially when the judge delivering the opinion is a renowned expert in the relevant area of law): consider, e.g., Lord Templeman's speech in *Street* v. *Mountford* [1985] AC 809, HL. Lord Reid, in the speech quoted at the outset of this chapter, argued that 'it is never wise' in the House of Lords 'to have only one speech ... dealing with an important question of law', because judges and jurists are

So far as precedents are concerned, authority does not necessarily equate with longevity. The authority of an old precedent might be attributable in part to the fact that the judge responsible for it is well remembered by history. But the fact that a judge is highly renowned is no guarantee that his precedents will endure, for even the wisest of judges may be responsible for precedents which, for one reason or another, quickly become dated. Blackstone warned against rushing to dismiss precedents created by judges long dead: 'though their reason be not obvious at first view, yet we owe such a deference to former times as not to suppose they acted wholly without consideration'.[20] But more often than not the authority of a precedent will diminish rather than ripen with age. 'Precedents drawn from the days of travel by stage coach', Justice Cardozo observed in *MacPherson* v. *Buick*, 'do not fit the conditions of travel today.'[21] He might well have been overstating the case – some such precedents could still be relevant to today's travel conditions – but the possibility of precedents losing authority owing to obsolescence seems obvious. Yesterday's easy case may be today's hard case.[22] Contemporary English judges, for example, are far more inclined to consider tortious liability for psychiatric harm a genuine and complex problem than were their Victorian counterparts.[23] Social conditions change, Lord Watson observed in 1894, and it is to be expected that courts will reflect this fact: '[t]heir function ... is ... not necessarily to accept what was held to have been the rule of policy a hundred or a hundred and fifty years ago, but to ascertain, with as near an approach to accuracy as circumstances permit, what is the rule of policy for the then present time.'[24] For Justice Holmes, writing around the same time, the

---

likely to reduce that speech to its enactment force, interpreting words and phrases within the speech rather as they might interpret the wording of a statute. *Cassell & Co. Ltd* v. *Broome* [1972] AC 1027, 1084–5. His point is not that single-opinion judgments may have insufficient, but that they may be accorded too much, authority.

[20] William Blackstone, *Commentaries on the Laws of England*, 4 vols. (Chicago: University of Chicago Press, 1979 [1765–69]), I, 70.

[21] *MacPherson* v. *Buick Motor Co.*, 217 NY 382, 391; 111 N.E. 1050, 1053 (N.Y. 1916).

[22] See Kenneth S. Abraham, 'Three Fallacies of Interpretation: A Comment on Precedent and Judicial Decision' (1981) 23 *Arizona L. Rev.* 771–83 at 772.

[23] Cf., e.g., *Victorian Railways* v. *Coultas* (1888) 13 App. Cas. 222, PC with *White* v. *Chief Constable of South Yorkshire Police* [1999] 2 AC 455, HL.

[24] *Nordenfelt* v. *Maxim Nordenfelt Guns & Ammunition Co. Ltd* [1894] AC 535, 554, HL. Lionel Smith has argued that when a court concludes that an 'earlier decision, which on its face is a binding precedent, was made in and for societal conditions that no longer exist', although the court 'may conclude that the decision need not be followed' this 'does not correspond to disagreeing with the decision'. The court is not disagreeing with the earlier decision, but

mere fact that a precedent is old should be of no consequence. An ancient precedent which is relevant to the problem facing us today ought not to be dismissed as without authority simply because of its age. By the same token, however, '[i]t is revolting to have no better reason for a rule of law than that so it was laid down in the time of Henry IV. It is still more revolting if the grounds upon which it was laid down have vanished long since, and the rule simply persists from blind imitation of the past.'[25]

concluding that while it may have been the correct decision for its time 'the earlier judge would not have decided as he or she did, had he or she been operating in the conditions of today'. Lionel Smith, 'The Rationality of Tradition', in *Properties of Law: Essays in Honour of Jim Harris*, ed. T. Endicott, J. Getzler and E. Peel (Oxford: Oxford University Press, 2006), 297–313 at 307, 309. The fact that today's court decides not to follow a prior decision certainly does not mean that the court must be disagreeing with that decision. But it might be disagreeing with the decision. There are, I think, three problems with the argument as Smith frames it. First, it is not inconceivable that a judge today might argue that a decision from the past is not only inappropriate to today's conditions but was inappropriate to its time. In such circumstances, it is difficult to know how to characterize the current judge's stance other than as one of disagreement. Secondly, judges do indeed sometimes express themselves to be in disagreement (albeit usually respectfully so) with the anachronistic statements of their forebears. The argument as set out by Smith suggests that judges may profess to be in disagreement with such statements and yet not be, as if they do not know their own minds. Thirdly, the claim that 'the earlier judge would not have decided as he or she did, had he or she been operating in the conditions of today' is necessarily speculative. Even if it is fair to assume that a nineteenth-century judge relocated to a twentieth-century court – whatever that might entail – would deliver opinions different from those which he would have delivered a century earlier, it might be that the difference would extend only to the wording rather than to the sentiments of the judge's opinions. Whether, say, Lord Halsbury would have been of a genuinely different cast of mind had he been on the bench today, and how his views might differ were we to take it for granted that they would, are matters which we can only meet with guesswork, because we simply cannot know what old judges would think and say were they alive and in office now.

[25] Oliver Wendell Holmes, Jr, 'The Path of the Law' (1897) 10 *Harvard L. Rev.* 457–78 at 469. Holmes did not believe that old rules are commonly followed in such an unreflective fashion. Even though the reason which first gave rise to a rule may have been forgotten, it might remain in force owing to adaptation: 'ingenious minds set themselves to inquire how it is to be accounted for. Some ground of policy is thought of, which seems to explain it and to reconcile it with the present state of things; and then the rule adapts itself to the new reasons which have been found for it, and enters on a new career. The old form receives a new content, and in time even the form modifies itself to fit the meaning which it has received.' O. W. Holmes, Jr, *The Common Law* (Boston: Little, Brown & Co., 1881), 5.

Sometimes, the past is not so much blindly imitated as misunderstood. That is, modern lawyers will now and again assume a precedent to stand for something that it was never intended to stand for: one nineteenth-century Scottish judge expressed the problem as an inter-jurisdictional rather than an inter-temporal one when he observed that '[t]he more I am able to collect of English law, I am only the more confident that we do not understand nine out of ten of the cases which are quoted to us, and that, in attempts to apply that law, we

The attention which later courts pay to a precedent will depend very much on how judges and lawyers assess it as an effort at legal reasoning. Much of the last two paragraphs could be reformulated to support this contention: the most authoritative precedents are likely to be those which represent unanimous reasoning, the reasoning of the most senior judges or (what is often the same thing) the very best legal minds or reasoning which has been tried and tested. '[W]hen confronted with a difficult case', one civil-law professor has observed, 'any lawyer in any country, any judge and any advocate ... tries to find, if not some support, at least some enlightenment and some inspiration, from what judges, and particularly the best judges, have found in similar cases'.[26] In English law, law reporters can increase the likelihood that a decision will be treated as especially authoritative by signalling – through the insertion of *cur. adv. vult* after the arguments of counsel – that judgment was reserved (i.e., only delivered after some reflection) rather than delivered extempore at the conclusion of the case.[27] Judicial precedents, we saw in the previous chapter, existed before reasoned decision-making was the norm, and to this day there is no absolute rule in English law requiring that judicial decisions be supported by reasons;[28] yet it is unlikely that a modern decision unaccompanied by reasoning would ever be considered much of a precedent.[29] A precedent does not have to be reasoned – a panel of judges could, in theory at least, explicitly cast a vote to determine the outcome in case *A*, thereby creating the precedent to be followed in materially identical case *B*. But the absence of reasons tends

---

run the greatest risk of spoiling our own by mistaking theirs.' *M'Cowan* v. *Wright* (1852) 15 D. 229, 232, *per* Lord Justice-Clerk Hope.

[26] M. I. Kisch, *ICJ Pleadings, Application of the Convention of 1902 Governing the Guardianship of Infants (Netherlands v. Sweden). Judgment of 28 November 1958* (Hague: International Court of Justice, 1958), 169, cited in Mohamed Shahabuddeen, *Precedent in the World Court* (Cambridge: Cambridge University Press, 1996), 237.

[27] *Cur. adv. vult.* = *Curia advisari vult* (the court wishes to consider the matter). The convention is, of course, not used in those common-law jurisdictions where there is an expectation that judgments will be reserved. For judicial endorsement of the claim that reserved judgments generally carry more weight than those delivered on the spur of the moment, see Charles Russell, *Behind the Appellate Curtain* (Birmingham: Holdsworth Club, 1969), 3 ('It is important in considering appellate judgments to differentiate between reserved judgments and unreserved judgments. The quality of the former is, or should be, better than that of the latter'), though cf. *ibid.* at 8–9 where it is emphasized that even *cur. adv. vult* is not a guarantee of authoritativeness.

[28] See *Halsbury's Laws of England*, 4th edn, vol. 1(1) (London: Butterworths, 1989), 156–7, 190–2, paras. 83, 99.

[29] Although there might be in a court's decision points which are accepted without argument yet treated as part of a strong precedent.

to make precedents weak. Even if litigants accept unreasoned decisions in their favour, they are likely to feel uneasy about them, not least because they might expect them to be vulnerable to appeal; whereas there is a greater likelihood that unsuccessful litigants will accept decisions against them if those decisions are well reasoned.[30] Almost any reasoning is likely to be better than none.

The argument set out in the previous paragraph – that precedents do not have to be reasoned but tend to be more authoritative when they are – is, we have seen, supported by English common-law history. While the purpose of this chapter is to examine the relationship between precedent and reason, it is worth emphasizing not only that unreasoned decisions can be precedents but also that even the most carefully reasoned decisions need not be. Joseph Raz has observed that an adjudicative system could imaginably be one of absolute discretion, in the sense that the judicial convention may be to decide each case on the basis of reasons and taking into account whatever considerations seem relevant.[31] Such a system would not be arbitrary – judges would decide according to reasons, and because of this 'we could expect some regularity in the decisions of the courts'[32] – but neither would precedents constrain. 'It is unlikely', Raz observes, 'that such a system has ever existed or will ever exist', not only because 'the decisions of the courts over a period of time are unlikely to reflect any consistent line on any issue'[33] but also because it is inefficient to adjudicate every problem afresh each time it arises. Imagining the system nevertheless helps us to recognize that the relationship between precedent and reason is a contingent one. Precedents usually embody reasons, and precedent-following is often a good way to avoid reinventing the wheel; but within the common law tradition there is a discernible line of thought which has it that we must not assume precedents to be nothing more than reasons. Sometimes, so the argument goes, we may refer to the reason for a decision as if it were somehow the essence of that decision, but identifying the essence of the decision may in fact require that we do more than look to the judicial reasoning.

---

[30] See Neil Duxbury, *Random Justice: On Lotteries and Legal Decision-Making* (Oxford: Clarendon Press, 1999), 114–39.
[31] See Raz, *AL*, 112.   [32] *Ibid.*
[33] *Ibid.* Unlikely, but not impossible: for an account of a system perhaps not very far removed from that which Raz imagines, see Rebecca Redwood French, *The Golden Yoke: The Legal Cosmology of Buddhist Tibet* (Ithaca, NY: Cornell University Press, 1995).

1. Looking for a certain *ratio*

The most obvious reason we achieve little by saying that the essence of a judicial decision might be found by looking to the reasons supporting it is that decisions are often accompanied by various reasons of varying importance. As early as 1600, William Fulbeck drew a distinction between 'the principal points' and the 'bye-matters' to be found in case-law.[34] Three quarters of a century later, Vaughan C.J. argued in the Court of Common Pleas that the 'bye-matters' are of little or no consequence. 'An opinion given in Court, if not necessary to the judgment given of record, but that it might have been as well given if no such, or a contrary, opinion had been broach'd is no judicial opinion, nor more than a gratis dictum.'[35] One knows one is dealing with 'bye-matter', in other words, if a point can either be taken out of a decision or the meaning of the point reversed without the decision itself being altered. The test, we will see, is not especially reliable. And to dismiss the peripheral judicial opinion as no judicial opinion at all seems rather harsh. But what is most significant is the fact that, by the seventeenth century, the distinction between what is central and what is tangential to a decision was in the making.[36]

Today, it is difficult to imagine a common lawyer being unaware of this distinction – the distinction, that is, between the *ratio decidendi* of and the *obiter dicta* within a case. *Ratio decidendi* can mean either 'reason for the decision' or 'reason for deciding'.[37] It should not be inferred from this that the *ratio decidendi* of a case must be the judicial reasoning. Judicial reasoning may be integral to the *ratio*, but the *ratio* itself is more than the reasoning, and within many cases there will be

---

[34] William Fulbeck, *Direction, or Preparative to the Study of Law*, 2nd edn (London: Clarke, 1829; orig. publ. 1600), 237–8.
[35] *Bole* v. *Horton* (1673) Vaugh. 360, 382.
[36] The distinction seems to have emerged as decisions on demurrer became less common. A connection between the two developments would make sense, because it might be expected that as judges became less inclined to give official opinions on hypothetical problems (such as when a defendant contended that there would still have been no cause of action even if all the facts alleged by the plaintiff had been true) they would develop some criterion which minimizes the significance of hypothetical judicial pronunciations. See Simpson, 'The *Ratio Decidendi* of a Case', 160–1.
[37] See *Halsbury's Laws of England*, 4th edn, vol. 26 (London: Butterworths, 1979), 292, para. 573 ('The enunciation of the reason or principle upon which a question before a court has been decided is alone binding as a precedent. This underlying principle is called the *ratio decidendi*').

judicial reasoning that constitutes not part of the *ratio*, but *obiter dicta*. An *obiter dictum* is literally a 'saying by the way'. In judicial opinions, passages which are *obiter* come in various forms – they might be unnecessary to the outcome, or unconnected to the facts of the case or directed to a point which neither party sought to argue – and may have been formulated by the judge with less care or seriousness than would have been the case had the passage been part of the reason for the decision.[38] Common-law jurists and judges have occasionally tried to pile distinctions upon the basic *ratio-obiter* distinction – arguing that a case might contain a 'holding' which is more authoritative than a *ratio decidendi*, and that there can be 'judicial dicta' which are less authoritative than *rationes decidendi* but more authoritative than any *obiter dictum*.[39] But it is the basic distinction that has endured.[40] That it should have done so is hardly surprising. There are, we will see, good reasons for distinguishing *rationes decidendi* from *obiter dicta*. But before turning our attention to those reasons we ought to address various other matters.

a. The complexity of case-law

First, there is the fact that the distinction between *ratio decidendi* and *obiter dicta*, although important, is not easily made. '[T]he argumentative weight of the *ratio* of a case', one civil law theorist has observed, is partly determined by 'the relatively well-defined meta-rules of how to read precedents among judges and the legal profession.'[41] The greater the effort devoted to distinguishing what is the *ratio* and what is *obiter*, however, the more likely it will seem that no such meta-rules could ever exist. In *The Common Law Tradition*, Karl Llewellyn dismissed the search

---

[38] See *Flower* v. *Ebbw Vale Steel, Iron & Coal Co. Ltd* [1934] 2 KB 132, 154, CA, *per* Talbot J.; *United States* v. *Crawley*, 837 F.2d 291, 292–3 (7th Cir. 1988) (Posner J.).

[39] See, e.g., Karl Llewellyn, *The Case Law System in America*, ed. P. Gewirtz, Eng. trans. M. Ansaldi (Chicago: University of Chicago Press, 1989 [1933]), 14–15; *Richard West & Partners (Inverness) Ltd* v. *Dick* [1969] 2 Ch. 424, 431–2, CA, *per* Megarry J. ('But there are *dicta* and *dicta*'); *Brunner* v. *Greenslade* [1971] Ch. 993, 1002–03, CA, *per* Megarry J.; Cross and Harris, *Precedent in English Law*, 81; Robert Megarry, *A New Miscellany at Law: Yet Another Diversion for Lawyers and Others*, ed. B. A. Garner (Oxford: Hart, 2005), 254–5.

[40] Though the language used to articulate the distinction can vary. In the United States, for example, lawyers tend to distinguish the 'holding' of a case from *dicta* contained in it.

[41] Raimo Siltala, *A Theory of Precedent: From Analytical Positivism to a Post-Analytical Philosophy of Law* (Oxford: Hart, 2000), 148.

for the *ratio decidendi* of a case as the futility of 'providing a Never-Never Single Answer' and, as for meta-rules for handling precedents, claimed that there are at least sixty-four that judges and lawyers might use.[42] Jurists, we will see, have been unable to agree on either a definition of or a test for identifying the *ratio decidendi*, and the use of the concept in the courts has been, in the words of one legal philosopher, 'both unprincipled and inconsistent'.[43]

Why has the concept of the *ratio decidendi* left legal thinkers so confounded? There seem to be six principal answers to this question. First, the *ratio decidendi* and *obiter dicta* often blur into one another. *Obiter dicta*, Cardozo remarked, 'are not always ticketed as such, and one does not recognize them always at a glance'.[44] Much the same could be said about the *ratio decidendi*. A rough and ready way of separating the two would be to say that statements which form part of a dissenting judgment cannot be part of the *ratio*. But this test is patently unsatisfactory. A dissenting judge might disagree with some parts of a majority judgment while explicitly approving of others; in such instances, statements by dissenting judges which show them to be in partial agreement with the majority contribute to the *ratio decidendi*. A judge in the majority might wish to give supplementary reasons for his or her decision, furthermore, without making those reasons part of the *ratio*.[45] In some instances, a judge might believe, or be persuaded by counsel, that an *obiter* statement in an earlier case – whether it appears in a dissenting or in a majority opinion – now ought to be treated as if it were a *ratio decidendi*.[46] In others, a judge might recognize a statement in an earlier decision of a higher court to be technically *obiter* but, given

---

[42] Karl N. Llewellyn, *The Common Law Tradition: Deciding Appeals* (Boston: Little, Brown & Co., 1960), 14 n. 9, 77–91.

[43] Gidon Gottlieb, *The Logic of Choice: An Investigation of the Concepts of Rule and Rationality* (London: Allen & Unwin, 1968), 78.

[44] Benjamin N. Cardozo, *The Nature of the Judicial Process* (New Haven: Yale University Press, 1921), 30.

[45] See, e.g., *Behrens v. Bertram Mills Circus Ltd* [1957] 2 QB 1, 24, *per* Devlin J. ('A judge may often give additional reasons for his decision without wishing to make them part of the *ratio decidendi*; he may not be sufficiently convinced of their cogency as to want them to have the full authority of precedent, and yet may wish to state them so that those who later may have the duty of investigating the same point will start with some guidance'). This in part explains why it is an oversimplification to say that '[e]ssentially the *ratio* is the reason(s) by which the court justifies its decision', and a mistake to 'assume that all the court's reasons of whatever generality are part of the *ratio*'. Raz, *AL*, 184.

[46] Cf. those instances in which later courts recognize *obiter dicta* in a particular case to be indeed just that (i.e., there is no blurring), but nevertheless now consider the *dicta* to

the relevance of the statement to the problem at hand and the eminence of the judge who made it, determine that it ought to be followed, perhaps even in preference to the *ratio decidendi* of an inferior court.[47] ('It may be that those statements in the judgments of those two learned judges were *dicta* in the sense that they were not necessary for the determination of that case', one Chancery judge observed in 1935 apropos of complementary utterances by two Lords Justices of Appeal, 'but they are *dicta* which I think I ought to follow'.[48]) The most compelling *dicta* will often, for all practical purposes, be indistinguishable from pronouncements which form part of the *ratio*.[49] All five of the Law Lords sitting in *Hedley Byrne* v. *Heller* agreed that it is possible to be liable in tort for negligent misrepresentation, even though there was in that case no such liability because the representations to the plaintiffs were expressly made without responsibility.[50] Since the claim was not that there was negligent misrepresentation in *Hedley Byrne*, but only that liability for such misrepresentation was a possibility (i.e., there would have been liability but for the fact that there was a disclaimer), it is at least arguable that their Lordships' observations about this type of

---

be more authoritative than the *ratio decidendi* of the case. Although it would seem that dissenting opinions by definition do not form part of the *ratio decidendi* they can, as we have noted already, sometimes take on a life, and accumulate authority, of their own.

[47] See G. W. Paton and G. Sawer, '*Ratio Decidendi* and *Obiter Dictum* in Appellate Courts' (1947) 63 *LQR* 461–85 at 475–6. MacCormick has observed more generally that '*obiter dicta* are not to be dismissed merely because they are not binding. These after all include judges' discussion of the inherent values of the law, their weighing of principles, and indeed their attempts to formulate principles hitherto more implicit than explicit in the law. Much legal argument concerns matters such as these, and the absence of strictly binding force in such dicta is irrelevant to their broader value as an element in legal discourse. Moreover, it is not only as binding precedents that lawyers read cases. Precedents play a great part in argument by analogy in law, and argument by analogy is an important form of argument in the law.' Neil MacCormick, *Rhetoric and the Rule of Law: A Theory of Legal Reasoning* (Oxford: Oxford University Press, 2005), 160.

[48] *Tees Conservancy Commissioners* v. *James* [1935] Ch. 544, 560, *per* Farwell J. The judge was paying deference to statements by Lord Esher, M.R. and Lopes L.J. in *Salford Corporation* v. *Lancashire County Council* (1890) LR 25 QBD 384, CA. The prolix rendering of the passage in the *Times Law Reports* makes the deference more vivid: 'It may be that those statements were *dicta* in the sense that it [*sic*] was not necessary for the determination of that case, but they are *dicta* which I cannot possibly disregard of two learned judges whose experience in matters of that kind was so great and of such high authority that it would be quite wrong of me to treat them as *dicta* and disregard them.' *Tees Conservancy Commissioners* v. *James* (1935) 51 TLR 219, 223.

[49] Cross and Harris, *Precedent in English Law*, 77.

[50] *Hedley Byrne & Co.* v. *Heller & Partners, Ltd* [1962] 1 QB 396.

liability were merely *obiter* and that the law remained that there could be no liability for negligent misrepresentation unless there was a contractual duty of care.[51] But, as Cairns J. observed in *Anderson v. Rhodes*:

> that would be an unrealistic view to take. When five members of the House of Lords have all said, after close examination of the authorities, that a certain type of tort exists, I think that a judge of first instance should proceed on the basis that it does exist without pausing to embark on an investigation of whether what was said was necessary to the ultimate decision.[52]

The second difficulty with the *ratio decidendi* is that in some decisions it will be impossible to locate, let alone separate from *obiter dicta*. For the simple fact is that not every case will yield a *ratio*.[53] In *Central Asbestos Ltd v. Dodd*,[54] the House of Lords held by a majority of three to two that the respondent, who had contracted asbestosis owing to the defendant's negligence, sued for damages within the relevant limitation period. This period began, Lords Reid and Morris of Borth-y-Gest contended, from the moment the respondent discovered he had a worthwhile cause of action. Lords Salmon and Simon of Glaisdale dissented, arguing that time had begun to run some two years earlier, by which point the respondent had not only given up work because of the effects of the asbestosis but was aware of the facts constituting the alleged negligence. Lord Pearson agreed with Lords Salmon and Simon that the respondent's lack of knowledge that he had a worthwhile cause of action was not a material fact which prevented time running against him, but nevertheless concluded that, even if the limitation period had run as Lords Salmon and Simon argued, the respondent had only become aware of the alleged negligence within that period. In *Harper v. N.C.B.*,[55] the plaintiff discovered he had a cause of action within the limitation period but became aware of the material facts before that period began. At first instance it was held that he should be refused leave

---

[51] In other words, that *Candler v. Crane, Christmas & Co.* [1951] 2 KB 164 remained an authoritative precedent.
[52] *W.B. Anderson & Sons Ltd v. Rhodes (Liverpool) Ltd* [1967] 2 All ER 850, 857.
[53] See Cross and Harris, *Precedent in English Law*, 91–2; Raz, *AL*, 184; J. L. Montrose, 'Judicial Law Making and Law Applying' (1956) 3 *Butterworth's South African L. Rev.* 187–205 at 202–3. Indeed, not every case is intended to yield a *ratio*. Generally, for example, the decisions of the European Court of Justice contain no *ratio* and will bind only the parties to the case.
[54] *Central Asbestos Co. Ltd v. Dodd* [1973] AC 518.
[55] *In re Harper and others v. National Coal Board (Intended Action)* [1974] QB 614.

to issue a writ because, in *Dodd*, Lords Pearson, Salmon and Simon had contended that time ran from the moment the respondent became aware of the facts founding his cause of action. But the Court of Appeal reversed this decision on the basis that it was wrong to adopt a line of reasoning which led to a conclusion contrary to that reached by the House of Lords. *Dodd* might have been settled by a majority of three to two, but in terms of reasoning the judgment resembled a Venn diagram, with Lord Pearson agreeing with Lords Reid and Morris that the respondent had issued a writ for damages within the limitation period but taking a view similar to that of Lords Salmon and Simon regarding the state of affairs that marked the beginning of that period. In these circumstances, Stephenson L.J. argued, 'I do not think that we can treat the reasoning of the majority – Lord Reid and Lord Morris of Borth-y-Gest – as the *ratio decidendi* of the House. It is the *ratio* given by only two out of five.'[56] 'We ought to accept the reasoning of the three in the majority *if* we can discover it', Lord Denning elaborated:

> [b]ut it is not discoverable. The three were divided. Lord Reid and Lord Morris of Borth-y-Gest took one view of the law. Lord Pearson took another. We cannot say that Lord Reid and Lord Morris of Borth-y-Gest were correct: because we know that their reasoning on the law was in conflict with the reasoning of the other three. We cannot say that Lord Pearson was correct: because we know that the reasoning which he accepted on the law led the other two (Lord Simon of Glaisdale and Lord Salmon) to a wrong conclusion. So we cannot say that any of the three in the majority was correct ... The result is that there is no discernible *ratio* among the majority of the House of Lords.[57]

The conclusion of the Court of Appeal in *Harper* v. *N. C. B.* was that *Central Asbestos Ltd* v. *Dodd* yielded no discernible *ratio decidendi* common to the majority of the House of Lords. The problem more commonly raised by decisions composed of a plurality of judgments – and the third of our six answers as to why the concept of the *ratio decidendi* has proved so perplexing – is that they yield multiple *rationes* rather than no *ratio*. A decision based on only one judgment may contain more than one *ratio*. '[T]here is in my opinion', Lord Simonds observed in *Jacobs* v. *London County Council*, 'no justification for regarding as *obiter dictum* a reason given by a judge for his decision,

---

[56] *Ibid.*, 623.   [57] *Ibid.*, 621–2.

because he has given another reason also'.[58] Multiple *rationes* are more usually discernible, nevertheless, in decisions composed of more than one judgment – where an evenly composed court is equally divided, for instance, or where a majority of judges reaches the same conclusion but for different reasons. In *London* v. *Attenborough*, Greer L.J. argued that such instances should not pose a problem, for 'we are not entitled to pick out the first reason as the *ratio decidendi* and neglect the second, or to pick out the second reason as the *ratio decidendi* and neglect the first: we must take both as forming the ground of the judgment'.[59] But this makes light of the difficulty. Should a court reach a decision on three different and incompatible grounds, *A*, *B* and *C*, each of which alone would suffice to support the decision, then, if a later court accepts ground *A* but rejects grounds *B* and *C*, it would appear to be following not the *ratio decidendi* of the case but one of the *rationes decidendi* of the case. Furthermore, if ground *A* – or either of the other grounds – is selected as the *ratio decidendi* to be followed it might, within the decision for which it is considered to be the reason, be a rather fragile authority. If grounds *A*, *B* and *C* were offered by three different judges who composed the majority in a five-member court, for example, the fact that, say, ground *A* was selected as the *ratio* does not preclude the possibility of that ground having been accepted by none of the other four judges.[60] Where a majority of judges agree as to the decision but disagree as to the correct grounds for the decision, extracting a *ratio decidendi* from the case may be an arbitrary exercise.[61] Perhaps we should not be surprised occasionally to encounter the argument that *rationes decidendi* might be more unequivocal and easily definable within a system of case law when judges sitting on multi-member panels are in the habit of voicing doubts and disagreements only for good reasons, such as to affect an outcome.[62] And perhaps we should not be surprised to find courts concluding now

---

[58] *Jacobs* v. *London County Council* [1950] AC 361, 369, HL.
[59] *London Jewellers Ltd* v. *Attenborough* [1934] 2 KB 206, 222, CA.
[60] See A. M. Honoré, '*Ratio Decidendi*: Judge and Court' (1955) 71 *LQR* 196–201 at 198.
[61] See *ibid.*, 201 ('The notions of a *decision* and a *reason for a decision* apply primarily to individuals. When they are applied to a group, such as a court consisting of several judges, artificial rules are needed to determine what shall count as a decision or reason of the group'); Cross and Harris, *Precedent in English Law*, 85 ('The *ratio decidendi* is a conception which is peculiarly appropriate to a single judgment. Accordingly it is probably impossible to avoid something in the nature of arbitrary rules to meet cases in which several judgments are delivered').
[62] See, e.g., Rupert Cross, 'The *Ratio Decidendi* and a Plurality of Speeches in the House of Lords' (1977) 93 *LQR* 378–85 at 383 ('[I]n the interests of a coherent system of law, it is

and again that what had been assumed to be the *ratio* of an earlier decision in fact was not.[63]

In the type of instance described in the last paragraph, it is unlikely to be clear what a precedent is authority for until a later court has decided which *ratio* within the precedent should be followed.[64] The fourth way in which the concept of the *ratio decidendi* has perplexed legal thinkers concerns its coming into being. Is the *ratio* of a case 'the court's own version of the rule of the case' or what the case 'will be made to stand for by another later court'?[65] It is doubtful that there is any common law court which would accept as a convention the blunt proposition that the *ratio* of a case is created retrospectively. One reason judges might be expected to resist such a convention is that accepting it would make it difficult to argue that a court had misunderstood the *ratio* of an earlier case. Unless that case has already had a *ratio* imposed on it, after all, how could it be said that there exists a *ratio* to be misunderstood? Nevertheless, there clearly are instances where the matter of what constitutes the *ratio* of a case is up for grabs and will not be settled until another court has addressed it. The difficulty of the issue can easily be exaggerated; the *ratio decidendi* of a case is often not so much interpreted as repeated, for one need look no further than the headnote of most cases to know that the case yields a *ratio* which will be unambiguous to any later court. But the fact that a *ratio* can be contested illustrates how judicial precedents may prove malleable, for in those instances where later courts select a *ratio* from two or more possible *rationes* within a case, they are determining for what authority the precedent should stand.

---

surely possible for a judge to suppress an occasional doubt than to give a separate judgment ...'); Megarry, *A New Miscellany at Law*, 254.

[63] In the case of *Beedie* in 1998, the Court of Appeal concluded that Lord Morris of Borth-y-Gest's articulation of double-jeopardy principles in *Connelly* v. *DPP* [1964] AC 1254, HL was not the *ratio decidendi* of the decision, as it is assumed to be in the 1997 edition of *Archbold's Criminal Evidence, Pleading and Practice*, but rather a dissent from the majority judgment. See *R* v. *Beedie* [1998] QB 356, 360–1.

[64] See R. E. Megarry, 'Precedent in the Court of Appeal: How Binding is "Binding"?' (1958) 74 *LQR* 350–2 at 351 ('In such cases the rule that the Court of Appeal is bound by its own decisions appears to mean that it is only fractionally bound by its own decisions, and that it is entitled to select which fraction to be bound by'); also Neil MacCormick, 'Why Cases Have *Rationes* and What These Are', in *Precedent in Law*, ed. L. Goldstein (Oxford: Clarendon Press, 1987), 155–82 at 171.

[65] K. N. Llewellyn, *The Bramble Bush: On Our Law and Its Study* (New York: Oceana, 1930), 53 (emphasis omitted).

The question of whether the *ratio* is created through the judge's words or through the interpretation of the judge's words perhaps need not exercise us all that much. The only significant points to emerge from this puzzle seem to be that the *ratio* can be determined as much by the interpreter as by the speaker, and that when judges excavate *rationes* from past decisions they are likely to influence if not determine how that precedent is conceived as authority in the future. Certainly, some legal theorists take the room for manoeuvre that comes with the retrospective determination of *rationes* very seriously.[66] If courts do sometimes impose *rationes* retrospectively, MacCormick observes, it might be argued that in those instances they take 'some proposition of law' which they 'find it expedient to ascribe to an earlier decision as the ground of that decision which may then be used to help justify some later decision'.[67] When judges identify the *ratio* of an earlier case in which more than one possible *ratio* presents itself, in other words, they may in fact be making rather than following law. While this is a fair point, it is worth bearing in mind – particularly since the argument will be pursued in the next chapter – that the selection of the *ratio* is unlikely to be an act of unconstrained discretion. Judges invariably feel compelled to provide cogent reasons for the constructions they place on past decisions, and may well consider themselves bound by particular rules of practice; and in any event, the available range of *rationes* in an earlier case will be limited.

The final two difficulties posed by the concept of the *ratio decidendi* go hand in hand. First, there is a definitional problem. So far, this issue has been skirted because '*ratio decidendi*' has been taken simply to mean 'reason for the decision' or 'reason for deciding'. We will see presently, however, that this is by no means the only definition of the *ratio decidendi*, and that to rely on this definition alone is to risk oversimplifying the concept. Secondly, there is the problem of determining the *ratio decidendi*. By defining the *ratio* we settle on what to look for. But this still leaves unaddressed the task of settling on a method by which to look. Looking for something that has been defined in a variety of ways is likely to prove difficult. Although the problem of defining the *ratio* is not the same as that of determining it, there is some sense in dealing with the problems together, not only because many jurists have addressed the

---

[66] See, e.g., Julius Stone, *Precedent and Law: Dynamics of Common Law Growth* (Sydney: Butterworths, 1985), 2; Siltala, *A Theory of Precedent*, 243–4.
[67] MacCormick, 'Why Cases Have *Rationes*', 157.

problems as if they are all of a piece but also because the difficulties with efforts to devise a method of locating the *ratio decidendi* are often connected to the problem of formulating a satisfactory definition of the concept.

b. Definitions and tests

There are some things that can be said about the *ratio decidendi* with certainty. It is certainly wrong, for example, to define the *ratio decidendi* as a proposition in a judgment which, were its meaning to be inverted, would have altered the decision. '[T]he beginner can determine whether a given proposition of law is involved in a given case', Eugene Wambaugh argued in 1892, by 'first fram[ing] carefully the supposed proposition of law'.

> Let him then insert in the proposition a word reversing its meaning. Let him then inquire whether, if the court had conceived this new proposition to be good and to be the point upon which the case ought to turn, the decision could have been the same. If the answer be affirmative, then, however excellent the original proposition may be, the case is not a precedent for that proposition ...[68]

Although Wambaugh found something resembling this test in a United States Supreme Court decision of 1853,[69] his argument is in fact closer to that which Vaughan C.J. had formulated in the seventeenth century.[70] It was intimated earlier that Vaughan's method for distinguishing *rationes decidendi* from *obiter dicta* is not especially reliable. In fact, the main reason for doubting Wambaugh's test and the reason for doubting Vaughan's are the same: where a court bases its decision on two alternative grounds, taking either ground and reversing its meaning does not alter the decision, for although the meaning of one

---

[68] Eugene Wambaugh, *The Study of Cases* (Boston: Little, Brown, & Co., 1892), 5–6.
[69] See *Carroll* v. *Carroll's Lessee*, 57 U.S. 275, 286–7 (1853) (Curtis, J.: 'If the construction put by the court of a State upon one of its statutes was not a matter in judgment, if it might have been decided either way without affecting any right brought into question, then, according to the principles of the common law, an opinion on such a question is not a decision. To make it so, there must have been an application of the judicial mind to the precise question necessary to be determined to fix the rights of the parties and decide to whom the property in contestation belongs').
[70] One commentator writes that Wambaugh's test 'seems to be based' on Vaughan's formulation: see R. E. Megarry (1948) *LQR* 29–31 at 31. There may be substance to the speculation, but I have not been able to find any.

of the grounds sufficient to support the decision has thereby been reversed, the other one is undisturbed and so the decision stands. Where a case contains two independent operative *rationes*, in other words, the inversion test decrees that there are only *obiter dicta*, for neither *ratio* is necessary to the decision.[71]

Other jurists, while not adopting the inversion test, have followed Wambaugh in treating the *ratio decidendi* as something that is necessary to a decision. 'In order that an opinion may have the weight of a precedent', according to John Chipman Gray, 'it must be an opinion the formation of which is necessary for the decision of a particular case'.[72] Gray's conception of the *ratio* is as easy to fault as is Wambaugh's, for it will never actually be necessary that a decision-maker form a particular opinion in order that a specific decision is reached.[73] Rupert Cross argued more precisely that the *ratio* 'is any rule of law expressly or impliedly treated by the judge as a necessary step in reaching his conclusion, having regard to the line of reasoning adopted by him.'[74] The *ratio*, in other words, is something that the judge believes to be necessary, rather than something that actually is necessary, to the decision. But what exactly does the judge treat as necessary to the decision? Cross's assumption – that the *ratio* is the 'rule of law' that a judge treats as necessary to a decision – does not seem quite correct. When, for example, a judge interprets a statute in the process of reaching a decision, the *ratio* is what the judge believes to be the best

---

[71] See Lord Justice Asquith, 'Some Aspects of the Work of the Court of Appeal' (1950) n.s. 1 *JSPTL* 350–62 at 359–61; also *United States* v. *Johnson*, 256 F.3d 895, 915 n. 8 (9th Cir. 2001) (Kozinski J.: 'Under [the] rationale ... that everything not necessary to the result is *dicta*, both alternative holdings are *dicta* because neither is necessary to the result. We can test this proposition by asking the question: Would the result change if either of the alternative holdings were removed? The answer, of course, is no. Since either could be removed without affecting the result, neither is necessary'). The fact that a case contains more than one *ratio* is not alone sufficient to undercut the inversion test, for the *rationes* within a case will sometimes be interdependent rather than independent. See Montrose, 'Judicial Law Making and Law Applying', 193–4. Where the *rationes* are interdependent, reversing one might alter the other, which in turn might affect the decision.

[72] John Chipman Gray, *The Nature and Sources of the Law* (New York: Columbia University Press, 1909), 246. In a similar vein, see Carleton Kemp Allen, *Law in the Making*, 3rd edn (Oxford: Clarendon Press, 1939), 227 ('Any judgement of any Court is authoritative only as to that part of it, called the *ratio decidendi*, which is considered to have been necessary to the decision of the actual issue between the litigants').

[73] See Sartorius, 'The Doctrine of Precedent and the Problem of Relevance', 348–50; Michael Abramowicz and Maxwell Stearns, 'Defining Dicta' (2005) 57 *Stanford L. Rev.* 953–1094 at 1060.

[74] Cross and Harris, *Precedent in English Law*, 72; see also *ibid*., 40.

interpretation of the statute – the judge's ruling, in other words, rather than the legal rule.[75] No doubt judges sometimes will expressly or impliedly treat particular rulings as necessary to particular conclusions; but it is just as likely that they will sometimes treat particular rulings as their preferred means by which to reach those conclusions. Necessity tests, however formulated, provide only inadequate conceptions of the *ratio decidendi*.

For many jurists, all that can be said with certainty about the *ratio decidendi* is that it is a concept riddled with uncertainty. Some early writers on the subject adopted a strategy of definition and avoidance, the implication behind this strategy being that if a particular definition of the *ratio decidendi* is considered satisfactory, all we need do, when trying to understand how particular decisions bind future courts, is read those decisions with a view to uncovering the *ratio decidendi* so defined.[76] But even though there was general agreement that the *ratio decidendi* is the binding part of a decision, there was little if any agreement about what the *ratio decidendi* is. Leaving aside the difficulties identified so far, nobody could say for sure whether the *ratio decidendi* is best characterized as the rule, the principle, or the reason embodied in a case, though there was little doubt that the principle of a case is not the same as either the reasons given in a judgment or the rule on which a court has relied.[77]

The slipperiness of '*ratio decidendi*' caused some jurists to despair. That it should have done so is somewhat puzzling. Our inability to define or agree upon a definition of something does not have to be a barrier to our identifying it and sharing in our identification of it. Yet these jurists seemed to think that if we cannot agree on how to define a *ratio decidendi*, we can never be sure of how to locate one in a case. In his introductory lectures for Columbia University law students, written at the end of the 1920s, Karl Llewellyn, having noted the difficulties of determining the *ratio* of 'the multi-point decision', added that 'our troubles with the *ratio decidendi* are not over', for 'the precise point you have up for study is how far is it safe to trust what the court says. The

---

[75] See Neil MacCormick, *Legal Reasoning and Legal Theory* (Oxford: Clarendon Press, 1978), 215, 221; 'Why Cases Have *Rationes*', 179.

[76] See, e.g., John W. Salmond, *Jurisprudence, or the Theory of Law* (London: Stevens & Sons, 1902), 176.

[77] See, e.g., Arthur L. Goodhart, 'Determining the *Ratio Decidendi* of a Case', in his *Essays in Jurisprudence and the Common Law* (Cambridge: Cambridge University Press, 1931), 1–26 at 2, 5–6. The essay was originally published at (1930) 40 *Yale L.J.* 161–83. References hereonwards are to the reprint in the *Essays*.

precise issue which you are attempting to solve is whether the court's language can be taken as it stands, or must be amplified, or must be whittled down.'[78] Around the same time another legal realist, Herman Oliphant, argued similarly that '[t]here can be erected upon the action taken by a court ... a gradation of generalizations', so that it is impossible to be sure 'what it is in prior decisions which is to be followed'; the 'student is told to seek the "doctrine" or "principle" of a case, but which of its welter of stairs shall he ascend and how high up shall he go?'[79] Nearly fifty years later, a very different legal realist sought to spell out the implications of Oliphant's argument: the *ratio decidendi* is supposedly the part of a precedent that binds, but 'the judge has considerable freedom of interpreting the *ratio decidendi* in such a way that a cited precedent need not stand in the way of the decision which from other motives he desires to give', and so the doctrine of binding precedent 'is in reality only an illusion'.[80]

Not everybody despaired so. There may be 'much difference of opinion' about the concept of the *ratio decidendi*, Paton and Sawer argued in the 1940s, but there is little doubt that *rationes* do exist and that, for the purpose of understanding the authority of precedents, they are important; and so it makes sense to devise tests that might enable us to identify them.[81] Paton and Sawer offered no new test of their own, but instead made a suggestion to the judiciary: if judges in majorities were to adopt the American practice of delivering joint opinions, the likelihood of courts issuing multiple *rationes*, or *rationes* which are difficult to distinguish from *obiter dicta*, might be reduced. The suggestion was decidedly hesitant – joint opinions, Paton and Sawer conceded, can militate against judicial independence and prolong the length of time between argument and judgment[82] – but at least it was intended to be constructive.[83]

---

[78] Llewellyn, *The Bramble Bush*, 46–8. The book, according to Llewellyn, 'grew out of an attempt in 1929 and 1930 to introduce the students at Columbia Law School to the study of law' (*ibid.*, vii).
[79] Herman Oliphant, 'A Return to *Stare Decisis*' (1928) 14 *ABAJ* 71–6, 107, 159–62 at 72–3.
[80] Alf Ross, *On Law and Justice* (London: Stevens & Sons, 1974), 86–8.
[81] Paton and Sawer, '*Ratio Decidendi* and *Obiter Dictum* in Appellate Courts', 471–2.
[82] See *ibid.*, 483–5. It would be a mistake, furthermore, to think that American judges composing a majority always deliver a joint opinion: see, e.g., *Furman* v. *Georgia*, 408 U.S. 238 (1972); *Regents of University of California* v. *Bakke*, 438 U.S. 265 (1978); *Hamdi* v. *Rumsfeld*, 542 U.S. 1 (2004).
[83] Possibly there is a stronger likelihood that appeal courts will not provide dissenting judgments where it is especially important that they give very clear guidance to lower courts. Dissents are eschewed, for example, by the Court of Appeal (Criminal Division),

Had there been a prize for constructively tackling the *ratio decidendi* problem, however, it would not have been awarded to Paton and Sawer. The jurist who would have received it, Arthur Goodhart, made a minor contribution to the jurisprudence of precedent in 1934, when he argued that 'from the English standpoint, the most important reason for following precedent is that it gives us certainty in the law'.[84] The argument was notable for drawing two responses – from William Holdsworth, who asserted that the doctrine of precedent generates neither rigidity nor flexibility in law but rather a 'golden mean' between the two,[85] and from C. K. Allen, who appeared to believe, but could not quite bring himself to say, that the malleability of precedents means that they cannot ever guarantee legal certainty.[86] Goodhart's principal contribution to the jurisprudence of precedent can be traced to an article he had written on possession, which had appeared in the *Cambridge Law Journal* six years earlier. In that article, Goodhart analyzed three cases dealing with rights to lost property – if, for example, A finds some money on the floor while browsing in B's shop, and neither A nor B knows to whom the money belongs, is A entitled to keep it or is it B's?[87] Goodhart was not

---

which needs to give clear guidance on principles to trial judges, so that they can provide clear instructions to juries.

[84] A. L. Goodhart, 'Precedent in English and Continental Law' (1934) 50 *LQR* 40–65 at 58.

[85] W. S. Holdsworth, 'Case Law' (1934) 50 *LQR* 180–95 at 193. In a similar vein, see Lord Reid, 'The Judge as Law Maker' (1972) n.s. 12 *JSPTL* 22–9 at 24–5. Holdsworth's response drew a rather withering response of its own: see W. Ivor Jennings, 'Judicial Process at Its Worst' (1937) 1 *MLR* 111–31 at 129.

[86] See Carleton Kemp Allen, 'Case Law: An Unwarrantable Intervention' (1935) 51 *LQR* 333–46. 'How can precedents be described as certain', Allen asked, 'when every day and all day in our Courts cases on which counsel confidently rely are rejected, distinguished, "not followed" and "held inapplicable"?' (*ibid.*, 335). The question is not surprising given, as we have already seen in this study, that Allen could not see how precedents can be considered genuinely binding. Yet, having asked this question, he proceeds to pull his punches, concluding not that the doctrine of precedent is uncertain but that he 'believes it to be ... a great and successful legal instrument ... because ... there does not seem to be any better way of applying legal principles to infinitely variable facts; and because ... our reports constitute an incomparable storehouse of legal reasoning, exposition, analogy, and learning' (*ibid.*, 346). Allen was famously dismissive of American legal realism: 'it has added nothing to the moderate sociological school, except an extreme dogmatism in repelling dogmatism, and a remarkable wealth of invented jargon. It was perhaps appropriate that the age of jazz should produce a Jazz Jurisprudence.' Allen, *Law in the Making*, 45. Yet, as Julius Stone observed, Allen's reflections on precedent suggest that realist jurisprudence ought to have drawn from him more approval than disdain: see Julius Stone, *Recent Trends in English Precedent* (Sydney: Associated General Publications, 1945), 41.

[87] See A. L. Goodhart, 'Three Cases on Possession' (1928) 3 *Cambridge L.J.* 195–208 at 197–8.

convinced that each of the three cases he considered contained a clear *ratio decidendi*.[88] But he was convinced that the only way to discover if they did was to uncover the reasons supporting the judgment in each case. Jurists sometimes misrepresent the *ratio* of a case, he argued, because they construct it from reasons which the deciding court never considered.[89] To discover the *ratio decidendi*, he urged, one must stick to the grounds on which a case was decided and leave aside those on which it could have been decided.

Goodhart's article had not long been published before it was subjected to serious critical scrutiny. Joseph F. Francis, a law professor at the University of Oklahoma, wondered if Goodhart was so much as aware of the arguments of Oliphant and other realists concerning the indeterminacy of any *ratio decidendi*. 'I fail to discern more than the faintest shadows of signs', Francis wrote, 'that indicate that Mr. Goodhart is even remotely conscious of these theories as a realistic description of legal concepts and of what is taking place in our court rooms'.[90] Francis himself was not shy of spouting routine realist sentiments, such as that we cannot take for granted that what judges have to say explains the decisions that they reach.[91] This last lesson in particular, he argued, Goodhart would have done well to heed; instead, Goodhart assumed that the *ratio* of a case must be found in the judicial reasoning when, in fact, the *ratio* need not even have been in the judge's mind when the decision was made.[92] There is no reason to think 'that a court must discuss a point or in some other manner clearly indicate that it had the point in mind before that point can be considered part of the doctrine of the case'; for no judge is 'wise enough to comprehend more than a few of the facts at a time that go to make up the infinite number of facts that any simple case presents'.[93]

It seems that Goodhart found this criticism persuasive. One commentator has argued that Goodhart 'made a huge concession to the

---

[88] See *ibid.*, 203.
[89] See *ibid.*, 198–9 and 201–2, where this criticism is levelled at Oliver Wendell Holmes, Frederick Pollock and John Salmond.
[90] Joseph F. Francis, 'Three Cases on Possession – Some Further Observations' (1928) 14 *St. Louis L. Rev.* 11–24 at 23.
[91] See *ibid.*, 22 ('The court is more likely to search legal theories and principles to back up a decision it has already arrived at before the argument is half finished than to look to them for the purpose of determining the decision'); and cf. 24 ('the effort to find the *ratio decidendi* of a case will soon be viewed in the same light as a physiologist trying to locate the soul').
[92] See *ibid.*, 14–15.   [93] *Ibid.*, 17.

Legal Realists' by accepting 'that what judges say in their legal opinions need not be taken to explain why they decide cases the way that they do'.[94] Whether the concession really was all that significant is debatable: in his Oxford inaugural lecture of 1932, Goodhart can be found bullishly defending the doctrine of precedent against realist claims of indeterminacy.[95] But there is no doubt that, not long after the publication of his *Cambridge Law Journal* article, Goodhart's perspective on the notion of *ratio decidendi* did change. In what is without doubt his main contribution to the jurisprudence of precedent, his essay on 'Determining the *Ratio Decidendi* of the Case', first published in 1930, Goodhart acknowledged the realist accounts of *ratio decidendi* that had been advanced by Oliphant and Francis. By Oliphant he was not persuaded at all.[96] But Francis – who, in contrast to Oliphant,[97] emphasized the importance not of the facts of a case to the formation of the *ratio* but, more precisely, the facts which the court chose to treat as material – appeared to lead him to rethink his position.[98] Whereas, in 1929, Goodhart had argued that the *ratio* of a case must be found in the reasons for the decision, by 1930 he was arguing, as Francis had, that there is no necessary connection between the *ratio* and the reasons. '[T]he first rule for discovering the *ratio decidendi* of case', he wrote in his essay on the subject, 'is that it must not be sought in the reasons on which the judge has based his decision'.[99]

Goodhart, it must be understood, was not arguing that judicial reasons have no relevance to the *ratio* of a case. In fact, he emphasized that 'the reasons given by the judge in his opinion . . . are of peculiar importance, for they may furnish us with a guide for determining which facts he considered

---

[94] Robert G. Scofield, 'Goodhart's Concession: Defending *Ratio Decidendi* from Logical Positivism and Legal Realism in the First Half of the Twentieth Century' (2005) 16 Kings' College L.J. 311–28 at 312.
[95] See Goodhart, 'Precedent in English and Continental Law', 59–60.
[96] See Goodhart, 'Determining the *Ratio Decidendi* of a Case', 9–10.
[97] 'But there is a constant factor in the cases which is susceptible of sound and satisfying study. The predictable element in it all is what courts have done in response to the stimuli of the facts of the concrete cases before them.' Oliphant, 'A Return to *Stare Decisis*', 159.
[98] Goodhart finds a 'fallacy' in Oliphant's argument ('Determining the *Ratio Decidendi* of a Case', 10), but declares that Francis's 'does not in any way conflict with my view that, in determining the principle of a case, we are bound by the judge's statement of the material facts on which he has based his judgment' (*ibid.*, 7, n. 20).
[99] Goodhart, 'Determining the *Ratio Decidendi* of a Case', 4.

material and which immaterial'.¹⁰⁰ Nevertheless, the *ratio decidendi*, the reason for the decision, is not the same thing as the reasons for the decision. A decision for which no reasons are given does not necessarily lack a *ratio*; furthermore, the reasons offered by a court in reaching a decision might be considered inadequate or incorrect, yet the court's ruling might be endorsed in later cases – a 'bad reason may often make good law'.¹⁰¹

But then, what is the *ratio decidendi* of a case? For Goodhart, it is whatever facts the judge has determined to be the material facts of the case, plus the judge's decision as based on those facts.¹⁰² 'It is by his choice of the material facts that the judge creates law.'¹⁰³ That a judge might treat the wrong facts as material is irrelevant: even if the 'finding of fact is probably incorrect, ... we cannot ignore it if we are to determine the true principle of the judgments based on it'.¹⁰⁴ This conception of the *ratio decidendi* links the doctrine of precedent with the principle that like cases be treated alike: any court which considers itself bound by precedent ought to come to the same conclusion as was reached in a prior case unless there is in the case in hand some further fact which it is prepared to treat as material, or unless some fact considered material in the previous case is absent.¹⁰⁵ If one accepts this conception of the *ratio decidendi*, furthermore, one has an explanation as to why hypothetical instances are unlikely to be accorded the same weight as judicial precedents: for hypothetical instances are by definition *obiter dicta* (i.e., '*if* the facts had been thus, then ...').¹⁰⁶

Although Goodhart's essay belongs to a different era – formulae for determining the *ratio decidendi* of a case tend to look rather fossilized today – it should be noted that many academics and judges did, and probably still do, accept the conception that he devised.¹⁰⁷ When Goodhart retired as editor of the *Law Quarterly Review* in 1975, his

---

¹⁰⁰ *Ibid.*, 18. The point is reiterated almost thirty years later in A. L. Goodhart, 'The *Ratio Decidendi* of a Case' (1959) 22 *MLR* 117–24 at 119.
¹⁰¹ Goodhart, 'Determining the *Ratio Decidendi* of a Case', 4.   ¹⁰² See *ibid.*, 25.
¹⁰³ *Ibid.*, 10 (emphasis omitted).   ¹⁰⁴ *Ibid.*, 13.   ¹⁰⁵ See *ibid.*, 21–2.
¹⁰⁶ 'If ... a judge in the course of his opinion suggests a hypothetical fact, and then states what conclusion he would reach if that fact existed, he is not creating a principle ... When a judge says, "In this case as the facts are so and so I reach conclusion *X*", this is not a *dictum*, even though the judge has been incorrect in his statement of the facts. But if the judge says, "If the facts in this case were so and so then I would reach conclusion *X*", this is a *dictum*, even though the facts are as given.' Goodhart, 'Determining the Ratio Decidendi of a Case', 22–3.
¹⁰⁷ See, e.g., *Al-Mehdawi* v. *Secretary of State for the Home Dept* [1990] 1 AC 876, 883, HL, per Taylor L.J.; *United Steelworkers of America* v. *Board of Education*, 209 Cal. Rptr. 16,

successor, Paul Baker, singled out the essay on the *ratio decidendi* as one of Goodhart's major jurisprudential achievements. 'No subsequent writer on this fundamental subject has been able to ignore it. It has been acclaimed, dissected, criticised, misrepresented and generally discussed *ad nauseam*.'[108] Baker was right to suggest that the essay was at least as well known for provoking disagreement as it was for receiving acclaim. Those who took issue with Goodhart's thesis fell broadly into three camps. First, there were those who simply did not accept that the *ratio decidendi* could be conceived as something separate from the reasons provided in a judgment. '[T]he reasons given in the judgment ... do constitute the *ratio decidendi*', one South African judge wrote in the course of disagreeing with Goodhart, so long as they are not 'merely subsidiary reasons' or 'reasoning on the facts', and provided 'they were necessary for the decision ... in the sense that along the lines actually followed in the judgment the result would have been different but for the reasons'.[109] Not everybody who contested Goodhart's divorcing of *ratio* and reasons took the questionable step of re-emphasizing the necessity test. 'Up to a point it is undoubtedly true', Cross and Harris concede, 'to say that the principle of a case is not found in the reasons given in the opinion', and indeed '[m]any of the judge's reasons for arriving at the proposition of law upon which he bases his decision are not part of the *ratio decidendi*'.[110] Goodhart erred, nevertheless, in neglecting 'the way which the case was argued and pleaded, the process of reasoning adopted by the judge and the relation of the case to other decisions'.[111] He appreciated, of course, that looking to the judicial reasoning may help us to determine which facts the judge considered material. 'But this is not the only ground on which the reasons given by a judge in his opinion or his statement of the rule of law are of importance', for it is

---

21 (Ct. App. 1984) ('The basic formula [for distinguishing holding from *dicta*] is to take account of facts treated by the judge as material and determine whether the contested opinion is based upon them'); Achen v. *Pepsi-Cola Bottling Co. of Los Angeles*, 105 Cal. App. 113, 124; 233 P 2d 74, 81 (1951); SZEEU v. *Minister for Immigration and Multicultural and Indigenous Affairs* [2006] FCAFC 2 paras 130–1, Fed. Ct. Australia, *per* Moore J.; Michael C. Dorf, 'Dicta and Article III' (2001) 142 *U. Pennsylvania L. Rev.* 1997–2069 at 2036–7 n. 143; Abramowicz and Stearns, 'Defining Dicta', 1052–5 esp. at 1055 ('Goodhart's central contribution is in recognizing that judges inevitably have some discretion in selecting the issues on which they will make law, and that discretion is constrained, although not eliminated, by the facts presented').

[108] P. V. Baker, 'A.L.G.: An Editor's View' (1975) 91 *LQR* 463–8 at 467.
[109] *Pretoria City Council* v. *Levinson* 1949 (3) SALR 305, 317, *per* Schreiner J.A.
[110] Cross and Harris, *Precedent in English Law*, 67.   [111] Ibid.

sometimes important to discover not just which facts were considered material but why they were considered material, and so we will look to the judicial reasoning in an effort to discover 'what portions of the law were in the mind of the court when the selection [of material facts] was made'.[112] Determining the *ratio* of a case, Cross and Harris insist, sometimes demands that judicial reasoning be accorded more attention than Goodhart would have us devote to it.[113]

The second general line of critique directed at Goodhart's thesis is perhaps the most predictable. That his concession to realist jurisprudence could not have been all that huge is most evident from the fact that his approach to determining the *ratio decidendi* of a case met with plenty of realist, and realist-inspired, criticism. 'Goodhart's later writing has made it very clear that he has long outgrown his indiscretion of 1930', Karl Llewellyn claimed in 1960.[114] The claim is thoroughly perplexing, not only because Goodhart's essay could not by any stretch of the imagination be described as indiscreet, but, more importantly, because he had not outgrown it: as late as 1959 he could be found reiterating his 'thesis concerning the essential importance of establishing the material facts on which a conclusion may be based'.[115] What is certainly clear from Llewellyn's remark is that he was not at all enamoured of Goodhart's method. Another realist was equally disparaging when he observed that Goodhart's 'search for a logical formula that will

---

[112] *Ibid.*, 70.
[113] In a similar vein, see D.P. Derham, 'Precedent and the Decision of Particular Questions' (1963) 79 *LQR* 49–62; and cf. D.H. Hodgson, *The Consequences of Utilitarianism: A Study in Normative Ethics and Legal Theory* (Oxford: Clarendon Press, 1967), 116–17. Hodgson argues that the determination of the *ratio* presupposes a connection not with the judicial reasons but with the relevant legal rules. Discovering which facts the judge considered material requires, on this account, that one knows the legal rule or rules upon which he based his decision, because it is according to the rule or rules that the judge formulated his description of the material facts: 'one can know this description only by formulating the rules upon which the judge based his decision. So it seems best to direct one's enquiry primarily towards these rules, having due regard in doing so to the facts of the case, and the judge's discussion of them' (*ibid.*, 117). Although Hodgson considers this to result in a conception of *ratio decidendi* different from Goodhart's – because it 'include[s] those rules of law which a judge expressly or impliedly treats as a basis for his decision or holding' (*ibid.*, 116) – it is at best only a minor modification of it, for Hodgson's point is that looking to the rules which the judge applied helps us to determine which facts the judge considered material. It might even be that adopting Hodgson's approach uncovers no *ratio decidendi*, for the relevant rules may actually fail to take account of the facts which the judge considered material.
[114] Llewellyn, *The Common Law Tradition*, 18, n. 11a.
[115] Goodhart, 'The *Ratio Decidendi* of a Case', 124.

determine precisely what rule each decision implies is a wild goose chase starting from a logical confusion'.[116] That realists should have been so dismissive of Goodhart's approach is not surprising: Oliphant's article of the late 1920s had set out their stall on the concept of the *ratio decidendi*; Goodhart's essay, in so far as they accorded it any attention, was an opportunity for sniper practice.

It was not a realist, but a follower in the realist tradition who would eventually subject the essay to a sustained – or rather, repeated – critique. In numerous books and essays, Julius Stone argued that Goodhart's insistence that we look to the judge's choice of material facts to determine the *ratio decidendi* will rarely generate an answer in which we might be confident, because every material fact in a case can be stated at different levels of generality, each level tending to yield a different ruling.[117] Later courts can only guess as to the level of generality at which an earlier court intended a material fact to be understood, and so there will be within any case not a definite *ratio*, but various possible *rationes*.[118] Goodhart in fact anticipated this line of criticism, though his response – that we can trust the English courts not to be 'disingenuous and arbitrary' when settling on the material facts of a

---

[116] Felix S. Cohen, 'The Problems of a Functional Jurisprudence' (1937) 1 *MLR* 5–26 at 20.

[117] '[I]t is possible to draw as many general propositions from a given decision as there are possible combinations of distinguishable facts in it. By looking at the facts it is impossible *logically* to say which are to be taken as the basis for the *ratio decidendi*.' Stone, *Recent Trends in English Precedent*, 39. Stone himself on various occasions illustrated the argument by reference to the 'facts' in *Donoghue* v. *Stevenson* [1932] AC 562, HL. The case, on Goodhart's theory, can, as Eisenberg explains in the process of summarizing Stone, 'stand for almost numberless rules constructed from permutations of the material facts at various levels of generality – for example, the rule that if a manufacturer of nationally distributed goods that are intended for human consumption produces the goods in a negligent manner, it is liable for resulting physical personal or emotional injury; or the rule that if a person working on goods for profit is negligent, he is liable for resulting physical personal injury if he packaged the goods in such a way that the defect was concealed.' Melvin Aron Eisenberg, *The Nature of the Common Law* (Cambridge, Mass.: Harvard University Press, 1991), 54. In a similar vein, see G. W. Paton, *A Text-book of Jurisprudence* (Oxford: Clarendon Press, 1946), 160–1. For Stone's own efforts at illustration see, e.g., Julius Stone, 'The *Ratio* of the *Ratio Decidendi*' (1959) 22 *MLR* 597–620 at 603–7; *Precedent and Law*, 123–39, 228–33.

[118] '[T]here is not (despite Professor Goodhart's theory) any one *ratio decidendi* which is necessary to explain a particular decision, and is discoverable from that decision.' Stone, 'The *Ratio* of the *Ratio Decidendi*', 607. See also William Twining and David Miers, *How To Do Things with Rules: A Primer of Interpretation*, 4th edn (London: Butterworths, 1999), 335 ('Talk of finding the *ratio decidendi* of a case obscures the facts that the process of interpreting cases is not like a hunt for buried treasure, but typically involves an element of choice from a range of possibilities').

case – was hardly satisfactory.[119] Perhaps the best that can be said in Goodhart's defence is that Stone does not appreciate the full import of the claim that courts can only guess as to an earlier court's understanding of the generality of a material fact. Absent special contrary indications, it seems reasonable to attribute to the earlier court the intention that its formulations be construed in accordance with the conventions on precedent which prevailed at the time that it made its decision, and by reference to which it would expect its formulations to be construed. Whether or not it is reasonable to attribute this intention, the reality is that judges do draw inferences regarding how earlier courts appear to have intended material facts to have been understood, and it is most likely as a consequence of this that particular precedents will yield particular *rationes decidendi*.[120]

Goodhart was trying to do something constructive – to move beyond definitions and devise a method for determining the *ratio decidendi*. Stone sought to expose the method as unsound, but suggested no method of his own – indeed, his point was that the *ratio decidendi* of a case is not susceptible to being determined by any method or formula, that such an approach really is a wild goose chase. Such negativity probably exasperated Goodhart, who was generally keen to help judges and lawyers with their problems rather than add to the confusion and complexity.[121] But at least Stone was deliberately and unapologetically unconstructive. The final response to Goodhart's thesis was intended to build upon rather than dismantle it. Yet it was probably the least fruitful response of all.

In the 1950s, an academic lawyer named J. L. Montrose produced a series of notes and essays in which, taking his cue from Goodhart, he sought to pin down the concept of the *ratio decidendi* once and for all. Montrose shared with Cross and Harris the view that Goodhart underestimated the importance of reasons within decisions. 'The term "reason for a decision"', Montrose asserted, 'may be a translation of "ratio decidendi" and mean the principle which, applied to the facts of the case, leads to the decision. On the other hand it may have a wider meaning and signify all the reasoning leading to the ultimate decision,

---

[119] Goodhart, 'Determining the *Ratio Decidendi* of a Case', 24. See also N. H. Andrews, 'Reporting Case Law: Unreported Cases, the Definition of a *Ratio* and the Criteria for Reporting Decisions' (1985) 5 *Legal Studies* 205–32 at 210–11.
[120] See Gottlieb, *The Logic of Choice*, 84.
[121] See Neil Duxbury, *Jurists and Judges: An Essay on Influence* (Oxford: Hart, 2001), 87–101.

and thus refer also to the reasons which have led a judge to accept the principle which constitutes the *ratio decidendi*.¹²² If it is correct to say that, when seeking to identify the *ratio decidendi* of a case, we must take account of all reasoning which bears upon the decision, is it possible to devise a method for determining what all the appurtenant reasons are? 'The pattern which judgments may take', Montrose answered, 'is more easily discerned by the adoption of a notation which permits of a generalization of the various reasoning processes'.¹²³ To this end, he devised 'a set of shorthand symbols' – 'a+ signifies that fact *a* exists; a= signifies no finding that fact *a* exists or not; a- signifies that fact *a* does not exist', and so on 'for facts *b*, *c*, etc' – so as to 'permit the statement of a complex set of propositions to be made in an abbreviated form, thereby enabling them to be seen and comprehended with less mental effort than would otherwise be required'.¹²⁴

When Montrose attempted to apply his system of notation to judgments involving multiple issues of fact and law, it became convoluted to the point of unintelligibility.¹²⁵ To use symbols to signify facts is to create another level of information to be processed; remembering which symbols stand for which facts is likely to increase rather than diminish the mental burden. Moreover, while creating symbols for the facts which were either found to exist or which remain undetermined in a particular case is at least feasible (a+ signifies that the bottle contained ginger beer, b+ that the ginger beer was poured over ice cream, c+ that the bottle also contained a snail, c= that it has been impossible to ascertain if any of the snail was consumed with the ginger beer and ice cream, etc), to devise symbols for the possible non-existent facts (a- signifies that the bottle did not contain lemonade, b- that the bottle did not contain a ladybird, c- that it did not contain a spider, etc) is to undertake an exercise which is potentially endless as well as pointless. Whereas Goodhart had striven to develop a straightforward formula for determining the *ratio decidendi* of a case, Montrose, throughout all his writings on precedent, seemed intent on splitting every hair so as to generate a tangled, fuzzy mass.¹²⁶ A. W. B. Simpson sought to demonstrate

---

[122] J. L. Montrose, 'The Language of, and a Notation for, the Doctrine of Precedent' (1952–3) 2 *Univ. Western Australia Annual L. Rev.* 301–29, 504–25 at 306.
[123] *Ibid.*, 509.   [124] *Ibid.*, 509, 523.   [125] See *ibid.*, 518–23.
[126] Montrose himself appears never to have abandoned faith in his proposal for a notation system and, in his later works, quite often refers to it as encapsulating his theory of precedent: see, e.g., J. L. Montrose, 'Reasoning, *Ratio Decidendi* and Denning L.J.' (1954) 17 *MLR* 462–4 at 462; 'Distinguishing Cases and the Limits of *Ratio*

that this constant retreat into complexity led to some mistaken conclusions about the meaning of *ratio decidendi*, though Montrose would have none of it.[127] The suspicion that the exchange between the two men was inconclusive was intensified by interventions from Goodhart, who argued that neither Montrose nor Simpson had understood his original argument, and from Julius Stone, who, as we have seen, insisted that the very idea of devising a method to determine the *ratio decidendi* of a case was foolhardy.[128] Anybody not directly involved in the debate might have wondered what the fuss was about. The parties to a case are primarily interested in the order of the court – the *ratio decidendi* supporting the order will, unless it is a cause for appeal, probably be of little or no concern to them – and even judges might wonder what harm is done by conceiving of the *ratio* impressionistically. The fact that we might struggle to state exactly what the *ratio* of a case is, Lord Dunedin observed in 1928, does not mean that we fail to see that it exists and constrains us: 'I do not think it is part of the tribunal's duty to spell out with great difficulty a *ratio decidendi* in order

---

Decidendi' (1956) 19 *MLR* 525–30 at 529; 'Ratio Decidendi and the House of Lords' (1957) 20 *MLR* 124–30 at 125. Nevertheless, the editor of a posthumous collection of his main essays did not see fit to include it: James Louis Montrose, *Precedent in English Law and Other Essays*, ed. H. G. Hanbury (Shannon: Irish University Press, 1968). Even though an essay by Andrew Phang, 'Exploring and Expanding Horizons: The Influence and Scholarship of Professor J. L. Montrose' (1997) 18 *Singapore L. Rev.* 15–57, is unremittingly charitable towards its subject, the impression of Montrose that emerges is one of 'an idealist' (*ibid.*, 28) who never 'fully unpacked his own ideas' (*ibid.*, 32) and tended not to reflect on the implications of his arguments. Although Montrose's work on precedent is more or less forgotten today, the type of project he attempted – specifically, the idea that the concept of the *ratio decidendi* is better explicated when the material facts of cases are modelled – has been revived in computer science: see, e.g., L. Karl Branting, 'A Reduction-Graph Model of *Ratio Decidendi*', in *Proceedings of the Fourth International Conference on Artificial Intelligence and the Law* (Amsterdam: ACM Press, 1993), 40–9; 'A Reduction-Graph Model of Precedent in Legal Analysis' (2003) 150 *Artificial Intelligence* 59–95; Henry Prakken and Giovanni Sartor, 'Modelling Reasoning with Precedents in a Formal Dialogue Game' (1998) 6 *Artificial Intelligence and Law* 231–87 at 249–50, 279–80.

[127] See A. W. B. Simpson, 'The *Ratio Decidendi* of a Case' (1957) 20 *MLR* 413–15; 'The *Ratio Decidendi* of a Case' (1958) 21 *MLR* 155–60. Cf. J.L. Montrose, 'The *Ratio Decidendi* of a Case' (1957) 20 *MLR* 587–95. Simpson, it should be mentioned, was responding as much to Goodhart's arguments as he was to Montrose's: see especially A.W. B. Simpson, 'The *Ratio Decidendi* of a Case' (1959) 22 *MLR* 453–7.

[128] See Goodhart, 'The *Ratio Decidendi* of a Case'; Stone, 'The *Ratio* of the *Ratio Decidendi*'.

to be bound by it'.[129] For an answer to the question of how to make the *ratio-obiter* distinction, Lord Asquith joked some years later:

> I consulted... one of our greatest judicial luminaries – one who has made classic contributions to this problem. I caught him in a light vein, and he told me this :– 'the rule is quite simple: if you agree with the other bloke, you say it's part of the *ratio*; if you don't, you say it's "*obiter dictum*," with the implication that he is a congenital idiot.'[130]

c. The point of the search

It might be assumed from all of this that the safest line to take as regards '*ratio decidendi*' is something akin to the realist one. But the difficulty with adopting such a perspective is that one risks neglecting a serious point: there are good reasons to try to determine the *ratio* of a case. One of the reasons immediately evident from much of the literature on the subject is that anyone studying law wants to know what to look for when reading cases; indeed, many of those writers seeking to devise a test for determining the *ratio decidendi* explicitly conceive the purpose of the enterprise to be one of enlightening law students.[131] A variant on this argument is to be found within the literature of law and economics. According to this perspective, distinguishing *rationes decidendi* from *obiter dicta* is an important strategy for managing information – not, primarily, so that students can know 'the law', but so that the very notion of judicial precedent as a source of law can be taken seriously. If, within the common law tradition, the distinction between *ratio decidendi* and *obiter dicta* was not recognized, judges would be able to create a more or less unlimited amount of new law and courts would be overwhelmed by precedent; everything within a previous decision – and not necessarily just the decision on materially identical facts – would be potentially relevant to the case in hand.[132]

---

[129] *The Mostyn* [1928] AC 57, 73, HL.
[130] Asquith, 'Some Aspects of the Work of the Court of Appeal', 359.
[131] See, e.g., Wambaugh, *The Study of Cases*, 5 ('the beginner ...'); Goodhart, 'Determining the *Ratio Decidendi* of a Case', 11 ('The following tentative suggestions may ... prove of some aid to the student faced with his first case book'), 22; Cross and Harris, *Precedent in English Law*, 48–9; also Oliphant, 'A Return to *Stare Decisis*', 73; R. N. Gooderson, '*Ratio Decidendi* and Rules of Law' (1952) 30 *Canadian Bar Rev.* 892–907 at 892.
[132] See Eric Rasmusen, 'Judicial Legitimacy as a Repeated Game' (1994) 10 *Jnl of Law, Econ. & Organization* 63–83 at 75.

A stronger formulation of this last argument is that *stare decisis* will be undermined where the distinction between *ratio decidendi* and *obiter dicta* is blurred. A test which makes the distinction credible is valuable, in other words, not primarily for the purpose of information-management but because it will help judges identify what it is within a precedent that actually constrains them.[133] The logical conclusion of this argument is that the concept of the *ratio decidendi* has to be taken seriously because the *ratio decidendi* triggers *stare decisis*: it is the binding part of a previous case. Before a court decides whether to follow a precedent it wants to know what the precedent establishes.[134]

Jurists of various persuasions – including some of those who are markedly sceptical about quests to locate *rationes decidendi* – recognize that this argument has considerable force.[135] It is, nevertheless, an argument that can be exaggerated, for the authority of precedent is not reducible to the *ratio decidendi*. Even decisions which are not valued as precedents – decisions of certain inferior courts, for example – can have a *ratio*. The identification of a *ratio* within a prior decision is therefore not necessarily evidence that a decision has constraining force. Exceptionally, furthermore, a court may consider itself bound by a prior judgment for reasons other than any *ratio decidendi* associated with the case. In English law, for example, an appellate court may be bound by a judgment at first instance, even though it would not be bound by the *ratio decidendi* of the case, in so far as it would have to apply the principles of *res judicata* arising from the judgment were the same parties to litigate the same issue again.[136] No doubt one reason the effort to devise a test by which to determine the *ratio decidendi* has been taken so seriously is the conviction of many jurists that formulating a workable and reliable test is the key to understanding the binding force of precedent. But it seems more likely that the real value of seeking such a test rests in its capacity to demonstrate something which has been

---

[133] Counsel, of course, may have some influence in determining whether a particular approach to identifying the *ratio decidendi* of a precedent carries any weight in a particular case.

[134] See *Nash v. Tamplin & Sons Brewery Brighton Ltd* [1952] AC 231, 250, HL, per Lord Reid ('It matters not how difficult it is to find the *ratio decidendi* of a previous case, that *ratio* must be found; and it matters not how difficult it is to reconcile that *ratio* when found with statutory provisions or general principles: that *ratio* must be applied to any later case which is not reasonably distinguishable').

[135] See, e.g., Wright, 'Precedents', 124; Smith, 'The Rationality of Tradition', 306; Stone, 'The *Ratio* of the *Ratio Decidendi*', 599; MacCormick, 'Why Cases Have *Rationes*', 157.

[136] See Cross and Harris, *Precedent in English Law*, 98.

remarked upon already in this study: that a judicial precedent can both vest discretion in and constrain future decision-makers. Judges might not be strictly bound by the *ratio decidendi* which a particular precedent is considered to yield, but, if their decision is not to follow the precedent, they will very likely at least consider themselves bound to explain why the *ratio* is not being adopted or how it is being distinguished. *Rationes*, we might say, beget *rationes*: the fact that an earlier decision provides reasons for deciding in a particular way on particular facts means that a court which does not follow that decision will recognize the importance of providing its own reasons for deciding differently. Thus it is that the common law's 'perpetual process of change can be reconciled with ... the rule of *stare decisis*.'[137] The concept of the *ratio decidendi* enables us to see how courts often consider themselves obliged to reckon with precedents even when they see no obligation to follow them.

2. Shortcuts to reason

The casual nature of judicial precedents – the fact that judges are generally free to say as much or as little as they like, the likelihood that there will be no canonical form of words capturing the *ratio decidendi* of a case, the difficulty of determining in many instances just what is the *ratio decidendi* as opposed to *obiter dicta* – means that they are not particularly efficient vessels for conveying important legal information. Anyone who has been a law student, or certainly a student of English law, is likely to recall the despair of reading a case composed of an unhelpful headnote, a convoluted summary of the facts and a series of labyrinthine judicial opinions, and being not only unsure as to which portion of the case should be kept in mind for class but confounded on discovering from the textbook that it was *that* opinion or passage which later courts treated as the principle of the decision. That distinguishing the wheat from the chaff is something at which we tend to get better with practice does not alter the fact that precedents do not always offer up

---

[137] Lord Wright, *Legal Essays and Addresses* (Cambridge: Cambridge University Press, 1939), xvi; see also Raz, *AL*, 183–4 ('Until fairly recently most of the writings on precedent in English law (and related systems) were preoccupied with devising ever more sophisticated tests for identifying the *ratio* of a case, which were designed to reconcile the binding force of precedents with the wide discretion judges often have when faced with them').

legal principles straightforwardly. As Frederick Pollock appreciated, precedents are decidedly awkward sources of law.[138]

But things could be worse. Precedents, it was argued earlier, could conceivably exist in the absence of supporting reasons – just as the common law once existed in the absence of a doctrine of precedent. A previous decision will more often than not be considered authoritative, nevertheless, precisely because it does provide a reason, or a set of reasons, for reaching a particular outcome on particular facts. If the reasons supporting the decision in a particular case are good reasons they should remain so in future similar cases, and so *prima facie* it makes sense to treat the reasons for the decision in the first case as reasons for replicating the decision in future similar cases. An adjudicator who eschews precedent is, in effect, declining the opportunity to piggyback on reasoning undertaken by his forebears.

Piggybacking is not necessarily easy. If judges are to follow earlier decisions, they must determine what the earlier decisions, and what the reasons for those decisions, are. A court's resolution to take account of – or, more likely, counsel's insistence that the court take account of – accumulated case-law suggesting more than one precedent applicable to the case at hand might require of judges greater mental investment than would have been necessary had they decided the case from the ground up. Always to decline the opportunity to piggyback, nevertheless, would be unwise judicial policy. As Cardozo observed, 'the labor of judges would be increased almost to the breaking point if every past decision could be reopened in every case, and one could not lay one's own course of bricks on the secure foundation of the courses laid by others who had gone before him'.[139] A strong prudential argument in support of precedent-following, in other words, is that replicating an earlier decision on an issue rather than deciding the issue afresh is a good way of

---

[138] See Frederick Pollock, *A First Book of Jurisprudence for Students of the Common Law* (London: Macmillan, 1896), 238–40; 'Introduction', in *The Progress of Continental Law in the Nineteenth Century*, J. H. Wigmore et al. (London: Murray, 1918), pp. xli-xlix at xliv; also A. W. B. Simpson, 'The Common Law and Legal Theory', in *Oxford Essays in Jurisprudence (2nd Series)*, ed. A. W. B. Simpson (Oxford: Clarendon Press, 1973), 77–99 at 84–91; Cardozo, *The Nature of the Judicial Process*, 29 ('Cases do not unfold their principles for the asking. They yield up their kernel slowly and painfully').

[139] Cardozo, *The Nature of the Judicial Process*, 149, and cf. *ibid.*, 20 ('precedents have so covered the ground that they fix the point of departure from which the labor of the judge begins'). See also *Planned Parenthood* v. *Casey*, 505 U.S. 833, 854 (1992) ('With Cardozo, we recognize that no judicial system could do society's work if it eyed each issue afresh in every case that raised it').

conserving adjudicative resources. Where there is no practice of precedent-following, courts will be regularly reinventing the wheel, adjudicating matters which really need not be litigated (or relitigated) and failing to address genuinely novel issues of principle while spending too much time deciding cases which, had notice been taken of earlier judicial endeavours, would have been recognized as comparatively straightforward.

Precedents, on this account, resemble what cognitive theorists term *availability heuristics*.[140] When decision-makers recognize that their capacity to obtain and assimilate information is limited, they tend to devise procedures and mechanisms which establish a link between a body of existing information they might confidently use and the decisions they have to make.[141] I know little about breeds of dog, but I do know that the labrador which was the family pet of my childhood was always placid, and so I think that if my children are to be allowed a dog then a labrador would be a good choice. Possessing sub-optimal information, I rely on a convenient analogy or rule of thumb – crude though it might be – in order to make a decision. Similarly, legal decision-makers, lacking the information to reach a fully informed and reasoned decision, are likely to establish procedures which perpetuate the influence of past cases on future ones. Since many judges, lawyers and jurists have spoken and written in praise of the decision in *Smith* v. *Jones*, today's court might resolve to follow it when dealing with what appear to be much the same facts, even though the very fact that there is a case being litigated suggests that not everybody considers *Smith* v. *Jones* to capture the entire problem. Relying on availability heuristics is, of course, risky: not all labradors are placid, and *Smith* v. *Jones* might indeed not be as similar to today's case as the court is inclined to think. But the temptation to resort to such strategies is entirely understandable, for if the analogy drawn is sound the likelihood is that we will reach a satisfactory decision without having to spend a considerable amount of time reasoning and seeking information. Precedents, *qua* availability heuristics, 'make it easier (or less costly) for judges to decide because they do not have to rethink each decision. Instead they can rely

---

[140] On the concept of the availability heuristic, see Timur Kuran, *Private Truths, Public Lies: The Social Consequences of Preference Falsification* (Cambridge, Mass.: Harvard University Press, 1995), 166–7.

[141] See Ronald A. Heiner, 'Imperfect Decisions and the Law: On the Evolution of Legal Precedent and Rules' (1986) 15 *Jnl Leg. Studs* 227–61.

on earlier analysis in the form of a stock of already accumulated experience from past cases.'[142]

There are other benefits, besides decisional economy, to be derived from treating precedents as ready-made reasons. Since reliance on a precedent is reliance on something tried or even, if the precedent has already been followed, tried and tested, a court, when following reasons given for an earlier decision on essentially the same facts, may well be deciding strongly as well as efficiently. Were an appeal court to consider its decision to be essentially 'a restricted railroad ticket, good for this day and train only',[143] it is difficult to see why anyone else should invest the decision with any greater significance; indeed, a court which did treat its decision thus – which, in deciding, attempted neither to learn from past judges nor leave a legacy for future ones – would probably be widely regarded as lacking self-esteem and unworthy of public confidence.[144] Cardozo, in the passage quoted above, offers a complementary line of reasoning: a decision which stands on what has already been built not only takes the benefit of the 'secure foundation' but also makes the building that bit more imposing, and so it is less likely to be successfully challenged than the decision which has no precedent underpinning it. Reliance on pre-formed reasons might not only make for strong decisions but also enhance the institutional strength of the judiciary itself. Following settled case-law should make that case-law seem yet more settled, and so make the judges responsible for that case-law seem all the more clear minded.[145] It might also reduce the likelihood of judicial error, for where courts rely on a precedent authored by a judge with

---

[142] *Ibid.*, 229. A twist on this justification of precedent-following is developed by Shapiro, who, utilizing communications theory, defends *stare decisis* as a form of repetition or 'redundancy' which functions to counteract the 'noise' (i.e., the potentially conflicting messages) generated by an organization with the complexity of a legal system, thereby enabling lawyers and judges accurately to receive information about how earlier courts have decided issues. 'A system that inevitably generates a great deal of noise,' Shapiro explains, 'and one in which high levels of random error would jeopardize coordination, fully employs the standard techniques for the reduction of noise-caused transmission error ... *Stare decisis* viewed as redundancy is a fully rational, probably indispensable, method of solving the problem of syntactic noise in a system with very high message loads – which any system that proceeds case by case inevitably is.' Martin Shapiro, 'Toward a Theory of *Stare Decisis*' (1972) 1 *Jnl Leg. Studs* 125–34 at 132, 133.

[143] *Smith* v. *Allwright*, 321 U.S. 649, 669 (1944) (Roberts J., dissenting).

[144] See Henry Paul Monaghan, '*Stare Decisis* and Constitutional Adjudication' (1988) 88 *Columbia L. Rev.* 723–73 at 753.

[145] See John Paul Stevens, 'The Life Span of a Judge-Made Rule' (1983) 58 *New York Univ. L. Rev.* 1–21 at 2.

particular expertise in the area of law at stake, they rely on reasons which not only have already been formulated but which, unless there has been subsequent legal change, are likely to be more or less incontrovertible, and so unlikely to be considered on appeal.[146] Furthermore, judges who refrain from constantly formulating their own reasons and who are willing to follow the reasoning of others might accrue respect for their commitment to what is, in effect, a form of judicial restraint.[147] Even if judges believe that a precedent does not decide an issue as well as it would be decided were it to be reasoned afresh, consideration of the efficiency and the robustness of the decision-process might still motivate a court to leave the precedent undisturbed, for judges are commonly and understandably of the view that it is better that the law be stable than that it be perfect.[148] A legal culture in which precedents are commonly treated as availability heuristics might, finally, encourage judicial responsibility: judges, that is, who think of precedents as pre-packaged reasons might feel a compulsion to develop their own reasoning carefully when they lack a precedent to follow, for they are likely to appreciate that their own decisions could be the ready-formed reasons of the future.[149]

---

[146] On precedent-following as a method of reducing error costs within the judicial system, see generally Jonathan R. Macey, 'The Internal and External Costs and Benefits of *Stare Decisis*' (1989) 65 *Chicago-Kent L. Rev.* 93–113.

[147] See *Florida Department of Health* v. *Florida Nursing Home Association*, 450 U.S. 147, 153–4 (1981) (Stevens J., concurring); Lewis F. Powell, Jr., '*Stare Decisis* and Judicial Restraint' (1990) 47 *Washington & Lee L. Rev.* 281–90 at 286–7.

[148] See, e.g., Cardozo, *The Nature of the Judicial Process*, 150 ('The situation would ... be intolerable if the weekly changes in the composition of the court were accompanied by changes in its rulings. In such circumstances there is nothing to do except to stand by the errors of our brethren of the week before, whether we relish them or not'); *Sheddon* v. *Goodrich* (1803) 8 Ves. Jun. 481, 497, *per* Lord Eldon ('[A]fter the doctrine has been so long settled ... it is better that the law should be certain, than that every Judge should speculate upon improvements in it'); *Fitzleet Estates Ltd* v. *Cherry (Inspector of Taxes)* [1977] 3 All ER 996, 999, HL, *per* Lord Wilberforce ('Nothing could be more undesirable, in fact, than to permit litigants, after a decision has been given by this House with all appearance of finality, to return to this House in the hope that a differently constituted committee might be persuaded to take the view which its predecessors rejected ... [D]oubtful issues have to be resolved and the law knows no better way of resolving them than by the considered majority opinion of the ultimate tribunal. It requires much more than doubts as to the correctness of such opinion to justify departing from it'); also John W. Salmond, 'The Theory of Judicial Precedents' (1900) 16 *LQR* 376–91 at 381–2.

[149] See Gely, 'Of Sinking and Escalating', 107.

The argument that precedents facilitate efficient and strong judicial decision-making is what might be termed a consequentialist justification of precedent-following. In chapter 5, some other such justifications of the practice will be considered. As consequentialist claims for precedent-following go, the argument that precedents are helpful for short-cutting the reasoning process and managing information is by no means negligible. Economy and strength in decision-making are certainly important qualities for the administration of justice. But this line of argument is clearly quite limited. While economy in judicial decision-making is desirable, it is rarely if ever the overriding concern. A system which did posit economy as the overriding concern would see more advantage in decision-makers casting, say, votes or lots to decide cases rather than wading through precedents. While relying on precedent may conserve judicial resources far more than would deciding every case afresh, in other words, there may be other decision-methods which would conserve those resources still more than does precedent-following.[150]

It might be argued that even if it is correct to say that precedent-following is not the most efficient method of decision-making available to judges, it is still more efficient than courts perpetually starting with a clean slate. This argument meets with two objections. First, to defend the efficiency of a method of decision-making by asserting that it appears not to be the most inefficient of such methods is curious, to say the least. The argument in favour of precedent on the basis of decisional efficiency invariably amounts to the claim that there is another method of deciding that is always more costly – that precedent-following is an efficient way to decide because it is definitely not the most inefficient way to decide. But showing that something is good requires more than just a claim that it is not as bad as the worst. Secondly, precedent-following might not always be a more efficient decision-method than is starting with a clean slate: there may be conflicting precedents, and multiple *rationes* within the precedents themselves, so that starting with a clean slate, should it be a viable option, might be less troublesome an option than following an earlier decision or series of decisions.[151]

---

[150] See Richard A. Wasserstrom, *The Judicial Decision: Toward a Theory of Legal Justification* (Stanford, Ca.: Stanford University Press, 1961), 73.
[151] See Earl Maltz, 'The Nature of Precedent' (1988) 66 *North Carolina L. Rev.* 367–93 at 370.

Sometimes, adjudicators might recognize that precedent-following facilitates efficient and strong decision-making and yet believe that precedents ought not to be followed because considerations of efficiency and strength are secondary to other concerns. Judges may be wary of treating a matter as settled by the reasons offered in an earlier decision because those reasons might not fully address what is at stake in the case before them. 'Finality is a good thing,' Lord Atkin declared in 1933, 'but justice is better'.[152] While stability in the law may be more desirable than perfection, there may sometimes be a danger of courts deciding cases unsatisfactorily if they rely too readily on the reasoning found in a well-established precedent or line of precedents. That justice might be compromised by judges who accept too quickly the reasoning of their forebears is an obvious concern, but by no means the only one. After the American War of Independence, some states took the view that although the most efficient way for their courts to settle disputes would be to apply the established principles of the English common law, citation of English authorities in court should nevertheless be statutorily forbidden so as to encourage the development of indigenous doctrine and an independent legal identity.[153] Deciding on the basis of already-available reasons might be efficient, but might equally be lazy. One of the common concerns about judgments based on availability heuristics is that they sometimes generate negative cascade effects: when examples are followed, that is, the likelihood increases that they will be followed further, even though in many of these instances the example-following is unreflective and fails to generate the right or the best decision.[154] Whether there is much genuine opportunity for the emergence of negative cascades in the judicial decision-making context seems doubtful: factors such as long judicial tenures, written judicial opinions and hierarchical appeals processes tend to reduce the likelihood of

---

[152] *Ras Behari Lal* v. *King Emperor* [1933] All ER Rep. 723, 726, PC.
[153] See Francis R. Aumann, 'American Law Reports: Yesterday and Today' (1938) 4 *Ohio State Univ. L.J.* 331–45 at 332–4. (Aumann indicates that the desire to develop indigenous common law was not the only factor motivating state bans on the citation of English precedents.) Some Canadian common-law provinces appear, for similar reasons, to have been reluctant to cite both English and US precedents: see H. Patrick Glenn, 'Persuasive Authority' (1987) 32 *McGill L.J.* 261–98 at 291–2.
[154] See Andrew F. Daughety and Jennifer F. Reinganum, 'Stampede to Judgment: Persuasive Influence and Herding Behavior by Courts' (1999) 1 *American Law & Economics Rev.* 158–89; Cass R. Sunstein, *Why Societies Need Dissent* (Cambridge, Mass.: Harvard University Press, 2003), 54–5, 59–60, 64–5.

precedent-following having adverse cascade effects.[155] But this does not discount the possibility that judges who emulate or replicate the reasoning of earlier courts might sometimes betray insufficient reflexivity or be rather too willing, in Holmes's words, to keep 'with what is then understood to be convenient.'[156] This general line of argument is easily exaggerated. Within common-law jurisdictions, the stock of available precedent is usually the product of generations of judges struggling with difficult questions, and to choose not to take account of that general body of wisdom when tackling those questions anew will probably be both foolhardy and arrogant.[157] This observation should not lead us to ignore the fact, none the less, that when the available precedent enables judges to economize on reasoning there is a danger that it is not only the unnecessary reasoning that is being avoided.

3. Pre-emptive precedent?

The basic point of this chapter is to consider the different ways in which precedents can be understood to encapsulate reason. The primary value of a precedent to a lawyer or a judge, we saw in the first section of the chapter, is not the decision reached but the reason for the decision or *ratio decidendi*. Thorny though this concept is, it is not surprising that it should have taxed jurists as it has, for identifying the *ratio decidendi* of a case is in most (though not all) instances the key to understanding the case as legal authority. Another way to think of precedents as a form of reason is to conceive of them as ready-formulated efforts at reasoning through particular problems which today's decision-makers, when faced with the same problems, might use instead of working through the issues afresh. To value precedents as essentially labour-saving devices is to value them consequentially. The basic feature of consequentialist valuations is that they only explain the authority of precedent in so far as they posit the ends of the doctrine (decisional efficiency, predictability, stability and so on) intelligibly and show that precedent-following does indeed support those ends.

---

[155] See Eric Talley, 'Precedential Cascades: An Appraisal' (1999) 73 *Southern California L. Rev.* 87–137.

[156] Holmes, *The Common Law*, 2.

[157] See Frank H. Easterbrook, 'Stability and Reliability in Judicial Decisions' (1988) 73 *Cornell L. Rev.* 422–33 at 422–3.

More will be said about consequentialist valuations of precedent in chapter 5. The remainder of this chapter is devoted to another conception of precedent as reason. Whereas the argument that precedents are labour-saving devices is a straightforwardly justificatory one, the third perspective to be considered is, as with the various quests to explicate the *ratio decidendi* of a case, essentially analytical, an effort not to justify precedent-following but to explain how the authority of precedent operates. This third perspective has it that precedents are best understood not in terms of the reason for the decision, or as summarized reasons which judges with an eye to efficiency or expediency might want to replicate, but as reasons which can preclude a decision-maker from ruling on the basis of his or her own reasons.

The genesis of this idea can be found in Hobbes's *Leviathan*. Hobbes, we have seen, was no votary for the doctrine of binding precedent. Like Bentham and Austin, he could not see why the judgment of any court should bind anyone other than the parties to the case decided.[158] Like Shakespeare and Swift (and again, Bentham), he recognized that with a culture of precedent-following comes the likelihood of repeated wrongs.[159] '[M]en's judgments have been perverted', Hobbes believed, 'by trusting to precedents' which contradict the demands of natural reason; 'if afterward in another like case' the judge finds it 'more consonant to equity to give a contrary sentence' rather than follow the precedent, then give contrary sentence is what he must do.[160] Indeed

---

[158] See Hobbes, *Leviathan*, II. 26. 24 ('[T]hough the sentence of the judge, be a law to the party pleading, yet it is no law to any judge, that shall succeed him in that office').

[159] See Gerald J. Postema, *Bentham and the Common Law Tradition* (Oxford: Clarendon Press, 1986), 278; Jonathan Swift, *Gulliver's Travels* (Harmondsworth: Penguin, 1967 [1726]), 296 ('It is a maxim among these lawyers, that whatever hath been done before, may legally be done again: and therefore they take special care to record all the decisions formerly made against common justice and the general reason of mankind. These, under the name of *precedents*, they produce as authorities to justify the most iniquitous opinions; and the Judges never fail of directing accordingly'); Shakespeare, *Merchant of Venice*, IV. i:

> ... there is no power in Venice
> Can alter a decree established;
> 'Twill be recorded for a precedent,
> And many an error, by the same example,
> Will rush into the state ...

Many others have recognized the same: see Christopher J. Peters, 'Foolish Consistency: On Equality, Integrity, and Justice in Stare Decisis' (1996) 105 Yale L.J. 2031–115 at 2033.

[160] Hobbes, *Leviathan*, II. 26. 24.

Hobbes, in his own way, appreciated that there is potential hazard in the resort to precedent as an availability heuristic: 'judges that condemn without hearing the proofs offered, are unjust judges; and their presumption is but prejudice; which no man ought to bring with him to the seat of justice, whatsoever precedent judgments, or examples, he shall pretend to follow'.[161]

But we have also seen that Hobbes's conception of adjudication as an exercise founded in natural reason helps us to understand why the doctrine of *stare decisis* should have made its way into the common law. Within *Leviathan* there is to be found another argument which bears upon our understanding of the authority of precedent, though it is certainly not an argument about precedent. For Hobbes, as we saw in chapter 2, law is a matter not of counsel but of command. 'Command is, where a man saith, *do this*, or *do not this*, without expecting any other reason than the will of him that says it.'[162] From this short sentence, Hart maintained, quite a lot can be inferred:

> By this Hobbes meant that the commander characteristically intends his hearer to take the commander's will instead of his own as a guide to action and so to take it in place of any deliberation or reasoning of his own: the expression of a commander's will that an act be done is intended to preclude or cut off any independent deliberation by the hearer of the merits pro and con of doing the act. The commander's expression of will therefore is not intended to function within the hearer's deliberations as a reason for doing the act, not even as the strongest or dominant reason, for that would presuppose that independent deliberation was to go on, whereas the commander intends to cut off or exclude it.[163]

The hearer submits to the commander's authority, then, by forfeiting his own judgment regarding the act in question and adopting instead the commander's will as a guide to action.[164] As Hart puts it, the commander's words are authoritative because they are accepted by the hearer as 'constituting a peremptory reason' for action, 'a reason for belief without independent investigation or assessment of the truth of what is

---

[161] *Ibid.*   [162] *Ibid.*, II. 25. 2.
[163] H. L. A. Hart, *Essays on Bentham: Studies in Jurisprudence and Political Theory* (Oxford: Clarendon Press, 1982), 253.
[164] See Richard B. Friedman, 'On the Concept of Authority in Political Philosophy', in *Concepts in Social and Political Philosophy*, ed. R. E. Flathman (New York: Macmillan, 1973), 121–46 at 129 ('In this sense, obedience to a command "simply because X gave it" ... entails abdication of one's own judgment as to the particular act in question and the adoption in its place of the judgment of someone else guiding one's conduct').

stated'.[165] If we think of the hearer as the judge on a later court, he suggests, we can see that precedents are an example of a peremptory reason for reaching a particular decision: 'in a system where there is a strict theory of precedent the judge's decision in a particular case or a sufficient line of cases may be recognized as a fact constituting a peremptory reason for deciding cases in the same way and so though not itself a command, as creating a general legal rule'.[166] Not for the first time, we see Hart attempting to demonstrate that the authority of precedent has to be explained by something other than the classical-positivist language of law as a system of coercive orders: when courts follow precedents, they treat them as the declarations of earlier judges who not only were concerned with materially identical facts but who also addressed those facts with sufficient knowledge, intelligence and wisdom for today's judge to consider it reasonable to treat the precedent, or the line of precedent, as authoritative, as cutting off the need for independent deliberation on the facts or the earlier judicial reasoning.

It would be a mistake to categorize Hart's argument as a variant on the proposition that precedents are a type of labour-saving device. Judges who accept a precedent as a peremptory reason for deciding in a particular way do not necessarily believe that the reasoning to be found in the precedent represents the reasoning that they themselves would have produced had they deliberated the matter afresh. The reasoning to be found in a precedent – or, more likely, a line of cases composing a precedent – might not capture the reasons those judges would have articulated on the same facts, but the weight of authority behind the precedent (the status of the deciding courts, the eminence of the earlier judges and so on) might still effectively preclude them from departing from it. A peremptory reason, Hart explains, is not a ready-made or even the strongest reason for deciding in a particular way, but rather something which cuts off or excludes the opportunity to decide on the basis of one's own reasons.

In arguing thus, Hart was taking his cue from Joseph Raz, who conceives of legitimate authoritative directives as providing exclusionary reasons for action. 'The whole point and purpose of authorities', according to Raz, 'is to pre-empt individual judgment on the merits of a case'.[167] '[W]here improving the outcome is more important than

---

[165] Hart, *Essays on Bentham*, 261. [166] *Ibid.*
[167] Joseph Raz, *The Morality of Freedom* (Oxford: Clarendon Press, 1986), 47–8.

deciding for oneself',[168] individuals ought, as a matter of rational choice, to act on the basis of not their own but the authority's judgment as to what is right on the balance of reasons: the authoritative directive is a 'second-order' reason for action which ought to pre-empt other reasons for action.[169] Just as Hart believed precedents can be peremptory reasons for action, so too Raz believes they can be exclusionary reasons for action. The exclusionary power of precedent 'is not total in scope', he concedes, for '[s]ometimes judges have discretion to overrule'.[170] The House of Lords' insistence, before July 1966, that it was generally bound to follow its own precedents 'included a strong exclusionary element',[171] as does the general rule that the Court of Appeal must follow its own decisions as well as those of the House of Lords.[172] But the exclusionary element in both instances cannot properly be described as absolute, for the House of Lords before 1966 was not, and the Court of Appeal is not, completely bound to follow its own decisions.[173]

The capacity of precedents to provide exclusionary reasons determining the considerations on which courts may act is, none the less, significant. The primary institutions of a legal system, the judiciary among them, are required to act on certain reasons to the exclusion of others, 'even if they do not think that on the balance of reasons they ought to do so'.[174] 'Judges rendering judgment from a legal point of view do not deny that there are other valid reasons applicable to the situation'[175] which they have to adjudicate, but in accepting the doctrine of precedent

---

[168] Ibid., 69.
[169] See ibid., 57–69; and in a similar vein, see G. J. Warnock, *The Object of Morality* (London: Methuen, 1971), 40–1, 68.
[170] Joseph Raz, *Practical Reason and Norms*, 2nd edn (Oxford: Oxford University Press, 1999), 144 n. *.
[171] Joseph Raz, 'Facing Up: A Reply' (1989) 62 *Southern California L. Rev.* 1153–235 at 1172.
[172] For the House of Lords' practice, see *Practice Statement (Judicial Precedent)* [1966] 1 WLR 1234. For the Court of Appeal's position, see *Young* v. *Bristol Aeroplane Co.* [1944] KB 718.
[173] See, e.g., Lord Halsbury's argument in *London Tramways* v. *London County Council* [1898] AC 375, 380–1 that the House of Lords would not be bound to accept its own prior decisions where there is evidence that judicial reasoning was based on 'a mistake of fact'. The House of Lords has held that the Court of Appeal will not be bound by its own erroneous precedents where deferring to the precedent would perpetuate legal error because the losing party declines to appeal to the House of Lords, or where deferring causes the losing party unnecessary cost or, owing to delay, an injustice precisely because an appeal has to be made to the House of Lords. See *Davis* v. *Johnson* [1979] AC 264.
[174] Raz, *Practical Reason and Norms*, 142.   [175] Ibid., 143–4.

as 'part of the rule of recognition'[176] – as one of the criteria, that is, by which they identify the rules of a legal system[177] – they treat a previous decision as an exclusionary reason requiring them not to act on reasons which do not belong to the doctrine or are not recognized by it.[178] That is, judges who accept the doctrine cannot depart from previous decisions because they think that this would be the best thing to do on the overall balance of reasons; rather, they must accept those decisions as authoritative directives which exclude reliance on their own judgment. The doctrine of precedent, we might say, is an exclusionary rule which requires courts to treat precedents as giving rise to exclusionary rulings.[179]

Is it plausible to account for the authority of precedent in terms of exclusionary reasons? Even Raz has some doubts.[180] It makes 'perfect sense', he contends, to conceive of precedents as having binding force.[181] But the 'special revisability of judge-made law' – the fact that precedents can be overruled and distinguished – means that it is 'metaphorically ... less "binding" than enacted law'.[182] The very possibility of precedents being overruled is, Gardner has argued, evidence that they have binding force: after all, a 'decision of an earlier court must be binding in law for it to be necessary for a later court to overrule it.'[183] Certainly the point of a court overruling a precedent is to strip the precedent of authority. But to point to the necessity of overruling as evidence that a precedent is 'binding in law' seems questionable: before 1966, for example, the House of Lords was technically incapable of overruling nearly all of its own precedents, yet some of those precedents were circumvented because inconvenient,[184] or passed over because social conditions change and, as Lord Macmillan put it, '[t]he criterion of judgment must adjust and adapt itself to the changing circumstances of life'.[185] Raz, in characterizing judge-made law as more loosely binding than enacted law, clearly appreciates that the notion of binding precedent has

---

[176] Raz, *AL*, 184 n. 8; also *Practical Reason and Norms*, 146–8.
[177] See generally Hart, *CL*, 100–23.
[178] See Raz, *Practical Reason and Norms*, 144–5.
[179] See Raz, *AL*, 114; Stephen R. Perry, 'Second-Order Reasons, Uncertainty and Legal Theory' (1989) 62 *Southern California L. Rev.* 913–94 at 957; 'Judicial Obligation', 231.
[180] See Raz, 'Facing Up', 1171–2.   [181] *Ibid.*, 1172.   [182] Raz, *AL*, 195.
[183] John Gardner, 'Some Types of Law', in *Common Law Theory*, ed. D. E. Edlin (Cambridge: Cambridge University Press, 2007), 51–77 at 74.
[184] J. W. Harris, 'Towards Principles of Overruling – When Should a Final Court of Appeal Second Guess?' (1990) 10 *Oxf. Jnl Leg. Studs* 135–99 at 135–6.
[185] *Donoghue v. Stevenson* [1932] AC 532, 619, HL.

to be approached with some care, that a precedent 'is constantly subject to potential (though modest) revision on all occasions on which its application is litigated.'[186] A court which resolves to reshape an area of law by creating a new precedent, he contends, adopts a strategy which will meet with only limited success.[187] Deliberately deciding a case in such a way as to leave the law 'underdetermined' makes good sense, none the less, where the objective is to establish 'a framework for further legal development'.[188] It seems correct to argue, as Perry does, that the techniques available to judges for revising common-law rules are more extensive than Raz concedes.[189] But there is no doubt that Raz appreciates that some such techniques exist, that 'judicial law-making' is, among other things, 'concerned with extending existing doctrines, successively adjusting them to gradually changing technological, economic, or social conditions and introducing small alterations to avoid the undesirable and unintended consequences of applying rules to circumstances which were not foreseen when those rules were laid down'.[190]

If, however, judges have considerable discretion to distinguish, overrule, extend or by other means avoid simply following 'binding' precedents, how can it be correct to conceive of those precedents as giving rise to exclusionary rulings? Raz's answer — as should be clear from what has been said already — is that a precedent might be 'partial and incomplete', in so far as it leaves it open for a judge to undertake some degree of revision but still 'includes an exclusionary reason requiring' him not to act on some first-order reasons which could be brought to bear on a case.[191] The very fact that a legal principle is underdetermined suggests that it is exclusionary only up to a point. If the *ratio decidendi* of a case has become settled over time, a judge may be able to tell not only where the precedent pre-empts him from dealing, but also where it permits him to deal, with a new case on the ordinary balance of reasons. Another answer derivable from Raz's philosophy of authority is that precedents might be theorized as 'protected' reasons. Sometimes, a first-order reason might be protected by a second-order, exclusionary reason. My brother buys me a shirt for my birthday and tells me that it is just my style and I should wear it, but I decline to wear it because I think it is ugly. My reason for not wearing the shirt might be reinforced by the fact that my wife says that I should never take my brother's instructions as

---

[186] Raz, *AL*, 195. [187] Ibid., 196, 200–1. [188] Ibid., 194.
[189] Perry, 'Judicial Obligation', 238–9. [190] Raz, *AL*, 200.
[191] Raz, *Practical Reason and Norms*, 144.

reasons for action: she therefore provides me with a reason for not acting on another reason (my brother's instruction), an exclusionary reason, we might say, which is different from but which supports my first-order reason for not acting, indeed protects my first-order reason against my brother's first-order reason for my performing that action. According to Lamond, a precedent is a protected reason, though it is protected 'in a highly selective manner'.[192] The *ratio* of a case provides 'the basis for the first-order part of the protected reason' – a first-order reason for, say, deciding 'in favor of *C* when certain conditions are satisfied' – and '[t]he other facts of the case provide the basis for the exclusionary reason' supporting that decision: that is, 'later courts are excluded from relying on reasons provided by features that were present in the precedent case to defeat the first-order reason for the result'.[193]

Whatever type of Razian reason we understand a precedent to be, exclusionary or protected, it is worth noting that it is the precedent, not its *ratio decidendi*, that does the work of excluding or protecting. Indeed, the *ratio* is deemed to constitute the first-order reason rather than the second-order (exclusionary) reason. Lamond neatly summarizes the point in working towards his account of precedents as protected reasons: '[w]hat binds later courts are *precedents*, not *rationes*'.[194] A court set on treating a precedent as an exclusionary or a protected reason would need to be able to recognize the *ratio* as something that is distinct from the precedent, 'intelligible against the background facts of a case'.[195] As we have seen in this chapter, nevertheless, there is often plenty of scope for disagreement about what the *ratio* of a particular case is. Courts, as Lamond notes, rarely do much 'to assist in the construction of *rationes* from their judgments',[196] and although judges 'frequently *do* adopt the arguments of their predecessors' there is also a tendency for this process 'to break down ... where authorities are very old ... or the area of law is a site of considerable controversy ... or a judge is very independently minded'.[197] If it is impossible to say for sure what the *ratio* of a particular case is, it will be impossible to disentangle the first-order portion of a protected reason from its second-order component.

---

[192] Grant Lamond, 'Do Precedents Create Rules?' (2005) 11 *Legal Theory* 1–26 at 19. Although I take issue with Lamond's characterization of precedents as protected reasons, it should be clear from what I have said so far in this study that I agree with his general strictures against conceiving of precedents as rules.
[193] Ibid.   [194] Ibid., 16.   [195] Ibid., 24.   [196] Ibid., 15.   [197] Ibid., 13.

This last objection is hardly earth-shattering. The fact that courts will sometimes have difficulty separating the exclusionary component of a precedent from the first-order reason for decision is no basis for concluding that judges cannot treat precedents as giving rise to exclusionary rulings. My general point, however, is not that precedents cannot operate but that they are not well suited to operating in an exclusionary fashion. If, for some reason, a court considered the exclusionary conception of precedent to be the preferable one in a given set of circumstances, presumably it could be adopted.[198] But for various reasons it seems unlikely that a judge, in deciding a case, would consider a precedent to be something quite as blunt as an authoritative directive excluding him from relying on his own independent judgment. Most of the relevant reasons why this should be so have been discussed in this chapter already. In particular, case-law often lacks a canonical form of words, and in the absence of such words it is at best a decidedly inefficient exclusionary resource. Furthermore, judges might follow precedents and yet still modify the balance of principles justifying them, or even formulate completely fresh justifications.[199] The Razian association of precedents with exclusionary reasons certainly should not be discounted: the notion that 'the most rational course and the right way'[200] for judges to discharge their responsibilities is, among other things, to follow precedents even when their own deliberations would lead them to a contrary outcome deserves our attention if only because it is such an ingenious way of conceptualizing precedential authority. It is important to keep in mind, furthermore, that Raz is not arguing that precedents completely pre-empt the possibility of judges deliberating on the balance of reasons. Taking account of these concessions, nevertheless, does not stop the exclusionary conception of precedent from buckling under the weight of the common law's complexity: the doctrine of precedent places some constraints on the revisability of judge-made law, but the fact that these constraints nevertheless leave plenty of room for judicial innovation means that the characterization of a

---

[198] See Perry, 'Second-Order Reasons', 968.
[199] See also Perry, 'Judicial Obligation', 235, 239.
[200] Raz, *The Morality of Freedom*, 69. The relevant passage begins: 'If another's reasoning is usually better than mine...' (*ibid.*). I think it is implicit in Raz's argument that it is not simply precedent, but precedent as accumulated judicial wisdom, that gives rise to exclusionary reasons.

precedent as giving rise to an exclusionary ruling will nearly always be too straightforward.[201]

4. Conclusion

A precedent, even a judicial precedent, need not be reasoned if it is to guide present action. Yet we saw in chapter 2 that only once common law courts begin consistently to provide reasons for their decisions does the doctrine of binding precedent become intelligible. The primary purpose of this chapter has been to show how judicial precedents might be understood as vectors for reason. There are at least three ways in which a precedent might be conceived thus: first, there is the idea that most case-law contains a 'reason for the decision' or *ratio decidendi*, and identifying this *ratio* (which is not the same thing as the judicial *reasons* offered) is the key to determining how a precedent binds future courts; secondly, there is the idea that a precedent may offer today's court a ready-articulated reason for reaching a particular decision, thereby providing that court with an opportunity to avoid the costs of reasoning a legal problem from the ground up; finally, there is the idea that the doctrine of precedent requires judges to treat precedents as authoritative directives giving rise to 'exclusionary reasons', thereby pre-empting or taking the place of individual judgments as to what ought to be done.

Each of these explanations of precedent as a particular type of reason has been criticized. The explanation of the binding force of precedent by reference to the *ratio decidendi* concept meets with various objections – not least that many cases yield more than one *ratio*, that sometimes they yield none, and that even if we accept that there are good reasons for determining the *ratio* of a case, there is likely to be considerable disagreement about how to do this. Using precedents as ready- or partly-constructed reasons is likely to result in robust and efficient (which is not to say optimally efficient) decision-making; nevertheless, judges sometimes consider the virtue of decisional efficiency to be outweighed by the need to go about deciding 'in the right way' – primarily with an eye, that is, to the values underpinning the system of justice rather than to its expedient administration. To conceptualize precedents as exclusionary reasons requires that we accept too tidy a picture of precedents as authoritative directives to later courts – that we assume them to be more rule-like and less amenable to alteration and adaptation than tends to be the

---

[201] See Perry, 'Judicial Obligation', 239; 'Second-Order Reasons', 976.

case. There is, it has been suggested, no satisfactory overarching theory of precedent, and the fact that there are limitations to all three of these efforts to explain the authority of precedent in terms of one or another concept of reason provides us with no cause to think that this claim is wrong.

But emphasizing this point is really a case of missing the point. Explanations of precedents as giving rise to particular types of reasons might not completely account for precedential authority. But they are very valuable accounts, nevertheless. Precedents often guide decision-making precisely because they operate as types of reasons. It is because they operate as reasons, furthermore, that they sometimes will *not* guide decision-making: a court, that is, might determine that the reason which a precedent offers for deciding a case in a particular way is defeated by a stronger contrary reason. Here, it seems, we discover the real meaning of 'binding precedent': courts might not be bound to follow the earlier decisions of (usually) superior courts on the same facts but, when confronted with such decisions, they are obliged to deal with them somehow.

In chapter 5, we will consider some other explanations for the authority of precedent. Perhaps the most obvious explanation – that precedent-following seems to satisfy the expectation that like cases be treated alike – has featured surprisingly little in this book so far. But before we turn to that explanation and others, we will take a slight detour and consider the question of just what it is that courts do when they decide not to follow a precedent. A court which wishes to circumvent a precedent will probably have a host of techniques at its disposal – the earlier decision might be considered unclear in its scope, inappropriate to modern social conditions or conventions, premised on a misinterpretation of a statute or on a wrongheaded reading of still earlier case-law, unreliable in the light of judicial pronouncements in subsequent case-law and so forth.[202] The main two ways in which courts avoid following a precedent are – to use

---

[202] See Stone, *Precedent and Law*, 175–6; Allan C. Hutchinson, *Evolution and the Common Law* (Cambridge: Cambridge University Press, 2005), 7; Charles Lewis, 'The Truth about Precedent' (1976) 73 *Law Society Gazette* 957 ('[T]he judge who dislikes being constrained by precedent has numerous . . . small arms at his disposal. He can "not follow" a precedent that points in a certain direction without necessarily covering his case explicitly. He can simply state that a previous case was decided on its own facts and does not help him in his present difficulty . . . For an old precedent, which some might think all the more respectable for that reason alone, he may state that he is satisfied that it is no longer the law. He may even, if he is bold, and if he can find the source material that was not considered by the earlier court, announce that their decision was given *per incuriam*, that is without due consideration . . . It can thus be seen that the binding force of precedent is whittled down to nothing more, in practice, than a persuasive authority').

the terminology of the English common law – (1) distinguishing it and (2) overruling it. Both actions require that judges explain themselves, as it were, though the activity of distinguishing permits of a fairly obvious (if simplistic) explanation: the earlier decision was not followed because its facts are distinct – materially different – from those in the case to be decided. Overruling, by contrast, is a bolder and more controversial action. If courts could overrule precedents whenever and for whatever reasons they liked, the doctrine of *stare decisis* would simply not exist; and so it seems safe to say from the outset that overruling cannot be a license for judges to do whatever they wish. But the fact that courts often have *some* power to overrule has proved particularly troubling for many jurists. For what is the limit to this power? From where, furthermore, does it derive? The answer to this second question is usually that it derives from the courts themselves. We have seen that some jurists within the English tradition struggled immensely with the questions of how to define and discover the *ratio decidendi* of a case. But this struggle was nothing as compared with the inability of others among their number to comprehend how a court that is supposed to be bound by its own precedents could legitimately declare that its precedents no longer always bind.

4

Distinguishing, overruling and the problem of self-reference

A precedent may be a guide to action, but decision-makers do not always accept the guidance. Moreover, expectations that decision-makers will accept the guidance tend to vary from one adjudicative system to the next. Such variance is obvious even among common-law jurisdictions: traditionally, for example, lower court judges in the United States have, for a variety of reasons, been far more willing than have their English counterparts not to follow a precedent, even when it is not within their power to overrule it.[1] When judges seem quite comfortable declining to heed precedent, it is no surprise to find legal theorists arguing that *stare decisis* has little constraining power.[2] That judges often will not follow, and will be entirely within their rights not following, precedents can make it seem odd (even if not technically incorrect)[3] to talk of a doctrine of *binding* precedent. It would be a mistake, nevertheless, to think that

---

[1] See P. S. Atiyah and Robert S. Summers, *Form and Substance in Anglo-American Law: A Comparative Study of Legal Reasoning, Legal Theory, and Legal Institutions* (Oxford: Clarendon Press, 1987), 118–27.

[2] Consider the fairly recent spate of literature claiming, among other things, that precedents rarely guide United States Supreme Court decision-making: e.g., Saul Brenner and Harold J. Spaeth, *Stare Indecisis: The Alteration of Precedent on the Supreme Court, 1946–1992* (Cambridge: Cambridge University Press, 1995); Harold Spaeth and Jeffrey Segal, *Majority Rule or Minority Will: Adherence to Precedent on the US Supreme Court* (Cambridge: Cambridge University Press, 1999); Jeffrey A. Segal and Harold J. Spaeth, *The Supreme Court and the Attitudinal Model Revisited* (Cambridge: Cambridge University Press, 2002). For the argument that the picture is considerably more complicated cf., e.g., Henry Paul Monaghan, '*Stare Decisis* and Constitutional Adjudication' (1988) 88 *Columbia L. Rev.* 723–73; Jack Knight and Lee Epstein, 'The Norm of *Stare Decisis*' (1996) 40 *American Jnl of Political Science* 1018–35; and Thomas G. Hansford and James F. Spriggs II, *The Politics of Precedent on the US Supreme Court* (Princeton, NJ: Princeton University Press, 2006).

[3] The fact that judges often do not follow precedents is not sufficient to show that precedents have no binding force – if it were, we would have to conclude that much of the criminal law similarly lacks binding force. The fact that judges are often within their rights not following precedents likewise does not show that precedents lack binding force. But it does show that the binding force of precedent is restricted.

the judicial capacity to act appropriately by not following a precedent necessitates the conclusion that precedents are a weak form of authority. Just as judges might be acting appropriately, so too they might be acting inappropriately, in not following a precedent: the precedent, that is, might be soundly decided and on all fours with the case at hand, so that there is no good reason for a court to avoid following it. A precedent might inhibit, furthermore, even where it is not followed. Anyone familiar with English case law knows that judges will sometimes not follow an earlier decision but nevertheless see fit to refer to or apply it, or accord it significance in some other, similarly subtle way in the course of a judgment. Although a judge might with good reason see no obligation to follow, and might explicitly claim not to follow, a precedent, its existence may nevertheless lead him to decide differently from how he would have done had it not existed. The precedent might remind him of the weight of the past, that he is deciding within a tradition, and the decision which he makes, though it might not accord with the precedent, might pay respect to or in some other way bear the marks of that tradition.

The very fact that a judge explicitly departs from a precedent might be considered evidence that the precedent has some authority, for explicit departure from a precedent invariably entails an explanation; judicial precedents would only be devoid of authority if judges felt no need to offer reasons for their actions in those instances when they choose not to follow them. Holmes once remarked that '[a] common-law judge could not say I think the doctrine of consideration a bit of historical nonsense and shall not enforce it in my court.'[4] The reason so summary a declaration would be unacceptable is that the precedent supporting the doctrine of consideration creates a rebuttable presumption as to what the law requires.[5] The precedent is something to be reckoned with: it is, in Schauer's language, an 'articulated characterization' which places on the judge an 'argumentative burden' – the burden, that is, of saying

---

[4] *Southern Pac. Co.* v. *Jensen*, 244 U.S. 205, 221 (1917) (Holmes J., dissenting).

[5] 'Rules of precedent are like rules of evidence for questions of law rather than fact. They give special, sometimes dispositive, strength to one particular indicator of what the law requires. Precedent means that prior decisions are taken as correct, or correct unless shown otherwise to some requisite degree, much as evidentiary presumption means that some fact is taken to be true, or true unless clearly shown not to be.' John Harrison, 'The Power of Congress over the Rules of Precedent' (2000) 50 *Duke L.J.* 503–43 at 512. The notion that precedents supporting the doctrine of consideration might be rebuttable is not fanciful: see Lord Wright, 'Ought the Doctrine of Consideration to be Abolished from the Common Law?' (1936) 49 *Harvard L. Rev.* 1225–53.

how the precedent ought to be treated.[6] If a judge says that the precedent should not be followed, it is expected that he will say why it should not be followed. Refusal to follow a precedent is thus analogous to refusal to comply with a moral obligation, such as keeping a promise: the obligation is not absolute, but a justifiable refusal to comply must be supported by certain kinds of reasons.[7] It helps, of course, to identify just what these reasons are: to say that precedents should be followed unless there are strong reasons for not following them is, in itself, hardly enlightening.[8] Fortunately, as we will see when we turn our attention to overruling, judges do tend to specify the exceptional instances. What is particularly interesting is the capacity of the exceptional to emphasize the norm: the authority of precedent is revealed to a significant degree, that is, when judges decide not to follow precedents.

1. Distinguishing

'Distinguishing' is what judges do when they make a distinction between one case and another. The point may seem obvious, but it deserves to be spelt out because we distinguish within as well as between cases. Distinguishing within a case is primarily a matter of differentiating the *ratio decidendi* from *obiter dicta* – separating the facts which are materially relevant from those which are irrelevant to a decision. Distinguishing between cases is first and foremost a matter of demonstrating factual differences between the earlier and the instant case – of showing that the *ratio* of a precedent does not satisfactorily apply to the case at hand. Since no two cases are exactly the same, distinguishing is always possible at one or another level, though *rationes* which are broadly formulated are likely to be less easily distinguishable than those which have a narrower range of application.[9] The consequences of distinguishing might vary according to the field of law: in some areas of law, for example, a body of consistent and largely undisturbed precedent or a well-established, landmark decision (a 'super-precedent', to

---

[6] See Frederick Schauer, 'Precedent' (1987) 39 *Stanford L. Rev.* 571–605 at 580–1.
[7] See Joseph Raz, *Practical Reason and Norms*, 2nd edn (Oxford: Oxford University Press, 1999), 140; *AL*, 114; also Hart, *CL*, 139.
[8] See Richard A. Wasserstrom, *The Judicial Decision: Toward a Theory of Legal Justification* (Stanford, Ca: Stanford University Press, 1961), 44–6.
[9] See Schauer, 'Precedent', 594–5.

adopt the currently-fashionable American terminology)¹⁰ might induce a particularly high degree of reliance on the part of prospective litigants, and so distinguishing in these areas might cause more discontent than it would in areas where the decision to litigate is less influenced by the predictability of outcomes.

Most courts will distinguish cases fairly routinely and without controversy. The task will not always be straightforward because, as we saw in the previous chapter, the discursiveness of common-law judgments can make the identification of *rationes* difficult. Nor would it be correct to think that a court distinguishes cases merely by drawing attention to factual differences between them: courts are not only drawing a distinction but also arguing that the distinction is material, that it provides a justification for not following the precedent. Not just any old difference provides such a justification: the distinction must be such that it provides a sufficiently convincing reason for declining to follow a previous decision.¹¹ Since it is for judges themselves to identify significant differences — to determine, as it were, their own criteria of relevance — is it not easy for them to distinguish away the authority of any precedent? Sometimes it will be easy, no doubt, but not usually so; for distinguishing appropriately is as much a judicial norm as is the doctrine of *stare decisis* itself. The judge who tries to distinguish cases on the basis of materially irrelevant facts is likely to be easily found out. Lawyers and other judges who have reason to scrutinize his effort will probably have no trouble showing it to be the initiative of someone who is careless or dishonest, and so his reputation might be damaged and his decision appealed. That judges have the power to distinguish does not mean they can flout precedent whenever it suits them.

In the most routine instances, the activity of distinguishing leaves the authority of precedent undisturbed, for a court is declaring an earlier decision not to be bad law, but to be good but inapplicable law.¹² It is not even clear that it is right to talk about distinguishing a precedent in

---

¹⁰ See Michael Sinclair, 'Precedent, Super-Precedent' (2007) 14 *George Mason L. Rev.* 363–411; Daniel A. Farber, 'The Rule of Law and the Law of Precedents' (2006) 90 *Minnesota L. Rev.* 1173–1203.

¹¹ See A. W. B. Simpson, 'The *Ratio Decidendi* of a Case and the Doctrine of Binding Precedent', in *Oxford Essays in Jurisprudence*, ed. A. G. Guest (Oxford: Oxford University Press, 1961), 148–75, at 174–5.

¹² Determining that a precedent is inapplicable to the case at hand does not necessarily leave the precedent undisturbed. Distinguishing in this fashion may lead lawyers and judges, many of whom might have expected the precedent to be applied, to consider its authority to have been weakened somewhat. As the old joke goes, a precedent might lack authority

such instances, for a court considers the earlier decision irrelevant to the case at hand, and therefore, for its present purposes, not really a precedent at all. The more interesting and subtle form of distinguishing between cases is to be found where a court departs from a precedent by making a particular ruling depend on the presence of a more extensive range of material facts.[13] If a court decided in *Black* v. *Black* that X should be the outcome when facts A, B and C obtain, then if A, B and C are the operative facts in *White* v. *White*, we can expect the outcome to be X. But imagine that in *Grey* v. *Grey* the court distinguishes *Black* v. *Black* by deciding that X should be the outcome when A, B, C and E obtain. If, in *Grey* v. *Grey*, A, B and C, but not E, obtain, then X will not be the outcome despite the presence of the material facts that led to it being the outcome in the earlier case-law. By adding to the conditions necessary for X, the court in *Grey* v. *Grey* has changed the law: the *ratio decidendi* of *Grey* v. *Grey* is narrower – it will be applicable in fewer instances, since it requires the presence of more material facts – than that of *Black* v. *Black*.

When we conceive of distinguishing in this last sense, we see that it provides judges with the power to make new law out of existing law. It is difficult to imagine, none the less, that judges will normally be seeking to develop the common law when they distinguish precedents. Judges tend to distinguish cases not because they have a law-making agenda but because following the precedent will not produce what they consider to be the right outcome.[14] Distinguishing is, in any event, necessarily a limited law-making power (notwithstanding that many instances of distinguishing alter the law considerably). When a court distinguishes between cases it is not repealing the *ratio* of a precedent but amending it so that the later case falls outside its scope.[15] The *ratio* of the new case

---

because it is 'very distinguished'. See further Patrick Devlin, *The Judge* (Oxford: Oxford University Press, 1981), 92–3.

[13] See Raz, *AL*, 185–7.

[14] Even when they are seeking to use their power to distinguish in order to develop the common law, this is unlikely to be obvious from the judicial opinion: see Earl Maltz, 'The Nature of Precedent' (1988) 66 *N. Carolina L. Rev.* 367–93 at 384 ('[I]t often is difficult to determine whether a court is deliberately altering pre-existing doctrine or making a good faith effort to interpret prior case law').

[15] Assuming the precedent is in need of amendment. Sometimes, the *ratio* of a precedent will be sufficiently narrow that a court need add no new conditions to it in order to ensure that it does not apply to the case at hand, but the court will go through the motions of distinguishing basically as a precautionary measure to ensure that a non-applicable precedent is not followed. See John Gardner, 'Some Types of Law', in

contains conditions (though not necessarily all the conditions) that the *ratio* of the precedent contains, but it will not be applied unless some further condition, or set of conditions, is also present.[16] The *ratio* can only be amended, furthermore, in a manner compatible with the order made in the precedent. In *Grey* v. *Grey*, *X* depended on the presence of *A*, *B*, *C* and *E*, thereby distinguishing *Black* v. *Black*. A court which sought to distinguish *Black* v. *Black* by deciding that *X* now depends on the presence of *A*, *B*, *C* and *not-D* would fail in its objective unless *not-D*, combined with *A*, *B* and *C*, constituted a justifiable modification of the *ratio*. *Not-D* could be *E*, in which case the modified *ratio* would be sufficient to justify the order of *X*. But *not-D* could be many other things besides *E*, and if it were something that requires a decision contrary to *X* then the *ratio* will not be appropriately amended. Distinguishing between cases may change the law, but the range of changes permissible through distinguishing is constrained.

2. Overruling

Stare decisis is usually not a constitutional or a statutory requirement, but one which courts impose on themselves. When a common law system adopts a doctrine of precedent – and the main point of chapter 2 was that the doctrine is indeed adopted, that it is not innate to the system – it effectively develops a strategy of self-binding to guard against the injustices, inefficiencies and other weaknesses that would beset the adjudicative process if judges reasoned every point of law afresh, with complete discretion and without any regard to hard-won judicial wisdom. Not without good reasons do judges speak of being bound by precedent. But for equally good reasons – not the least of which is that the court which rigidly adheres to precedent will sometimes be replicating errors – judges resist being bound by precedent absolutely.[17]

Common Law Theory, ed. D. Edlin (Cambridge: Cambridge University Press, 2006), 51–77 at 71.

[16] Cf. Nicola Gennaioli and Andrei Shleifer, 'The Evolution of Common Law' (2007) 115 *Jnl Pol. Econ.* 43–68 at 46 ('"distinguishing" ... endorses the existing precedent but adds a new material dimension to adjudication and holds that the judicial decision must depend on both the previously recognized dimension and the new one').

[17] On, e.g., the House of Lords' willingness exceptionally to depart from its precedents during the era when it professed to be bound by them, see Anon., 'Precedent' (1967) 131 *Justice of the Peace* 595.

Distinguishing is obviously one method by which judges loosen the grip of precedent. So too is overruling. When judges overrule a precedent they are declining to follow it and declaring that, at least where the facts of a case are materially identical to those of the case at hand, a new ruling should be followed instead. Sometimes a precedent is overruled because it has somehow outstayed its welcome. Sometimes a court may consider it unfortunate that the precedent was created in the first place. Overruling, like distinguishing, provides the courts only with limited law-creating power, for, as was noted at the end of the previous chapter, if courts could overrule precedents whenever they liked it would make no sense to speak of a doctrine of *stare decisis*. But if this is the case, just when will it be appropriate for courts to overrule precedents? The basic answer, we have seen, is that judges who wish to depart from precedents are expected to account for themselves: 'the overruling of precedents cannot simply be regarded as arbitrary; judges have, and publish, their reasons'[18] – indeed, judges quite often insist that, if a precedent is to be overruled, the reason for so doing must be especially serious or strong.[19]

---

[18] Theodore M. Benditt, 'The Rule of Precedent', in *Precedent in Law*, ed. L. Goldstein (Oxford: Clarendon Press, 1987), 89–106 at 101. In a similar vein, see Steven J. Burton, *Judging in Good Faith* (Cambridge: Cambridge University Press, 1992), 100–1.

[19] See, e.g., *Jones* v. *Secretary of State for Social Services* [1972] AC 944, 966, HL, per Lord Reid; *Knuller* v. *DPP* [1973] AC 435, 455, HL, per Lord Reid ('... we must be sure that there is some very good reason before we so act'); *Planned Parenthood of S.E. Pennsylvania* v. *Casey*, 505 U.S. 833, 864 (1992) ('a decision to overrule should rest on some special reason over and above the belief that a prior case was wrongly decided'); *Hubbard* v. *United States*, 514 U.S. 695, 716 (1995) (Scalia, J.: 'The doctrine of *stare decisis* protects the legitimate expectations of those who live under the law ... Who ignores it must give reasons, and reasons that go beyond mere demonstration that the overruled opinion was wrong (otherwise the doctrine would be no doctrine at all)'); *R* v. *Robinson* [1996] 1 SCR 683, para. 76 (Lamer C.J.C.: 'It is beyond doubt that this Court [the Supreme Court of Canada] has the power to overrule one of its previous decisions if there are compelling reasons for departing from the principle of *stare decisis*'). This manner of thinking is not the preserve of common-law judges: see, e.g., *Da Costa en Schaake NV* v. *Nederlandse Belastingadministratie (Cases 28, 29 and 30/62)* [1963] ECR 31, 42 (opinion of Mr Advocate General Lagrange: 'Clearly no one will expect that, having given a leading judgment, the [European] Court [of Justice] will depart from it in another action without strong reasons, but it should retain the legal right to do so'); Thijmen Koopmans, 'Stare Decisis in European Law', in *Essays in European Law and Integration*, ed. D. O'Keefe and H. G. Schermers (Deventer: Kluwer, 1982), 11–27 at 18; Mohamed Shahabuddeen, *Precedent in the World Court* (Cambridge: Cambridge University Press, 1996), 147–51, 239–40.

The most obvious reason for overruling a precedent is that the inferior court which created it made a mistake.[20] But overruling tends to be a more delicate matter when a court is considering a decision of its own or of a court of equal authority. In these circumstances, the overruling court – assuming the court has the capacity to overrule[21] – will at the very least want to be convinced that the impugned precedent is clearly wrong.[22] Sometimes a court might want a yet stronger reason for overruling: for example, it might want to be convinced that overruling the erroneous precedent will bring about an overall improvement to the law[23] (even if it only replaces one evil with a lesser evil),[24] or that it will not disturb the legitimate expectations of citizens who have arranged some of their affairs

---

[20] See, e.g., *Algama* v. *Minister for Immigration and Multicultural Affairs* (2001) 115 FCR 253, 263, Fed. Ct. Australia (French J.: 'The view which we prefer is that unless an error in construction is patent, or has produced unintended and perhaps irrational consequences not foreseen by the court that created the precedent, the first decision should stand').

[21] The general position in the United States, for example, is that a court might reject the decision of a court of equal authority as a precedent for itself, but it cannot overrule that decision.

[22] See, e.g., *Fitzleet Estates Ltd* v. *Cherry* [1977] 1 WLR 1345, 1350, HL, *per* Viscount Dilhorne ('If the decision in the *Chancery Lane* case was wrong, it certainly was not so clearly wrong and productive of injustice as to make it right for the House to depart from it'); *O'Brien* v. *Robinson* [1973] AC 912, 930, HL, *per* Lord Diplock ('[U]nless your Lordships are prepared to overrule *Morgan* v. *Liverpool Corporation* ... I think you are compelled to hold that this appeal must fail ... While it would be open to your Lordships to do so, this is not, I think, a suitable case in which to exercise the recently asserted power of this House to refuse to follow one of its own previous decisions. An examination of the reasoning in the judgments in the cases on this subject during the last hundred years suggests that the law might easily have developed on different lines from those which it in fact followed. But, for my part, I am not persuaded that this development was clearly wrong or leads to results which are clearly unjust'); *Ashwander* v. *Tennessee Valley Authority*, 297 U.S. 288, 352–3 (1936) (Brandeis, J.: 'This Court, while recognizing the soundness of the rule of *stare decisis* where appropriate, has not hesitated to overrule earlier decisions shown, upon fuller consideration, to be erroneous'); *Smith* v. *Allwright*, 321 U.S. 649, 665 (1944) ('[W]hen convinced of former error, this Court has never felt constrained to follow precedent'); Benjamin N. Cardozo, *The Nature of the Judicial Process* (New Haven: Yale University Press, 1921), 158 ('The United States Supreme Court and the highest courts of the several states overrule their own prior decisions when manifestly erroneous').

[23] See *President of India* v. *La Pintada* [1985] AC 104, 131, HL, *per* Lord Brandon.

[24] See *United States* v. *South Eastern Underwriters' Association*, 322 U.S. 533, 594 (1944) (Stone, C.J.).

on the understanding that the precedent is binding[25] or that the desired rectification cannot be achieved by legislative intervention.[26]

Overruling with strong reasons looks like a favoured strategy of the ideal-typical realist judge – the judge who, 'being merely on his way with a roving commission to find the just solution, will follow his hunch wherever it leads him',[27] no matter what precedent requires. Such a judge will be wary of following any precedent unreflectively, Max Radin contended, and should certainly have no doubts about overruling unjust precedents so that they can never be cited as authority again.[28] William O. Douglas, a judge who bore some resemblance to this ideal type, insisted that injustice is not all that is at stake. 'It is, I think, a healthy practice (too infrequently followed) for a court to re-examine its own doctrine', he observed. 'Respect for any tribunal is increased if it stands ready (save where injustice to intervening rights would occur) not only to correct the errors of others but also to confess to its own.'[29]

To assume that realist judges are invariably the ones who will be most inclined to overrule precedents is, however, simplistic. A court is unlikely to overrule a precedent merely because it does not like the way that an earlier panel thought about an issue; more likely it will overrule because, at the very least, it finds that the earlier panel misapplied or overlooked a relevant statutory provision, or that subsequent legislation has undermined the precedent or that the precedent in some other way

---

[25] See *Ross Smith* v. *Ross Smith* [1963] AC 280, 303, HL, *per* Lord Reid ('*Simonin* v. *Mallac* cannot now be supported ... Should it, then, be overruled? That is, to my mind, a very difficult question ... It would have been a compelling reason against overruling that decision if it could reasonably be supposed that anyone has regulated his affairs in reliance on its validity, but it would be fantastic to suppose that anyone has'); *Indyka* v. *Indyka* [1969] 1 AC 33, 69, HL, *per* Lord Reid ('[I]t is well recognised that we ought not to alter what is presently understood to be the law if that involves any real likelihood of injustice to people who have relied on the present position in arranging their affairs').

[26] See *Myers* v. *DPP* [1965] AC 1001, 1021–2, HL, *per* Lord Reid; *Khawaja* [1984] AC 74, 106 HL, *per* Lord Scarman ('[T]he House must be satisfied ... that a judicial departure by the House from the precedent is the safe and appropriate way of remedying the injustice and developing the law. The possibility that legislation may be the better course is one which ... the House will not overlook'). For other reasons for and against overruling, see Alan Paterson, *The Law Lords* (London: Macmillan, 1982), 156–7.

[27] Joseph C. Hutcheson, Jr., 'The Judgment Intuitive: The Function of the "Hunch" in Judicial Decision' (1929) 14 *Cornell L.Q.* 274–88 at 278.

[28] See Max Radin, 'The Trail of the Calf' (1946) 32 *Cornell L.Q.* 137–60 at 143, 157, 159.

[29] William O. Douglas, '*Stare Decisis*', in *The Supreme Court: Views from Inside*, ed. A. F. Westin (New York: Norton, 1961), 122–42 at 132.

misrepresents the law.[30] To use Hart's terminology, overruling is more likely the remedying tool of the 'formalist' judge who believes that an earlier court overlooked or misinterpreted a legal rule than the liberating tool of a 'rule-sceptic' seeking to make the law as he or she would like it. Certainly in the United States there is some evidence that, in modern times, the Supreme Court Justices most inclined to overrule the Court's own precedents are the ones most disposed to arguing that legal rules yield correct interpretations.[31]

The argument that overruling is a method more suited to the judge who wants to apply rather than make law will probably seem counter-intuitive to anyone who accepts what Hart calls the 'false dilemma' – precedents must either 'bind as fetters bind' or not bind at all[32] – as if it were a genuine dilemma. When judges exercise discretion they are commonly deciding not in whatever way they like but according to the options which the law permits – legislating not uninhibitedly but, as Cardozo put it, within the limits of their competence.[33] 'To avoid arbitrary discretion in the courts,' Alexander Hamilton observed in *Federalist 78*, 'it is indispensable that they should be bound down by strict rules and precedents, which serve to define and point out their duty in every particular case that comes before them'.[34] One could easily

---

[30] There is also the danger that the overruling of a precedent could put some citizens in the position of having committed an illegality. In *R v. Millis* (1844) 10 Cl. & F. 534 the House of Lords declined to uphold a charge of bigamy because at common law a valid marriage required the presence of a minister in holy orders, and in this case no such minister was present. In *Beamish v. Beamish* (1861) 9 HL Cas. 273 the House of Lords had the opportunity to rule differently, but somewhat reluctantly decided that it was bound to follow *R v. Millis*. Although the House was vague about why it considered itself so bound in this instance – in *R v. Millis* it had apparently been hurried into issuing an opinion, had mis-stated the facts and was far from unanimous in its judgment (see *Beamish v. Beamish*, 334–9, *per* Lord Campbell) – one reason might have been that, had it declared that marriages not performed in the presence of a minister in holy orders are valid, there would be the remote possibility that some people, having married believing that their first marriage was never valid because of *R v. Millis*, would become bigamists.

[31] See Caleb Nelson, '*Stare Decisis* and Demonstrably Erroneous Precedents' (2001) 87 *Virginia L. Rev.* 1–84 at 50–1.

[32] Hart, *CL*, 139.

[33] See Cardozo, *The Nature of the Judicial Process*, 113; also Kent Greenawalt, 'Discretion and the Judicial Decision: The Elusive Quest for the Fetters that Bind Judges' (1975) 75 *Columbia L. Rev.* 359–99 at 361–2, 366, 368. Greenawalt is less concerned with challenging the false assumption that discretion must be unconstrained discretion than he is with disproving the thesis that in some adjudicative contexts there can be no discretion.

[34] Alexander Hamilton, James Madison and John Jay, *The Federalist* (New York: Barnes & Noble, 2006 [1787–88]), 434. Cf. Devlin, *The Judge*, 181 ('[C]ase law . . . is . . . because of

be forgiven for thinking that Hamilton believed precedents bind as fetters bind. But note that he regards precedent-following as a means of curbing not all but only 'arbitrary' discretion. Judges, he argued, will sometimes have to use their discretion – for example, 'in determining between two contradictory laws'.[35] Indeed, the judicial exercise of enlightened and responsible discretion – 'sound discretion guided by law', as Hamilton's British contemporary, Lord Mansfield, put it[36] – could be seen as a matter of duty rather than necessity.[37] If it is accepted that judges should not exercise arbitrary discretion but should nevertheless use constrained discretion when deciding cases, it becomes clear that they might sometimes be considered not merely permitted but actually expected to overrule a precedent.

For an illustration of this point, consider a somewhat simplified example taken from US administrative law.[38] Imagine that a statute, X, lends itself to four possible constructions – constructions A, B, C and D. This means that X permits the courts some discretion, but the discretion is constrained. It may be that, in case P^1, a court creates a precedent to the effect that X should mean A. A later court might prefer that X mean B. Notwithstanding this preference, nevertheless, that court would have no basis for overruling P^1, for in doing so it would simply be substituting one permissible construction for another. If such overruling were possible, the certainty and predictability of the relevant law might be significantly diminished, for it is difficult to see how still later courts could be precluded from overruling further in favour of constructions C and D. Given the nature of X, in fact, the chances of P^1 ever being overruled are slim.

<blockquote>
the doctrine of precedent, a broad description of the way in which, unless Parliament intervenes, the judges intend to continue using their powers. Respect for precedent is exacted, not only to keep the law in good shape, but primarily as a safeguard against arbitrary and autocratic decision-making').
</blockquote>

[35] Hamilton, *The Federalist*, 431.
[36] 'But discretion, when applied to a Court of Justice, means sound discretion guided by law. It must be governed by rule, not by humour: it must not be arbitrary, vague, and fanciful; but legal and regular.' *R v. Wilkes* (1770) 4 Burr. 2527, 2559.
[37] See Nelson, '*Stare Decisis* and Demonstrably Erroneous Precedents', 9–10.
[38] See *Chevron U. S. A. v. Natural Resources Defense Council*, 467 U.S. 837 (1984). In using this example I follow Nelson, '*Stare Decisis* and Demonstrably Erroneous Precedents', 6–7. Under the so-called *Chevron* doctrine, when an administrative agency adopts a 'permissible' interpretation of a statute which it administers, courts are generally expected to accept that interpretation even if they would have construed the statute differently were they interpreting it in the absence of that agency's precedent. See generally Richard L. Pierce, Jr., 'Reconciling *Chevron* and *Stare Decisis*' (1997) 85 Georgetown L.J. 2225–63.

But now imagine instead that, in case P^2, a court creates a precedent to the effect that X should mean E. Since E is not a permissible construction of X, we might expect that a later court with the capacity to overrule P^2 will do so, unless it can demonstrate a special reason for adhering to the construction of X as E. If a later court does overrule P^2 the likelihood is that it will do so in order to create a precedent similar to P^1: that is, the court will overrule so as to ensure that X is interpreted within its range of permissible constructions. The crucial point is the difference between P^1 and P^2: in P^1, the court exercises discretion within the permissible range, and so there is a rebuttable presumption against the precedent being overruled by a later court; in P^2, the court exercises its discretion outside that range, and so there is a rebuttable presumption in favour of the precedent being overruled by a later court.[39] Whereas distinguishing, we saw, can be understood as a form of amending, overruling is a form of repealing – substituting one ruling for another – and so, not surprisingly, is often conceived to be a more radical judicial initiative. But this does not mean that overruling must undermine *stare decisis*. If precedent-following is valued as a means of curbing arbitrary and facilitating properly constrained judicial discretion, overruling might sometimes be considered an important remedial option where courts have exercised discretion inappropriately. To put the point somewhat crudely, overruling might be understood as a method by which a court negates a precedent in order to uphold the law.[40]

3. The power to overrule oneself

The fact is, nevertheless, that overruling often is considered to be radical judicial action, to be taken only as a last resort.[41] This is, for various

---

[39] See Nelson, '*Stare Decisis* and Demonstrably Erroneous Precedents', 8 ('One could recognize a rebuttable presumption *against* overruling decisions that are *not* demonstrably erroneous while simultaneously recognizing a rebuttable presumption *in favor of* overruling decisions that *are* demonstrably erroneous').

[40] Cf. J. H. Baker, *The Law's Two Bodies: Some Evidential Problems in English Legal History* (Oxford: Oxford University Press, 2001), 5 (once a court of last resort 'has formally accepted that its decisions may sometimes be wrong' it follows '– since a legal decision can only be wrong if it is contrary to law – that the law must be something higher than any decision').

[41] See, e.g., *Jones* v. *Secretary of State for Social Services* [1972] AC 944, 966, HL, *per* Lord Reid (the power should be 'used sparingly . . . it should only be in rare cases that we should reconsider questions of construction of statutes or other documents'). Though, as we have observed already, the degree to which courts are reluctant to overrule varies from one jurisdiction to another.

reasons, not surprising. A court might see no incompatibility between upholding *stare decisis* and allowing that precedents can be overruled, yet still see good sense in keeping to a minimum the number of instances in which it departs from decisions which it would normally consider binding. The costs generated by the overruling of a precedent, after all, might be significant: public bodies and private citizens might have to invest heavily to understand and conform to the new ruling, and may even have to litigate in order to force the courts to make the ruling clearer or more refined.[42] Moreover, the court which overrules will often be overruling a precedent of its own – declaring that its earlier decision is contrary to law. Even if none of the judges who produced that precedent is still alive, a court might still consider such outright overruling too tactless an option and try instead to rectify its past error by some subtler means.[43]

But the main reason overruling has generated controversy, certainly in England, has nothing to do with the dangers of the action proving costly or causing offence. If some English jurists seemed excessively troubled by the elusiveness of the *ratio decidendi* in much case-law, this was nothing as compared with the consternation generated in some quarters by the House of Lords' Practice Statement of 1966. In this Statement, as is well known, the House of Lords declared that it would henceforth be free, in some circumstances, to overrule its own decisions. Within common law jurisdictions, it was by no means unheard of before this date for a court of final appeal to assume the power to overrule its own precedents. The United States Supreme Court appears always to have assumed this power, and can be found exercising it as far back as 1844.[44] And even when supreme courts in other

---

[42] On adjustment costs associated with precedent change, see Lewis A. Kornhauser, 'An Economic Perspective on *Stare Decisis*' (1989) 65 *Chicago-Kent L. Rev.* 63–92 at 83; Thomas R. Lee, '*Stare Decisis* in Economic Perspective: An Economic Analysis of the Supreme Court's Doctrine of Precedent' (2000) 78 *N. Carolina L. Rev.* 643–706 at 651–2; Nelson, '*Stare Decisis* and Demonstrably Erroneous Precedents', 63. To some degree, public bodies and private citizens may be able to protect themselves against such costs through insurance and other market mechanisms – see Louis Kaplow, 'An Economic Analysis of Legal Transitions' (1986) 99 *Harvard L. Rev.* 509–617 at 543–60 – though the range of protection is likely to be limited. It may be impossible, for example, to insure against the costs that could accompany some instances of overruling: see Jill E. Fisch, 'Retroactivity and Legal Change: An Equilibrium Approach' (1997) 110 *Harvard L. Rev.* 1055–1123 at 1090–1.
[43] See Radin, 'The Trail of the Calf', 143.
[44] See *Louisville, Cincinnati, and Charleston RR* v. *Letson*, 43 U.S. 497 (1844). Although, in *Letson*, the Supreme Court overruled an existing constitutional doctrine (concerning the

jurisdictions have stopped considering themselves absolutely bound by their prior decisions, the development has generally been accepted in a matter-of-fact fashion.[45] But English courts of last resort have seemed peculiarly unsure of themselves when dealing with the question of whether they must follow, or are at liberty to depart from, their own precedents. In 1891 the divisional court of Queen's Bench decided that, in instances when it sat as a final appeal court, the Chief Justice has the power to appoint a specially constituted court specifically for the purpose of reviewing, and if necessary revising, the divisional court's own precedents on the same issue.[46] In 1947 a divisional court presided over by Goddard C. J. decided, apparently in ignorance of the earlier case, that in such instances the court should generally consider itself bound by

status of corporations for the purposes of diversity of citizenship jurisdiction under Article III), it did not state that it was departing from an earlier practice of absolute adherence to precedents. The Court appears always to have operated on the assumption that a departure from precedent requires some special justification, but never on the assumption that such a departure is *per se* forbidden. The High Court of Australia, likewise, appears never to have considered itself bound by its own decisions (though it is worth noting that until the second half of the twentieth century it was not, strictly speaking, a court of last resort because its decisions could be overturned on appeal to the Privy Council): see *Viro* v. *R* (1978) 141 CLR 88. At least one commentator has speculated – though it really is nothing more than speculation – that the High Court's gradual refusal to be absolutely bound by Privy Council decisions may have inspired the House of Lords' resolution to issue the Practice Statement. See Edward St. John, 'Lords Break from Precedent: An Australian View' (1967) 18 *ICLQ* 808–16.

[45] In the early years of the twentieth century, the Supreme Court of Canada determined that it was bound by its own precedents and then, in a series of decisions from 1949 onwards, adopted the practice of overturning its decisions when appropriate. The authority for the position established early in the twentieth century is *Stuart* v. *Bank of Montreal* (1909) 41 SCR 516, contextual discussion of which is provided by E. K. Williams, 'Stare Decisis' (1926) 4 *Can. Bar Rev.* 289–301 at 295–8. On the Court's gradual movement away from this position from the late 1940s onwards, see the judgment of Iacobucci J. in *R* v. *Salituro* [1991] 3 SCR 654 at 665–6. Academic commentators appear to have been troubled not by the Court's alteration of the status of its precedents, but by the fact that it should have bound itself so rigidly in the first place. See, e.g., Edward McWhinney, 'Legal Theory and Philosophy of Law in Canada', in *Canadian Jurisprudence: The Civil Law and Common Law in Canada*, ed. E. McWhinney (London: Stevens & Sons, 1959), 1–23 at 15–19; and Gordon Bale, 'Casting off the Mooring Slopes of Binding Precedent' (1980) 58 *Can. Bar Rev.* 255–79 at 259–61. The New Zealand Court of Appeal resolved no longer to be absolutely bound by its own precedents around the same time as did the Supreme Court of Canada: see *In re Rayner* [1948] NZLR 455; also The Hon. Justice E. W. Thomas, 'A Critical Examination of the Doctrine of Precedent', in *Legal Method in New Zealand: Essays and Commentaries*, ed. R. Bigwood (Wellington: Butterworths, 2001), 141–74 at 143–4.

[46] See *Fortescue* v. *Vestry of St. Matthew, Bethnal Green* [1891] 2 QB 170, 178–9; affirmed in *Kruse* v. *Johnson* [1898] 2 QB 91, 102.

its own previous decisions.[47] In 1985, Goff L.J. concluded that although 'it will be only in rare cases that a divisional court will think it fit to depart from a decision of another divisional court', such departures are permissible if today's court is convinced that the earlier decision was wrong.[48] Basically, the divisional court has swung backwards and forwards on the question of whether or not it can overrule itself.

The House of Lords has, likewise, failed to maintain a consistent line over the years. Sixty-eight years before the Practice Statement, in *London Tramways* v. *London County Council*, the House determined that despite the instances of individual hardship that might result in its being bound to follow its own decisions, it is better that highest courts close the door on specific legal problems once and for all, so that lower courts know that the case law on those problems is established and so that the lawyers of prospective litigants can confidently advise whether a particular legal action might meet with success.[49] This was not, as is sometimes suggested, a declaration of infallibility by the House.[50] Osbert Lancaster's cartoon in the *Daily Express* the day after the Practice Statement was issued – depicting one Law Lord complaining to another that he cannot accustom himself 'to the idea that we could ever, conceivably, have been wrong' – was humorous but misleading, for case law is subordinate to legislation.[51] But even though the decision in *London Tramways* was not quite as radical as is sometimes suggested, and even though it came as no surprise – the House had been edging towards the decision since the mid

---

[47] *Police Authority for Huddersfield* v. *Watson* [1947] KB 842; affirmed (again without consideration of *Fortescue* v. *Vestry of St. Matthew*), in *Younghusband* v. *Luftig* [1949] 2 JB 354. See generally, Stephen Sedley, *On Never Doing Anything for the First Time* (Reform Club, London. Atkin Lecture, 2001), 9–10.

[48] *R* v. *Greater Manchester Coroner, ex p. Tal* [1985] QB 67, 81.

[49] *London Tramways* v. *London County Council* [1898] AC 375. Cf. John H. Langbein, 'Modern Jurisprudence in the House of Lords: The Passing of *London Tramways*' (1968) 53 *Cornell L. Rev.* 807–13 at 810 ('The real incidence of the rule was preventive: it served throughout the twentieth century to deter the bringing of litigation that would have required the overturning of a previous decision'). The name of the appellant in *London Tramways* is mistakenly given as 'London Street Tramways' in the title of the case ([1898] AC contains a corrigendum slip). London Street Tramways, a different company, had been involved in an unrelated appeal to the House of Lords four years earlier: *London Street Tramways* v. *London County Council* [1894] AC 489.

[50] See, e.g., John P. Dawson, *The Oracles of the Law* (Buffalo: Hein, 1986 [1968]), 91 ('This self-declaration of infallibility by the House of Lords').

[51] *Daily Express*, 28 July 1966, p. 1, col. 3. Even before 1966, of course, most if not all Law Lords must have privately accepted that decisions of the House could be 'wrong'; the point is really that, when this is what they thought, they still considered themselves precluded from overruling.

nineteenth century[52] – it was still controversial, not least because the binding force of the decision appears to depend on a self-referential manoeuvre.[53] The reason that the precedent established by the House of Lords in *London Tramways* could not be overruled was that, in *London Tramways*, the House of Lords decided that it generally could not overrule its precedents: the decision was its own source of immunity from overruling. Was there really anything to stop the court from going back on its word?

The Practice Statement is evidence that the court could, and indeed did, go back on its word. To present the development in this way, however, is to give the impression that the House of Lords acted capriciously. The Practice Statement itself provides two strong reasons for departing from *London Tramways*: that rigid adherence to precedents can perpetuate injustices and can impede worthwhile legal development. Though the Statement is well known, it is worth quoting in full if only so that, in due course, we can remind ourselves of what all the fuss was about:

> Their Lordships regard the use of precedent as an indispensable foundation upon which to decide what is the law and its application to individual cases.

---

[52] See *Beamish* v. *Beamish* (1861) 9 HL Cas. 273; Jacob E. Landau, 'Precedents in the House of Lords' (1951) 63 *Juridical Rev.* 222–33; and cf. *R* v. *Millis* (1844) 10 Cl. & F. 534; *Bright* v. *Hutton* (1852) 3 HL Cas. 341; *Att. Gen.* v. *Dean of Windsor* (1860) HL Cas. 369; *Caledonian Railway Co.* v. *Walker's Trustees* (1882) LR 7 App. Cas. 259. See also John Chipman Gray, 'Judicial Precedents – A Short Study in Comparative Jurisprudence' (1895) 9 *Harvard L. Rev.* 27–41 at 39–40 where, three years before the appearance of *London Tramways*, it was already assumed that the House of Lords was bound to follow its own decisions.

[53] On the incapacity of precedent to pull itself up by its own bootstraps, see Glanville Williams's argument in *Salmond on Jurisprudence*, 11th edn ed. G. Williams (London: Sweet & Maxwell, 1957), 187 ('Clearly, the doctrine of precedent cannot be authoritatively supported by reference to precedent .... One can no more prove the doctrine of precedent by referring to precedent than one can prove that Parliament is sovereign by reading out a statute which declares that it is'). The manoeuvre is not self-referential, however, if it is accepted that the House of Lords is vested with the power to make rulings about the status of its own decisions. See Simpson, 'The *Ratio Decidendi* of a Case', 148. Williams himself proposed a way of circumventing the boot-strapping conundrum – decisions about the doctrine of precedent, he suggested, are not themselves precedents but *obiter dicta*, because any such decision 'is necessarily irrelevant to the issues of law and fact that have to be decided by the court' and so that court is not using precedent as authority for the rules of precedent when it makes such decisions. Glanville Williams, 'Decisions by Equally Divided Courts' (1954) 70 *LQR* 469–71 at 471. The difficulty with this solution is that, if a decision on a point about the doctrine of precedent is considered to be *obiter*, it cannot be binding; indeed, the problem of bootstrapping would never have arisen in the first place. The correct approach would appear to be to treat courts' decisions concerning the doctrine of precedent to fall outside the *ratio-obiter* distinction.

It provides at least some degree of certainty upon which individuals can rely in the conduct of their affairs, as well as a basis for orderly development of legal rules.

Their Lordships nevertheless recognise that too rigid adherence to precedent may lead to injustice in a particular case and also unduly restrict the proper development of the law. They propose, therefore, to modify their present practice and, while treating former decisions of this House as normally binding, to depart from a previous decision when it appears right to do so.

In this connection they will bear in mind the danger of disturbing retrospectively the basis on which contracts, settlements of property and fiscal arrangements have been entered into and also the especial need for certainty as to the criminal law.

This announcement is not intended to affect the use of precedent elsewhere than in this House.[54]

The proposal 'to depart from' previous decisions is decidedly timid.[55] Before 1966, the House of Lords had distinguished some of its own precedents to the point where they were effectively stripped of authority.[56] What had the House been doing in those instances, if not 'departing from' its previous decisions? And if the House had been departing from previous decisions, did this mean that the Practice Statement was a proposal that the House do something that it did already? What the Practice Statement ought to have said – what, indeed, it was taken to mean – was that the House of Lords would now *overrule* its previous decisions when it appeared right to do so. But overruling, as noted

---

[54] *Practice Statement (Judicial Precedent)* [1966] 1 WLR 1234. The Irish Supreme Court declared around the same time that it likewise had the capacity to depart from its precedents: see *Att. Gen. v. Ryan's Car Hire Ltd* [1965] IR 642; T. Cedric Jones, 'The Implications of the New Doctrine of *Stare Decisis* in the Irish Supreme Court' (1967) 101 *Irish Law Times* 281–3, 291–3, 301–2, 311–12, 321–2.

[55] See *Miliangos v. George Frank (Textiles) Ltd* [1976] AC, 443, 470, HL, *per* Lord Simon. None the less, the language persists. In *R v. G* [2004] 1 AC 1034, the House of Lords overruled its decision on the meaning of recklessness in *R v. Caldwell* [1982] AC 341. Occasionally, in *R v. G* reference is made to the earlier decision being overruled (e.g., pp. 1064, 1066), and in one instance departing from and overruling are used synonymously (p. 1055). More often than not, however, their Lordships speak of departing from *Caldwell* (e.g., pp. 1035, 1058, 1064), and the headnote states that *Caldwell* is 'departed from' (p. 1035). Likewise, in *Horton v. Sadler* [2006] UKHL 27, their Lordships speak of their decision to depart from rather than overrule *Walkley v. Precision Forgings Ltd* [1979] 1 WLR 606, HL.

[56] Consider, e.g., the reception of *Rylands v. Fletcher* (1868) LR 3 HL 330 and the 'non-natural' use of land requirement.

already, is a particularly bold judicial action, and so it is perhaps not surprising that the Practice Statement is worded as it is. Lord Wright predicted as early as 1942 that the House of Lords would rarely overrule its own precedents were it ever to assume the power to do so. 'The instinct of inertia is as potent in judges as in other people ... No court will be anxious to repudiate a precedent. It will do so only if it is completely satisfied that the precedent is erroneous.'[57] His prediction was sound. Overruling an earlier decision is something that the House of Lords has never done lightly. Even a decision widely considered wrong might continue to be followed if people have reasonably relied on it in arranging their affairs, if overruling it would make no difference to the outcome in the present case, if Parliament has enacted legislation on the assumption that the law is as stated in the earlier case or if overruling would involve nothing more than a differently constituted panel second-guessing the original one.[58] In fact, only rarely since 1966 has the House of Lords used the power that it created for itself;[59] and it seems reasonable to speculate that it will not use it very much in the future, for the convergence of UK and EU law, and in particular the increasingly prominent role of the European Court of Justice in domestic legal affairs, means that the House of Lords is not quite the court of final appeal that it was forty or so years ago.[60] But the power certainly exists, and the House of Lords, in line with the highest courts in most other jurisdictions, can today, if it so wishes, overrule its own precedents.

---

[57] Lord Wright, 'Precedents' (1942) 4 *UTLJ* 247–77 at 275–6; repr. (1943) 8 *Cambridge L.J.* 118–45 at 144.

[58] See J. W. Harris, 'Towards Principles of Overruling – When Should a Final Court of Appeal Second Guess?' (1990) 10 *Oxf. Jnl Leg. Studs* 135–99; also John W. Salmond, 'The Theory of Judicial Precedents' (1900) 16 *LQR* 376–91 at 381–2.

[59] Opportunities to use the power, it should be noted, diminished at the very time that it was created: the establishment of the Law Commission in 1965 led to an increase in legislative activity, which made the overruling of some unsatisfactory House of Lords precedents unnecessary. See M. D. A. Freeman, 'Precedent and the House of Lords' (1971) 121 *New L. J.* 551–2 at 551.

[60] Although in terms of statutory interpretation, the House of Lords is now more significant than it has ever been owing to its power to adopt teleological reasoning with respect to EC law – an example would be the responsibility of the House, under the Human Rights Act 1998, s. 3, to render statutes compatible with human rights norms: see, e.g., *R* v. *A (No. 2)* [2002] 1 AC 45. It is, of course, possible that the House of Lords might henceforth use its power to overrule itself more frequently in order to bring UK law in line with EC law; but were it to do this, it would effectively be acknowledging that the European Court of Justice is a superior jurisdiction (for so long as the UK is a member of the EU), and so would not be regarding itself as a court of last resort.

4. The authority of the Practice Statement

The Practice Statement was the Ulysses strategy in reverse. In issuing it, the House of Lords undertook an act of self-liberation to combat the possibility that, so long as *London Tramways* prevailed, it might occasionally lack the motivation or imagination to find its way out of following precedents that compound injustices or fail to move with the times. Whatever the House of Lords' thinking in performing this act by issuing a Practice Statement, the method of execution made good sense not only because it expressed the House's intention simply and clearly but also because it was a peculiarly visible declaration – by issuing something akin to a legal press release,[61] the House drew far more attention to its action than would likely have been the case if it had departed from *London Tramways* in the course of a judgment – and so any future composition of the House would be making a massive climb-down were it to change the status of its precedents again.[62] In the language of modern constraint theory, by issuing the Practice Statement the House of Lords committed itself to a course of action by acting on its environment.[63]

Academic attitudes to the Practice Statement have been interesting. Before 1966, some jurists were plainly dissatisfied with the state of affairs that had been established by *London Tramways*.[64] Arthur Goodhart viewed a final court's willingness to overrule its own precedents much as did William O. Douglas. Where the most senior judges bind themselves to follow their own precedents, Goodhart suggested in 1934, they display a lack of confidence in their own abilities, and the abilities of

---

[61] Besides appearing at [1966] 1 WLR 1234, the Practice Statement can also been found at [1966] 3 All ER 77, [1966] 2 Lloyd's Rep. 151, (1966) 110 Sol. Jo. 584, (1966) 82 *LQR* 442 and HL Debs vol. 276, col. 677 (26 July 1966). The Statement is also replicated in its entirety in 'Lords relax judicial precedent rule', *Times*, 27 July 1966, p. 10 col.1.

[62] Though it is perhaps worth bearing in mind that the Practice Statement has not yet been around as long as was *London Tramways*!

[63] See Jon Elster, *Ulysses and the Sirens: Studies in Rationality and Irrationality*, rev. edn (Cambridge: Cambridge University Press, 1984), 36–111; *Ulysses Unbound: Studies in Rationality, Precommitment, and Constraints* (Cambridge: Cambridge University Press, 2000), 11–19.

[64] See, e.g., Dennis Lloyd, *Introduction to Jurisprudence with Selected Texts* (London: Stevens & Sons, 1959), 391–2; R.W.M. Dias, *Jurisprudence* 2nd edn (London: Butterworths, 1964), 75. For post-Practice Statement reactions see, e.g., R. W. M. Dias, 'Precedents in the House of Lords – A Much Needed Reform' [1966] *Cambridge L.J.* 153–6 (which begins with an unambiguous exclamation: 'At Last!'); and, in the same vein, B. A. Wortley, *Jurisprudence* (Manchester: Manchester University Press, 1967), 82–9, 457.

their successors. The judge who acts fairly and reasonably, and who performs his duties with professionalism and skill, need not be 'a slave to the past and a despot for the future, bound by the decisions of his dead predecessors and binding for generations to come the judgments of those who will succeed him'.[65] Rupert Cross, in the first edition of *Precedent in English Law*, was less negative, arguing that critics of *London Tramways* were often too quick to see it as a source of unfairness. Although the requirement that the House of Lords follow even erroneous precedents could perpetuate injustices, he argued, treating like cases alike will normally serve the cause of fairness.[66] He took the view, nevertheless, that even if *London Tramways* might be generally defensible, the House of Lords was entirely at liberty to change its practice.[67] Once the House of Lords had changed its practice, some jurists resolved to demonstrate that the Practice Statement was no less troublesome, and was perhaps even more troublesome, than the decision in *London Tramways*. If, in mid-twentieth-century England, senior judges did pay any attention to academic commentary, they might well have concluded that in the world of the university lawyer the House of Lords was damned either way.[68]

---

[65] A. L. Goodhart, 'Precedent in English and Continental Law' (1934) 50 *LQR* 40–65 at 61. Cf. Salmond, 'The Theory of Judicial Precedents', 386 ('The growth of case law involves the gradual elimination of that judicial liberty to which it owes its origin. In any system in which precedents are authoritative the courts are engaged in forging fetters for their own feet').

[66] Rupert Cross, *Precedent in English Law* (Oxford: Clarendon Press, 1961), 107–8.

[67] *Ibid.*, 249–50.

[68] At least one jurist thought that the Practice Statement most likely came about because of academic criticism of *London Tramways*: see D. N. MacCormick, 'Can *Stare Decisis* be Abolished?' [1966] *Juridical Review* 197–213. (Speculations about what motivated the issuing of the Practice Statement, it is worth observing, were not unforthcoming. We have noted already the argument of St. John, in 'Lords Break from Precedent', that the House of Lords was following the example of the High Court of Australia. Another view, no less difficult to substantiate, was that the Statement was illustrative of how 'American realist influence had begun to work through the British system'. P. B. Kavanagh, '*Stare Decisis* in the House of Lords' (1973) 5 *New Zealand Universities L. Rev.* 323–47 at 323.) MacCormick himself welcomed the Practice Statement but wondered whether it would have been better if lower courts had been allowed to follow the House of Lords' lead: '[i]f we go no farther than the new rule that the House of Lords alone will cease to be bound by its past decisions, we shall be faced with the ludicrous spectacle of litigants being forced to take all the expense of appeals to the highest tribunal ... [W]ould it not be cheaper, more efficient and more just if the precedent were rejected at first instance?' ('Can *Stare Decisis* be Abolished?', 199). Allowing lower courts to overrule the precedents of higher courts might seriously undermine the common law system of authority and appeals. A system which generally allows courts of first instance to overrule their

So, how did English academics react to the Practice Statement? They did not speak with one voice, and were not entirely critical of what the House of Lords did. But, in so far as they were critical, what did they hope to achieve? There seem to have been two main objectives.

a. Constitutional impropriety

The first was to demonstrate that the Practice Statement was constitutionally improper. Julius Stone presented the least convincing version of this argument. The Practice Statement cannot be binding, Stone argued, because it appeared that the Lord Chancellor (Lord Gardiner) 'and the other judges concerned in making the Statement were not acting "juridically" in the sense that the Statement was the act of a court of law, of judges acting in their curial capacity ... If their Lordships were not acting in a curial capacity, then the rule enunciated could not have any *legal* force as part of the precedent system'.[69] If rules of precedent have legal force, he elaborated, it is because they have 'emerged ... from strictly judicial activities'.[70] Any rule purporting to modify the rules of precedent 'would itself *have to have legal force*',[71] but the Practice Statement was not the product of strictly judicial activity and so legal force cannot be attributed to it. Constitutional convention requires that judges must speak in their capacity as judges, in other words, if they are authoritatively to alter their own practices regarding precedent-following.[72]

Stone's argument might be criticized on three grounds. The first is that it is wrong to conclude that the Practice Statement was not the declaration of a court of law. While judicial statements about the legal rights and duties of litigants must, if they are to have legal effect, be made in the course of judgments, there is no requirement that statements by courts regarding their own practices be made in the same context.[73] The second is that even if Stone were right – even if it were true that the

---

own precedents risks generating unpredictability: if lawyers of potential litigants cannot predict, or cannot make a decent attempt at predicting, their clients' chances of success, there is likely to be an increase in litigation, including a fair number of cases that should not have made it to court in the first place.

[69] Julius Stone, '1966 And All That! Loosing the Chains of Precedent' (1969) 69 *Columbia L.Rev.* 1162–1202 at 1163.
[70] Ibid.   [71] Ibid.
[72] The argument is developed further in Julius Stone, 'On the Liberation of Appellate Judges: How Not to do it!' (1972) 35 *MLR* 449–77.
[73] See Rupert Cross, 'The House of Lords and the Rules of Precedent', in *Law, Morality, and Society: Essays in Honour of H. L. A. Hart*, ed. P. M. S. Hacker and J. Raz (Oxford: Clarendon Press, 1977), 145–60 at 157.

House of Lords was not acting in its curial capacity when it issued the Practice Statement – it would not follow that the Statement carried no authority. The Judicial Committee of the House of Lords is, after all, a committee of a legislative chamber, and there is no obvious reason for considering its proposals less authoritative than other proposals that this chamber makes. The third criticism is that Stone's argument depends on a conception of binding force no less crude than the classical positivist conception which we encountered earlier in this study. The Practice Statement can only be binding, according to Stone, so long as it has technical validity, but it cannot have technical validity because it was not delivered in a curial capacity. If one accepts, for the sake of argument, that the Practice Statement was made in a non-judicial context the interesting question which then arises is why it should nevertheless have legal force. Stone simply emphasizes the oddness of the House of Lords' willingness to treat the Practice Statement – 'a mere extra-curial *ipse dixit*,'[74] he would have us believe – as binding. It matters not at all to him that the House does consider itself bound by, and that the legal profession does accept the authority of, the Practice Statement. Yet this is the real source of curiosity.

Defenders of the Practice Statement, and of *London Tramways* as well, usually argue from the premise of inherent jurisdiction: since appellate courts invariably have the power to regulate their own procedures and practices so as to prevent those procedures and practices being used as instruments of injustice, so this argument goes, it was not constitutionally inappropriate for the House of Lords to determine its own practice on precedent-following. Rupert Cross seemed in no doubt that 'the constitutional validity of the Practice Statement ... owes its validity to the inherent power of any court to regulate its own practice'.[75] The difficulty with this observation is simply that it is wrong to say that any court has the power to regulate its own practice. Around the time that Cross made the observation, Lord Denning was looking to establish that the Court of Appeal has the power to overrule its own past decisions; but Denning's crusade ultimately foundered, and the Court remains bound by its own decisions in all but exceptional circumstances (such as where an earlier decision given *per incuriam* took no account of a relevant statutory rule).[76] Cross's observation is correct in the sense that superior

---

[74] Stone, '1966 And All That!', 1168.
[75] Cross, 'The House of Lords and the Rules of Precedent', 157.
[76] See *Davis* v. *Johnson* [1979] AC 264, HL; also C. E. F. Rickett, 'Precedent in the Court of Appeal' (1980) 43 *MLR* 136–58; Hazel Carty, 'Precedent and the Court of Appeal: Lord

courts have the power to issue practice directions regarding litigation procedure, but this is something different from courts assuming the power to alter their practices regarding precedent-following.

The essence of the argument against the constitutionality of the Practice Statement is that it purported to change the law without recourse to any rule authorizing the change. Such a rule would have to be the work of Parliament: legislative action was needed, that is, if the House of Lords was no longer to be bound to follow its own precedents. The fact that the motivations of the House in issuing the Statement may have been laudable does not make its action any less constitutionally dubious. In stark Kelsenian language, the action was a 'revolutionary' one which, though leaving the basic norm of the legal system unaltered,[77] changed the identity of the system in a way which the system itself neither provided for nor permitted.[78] The Statement 'was and is generally welcomed', Francis Mann noted in 1983, but:

> the lack of clear constitutional foundation is worrying. If lawyers fail strictly to obey the law, if a new legal development is initiated by them without any attempt at juristic justification, if the legal basis of the new turn is far from obvious, then there results a degree of constitutional dubiousness which is liable to undermine the legal order and cannot be overcome by support for the new rule. If law rests on the respect it commands then the statement of 1966 may have done a disservice.[79]

The idea of the Practice Statement undermining the legal order may seem far-fetched, but it should be borne in mind that Mann witnessed at first hand just how quickly the rule of law was hijacked in Nazi Germany during the early 1930s.[80] His experiences probably positioned him well

---

Denning's Views Explored' (1981) 1 *Legal Studies* 68–76; Peter Alldridge, 'Precedent in the Court of Appeal – Another View' (1984) 47 *MLR* 187–200. (Anyone searching for this last article online should note that the *Modern Law Review* mistakenly spelt the author's surname 'Aldridge'.)

[77] See J. W. Harris, 'When and Why Does the Grundnorm Change?' (1971) 29 *Cambridge L.J.* 103–33 at 116–18.

[78] See Hans Kelsen, *Pure Theory of Law*, 2nd edn, trans. M. Knight (Berkeley: University of California Press, 1967; orig. German publ. 1960), 209; also John Finnis, 'Revolutions and Continuity of Law', in *Oxford Essays in Jurisprudence*, 2nd ser., ed. A. W. B. Simpson (Oxford: Clarendon Press, 1973), 44–76.

[79] F. A. Mann, 'Reflections on English Civil Justice and the Rule of Law' (1983) 2 *Civil Justice Quarterly* 320–36 at 331–2. See also D. H. Laird, 'The Doctrine of *Stare Decisis*' (1935) 13 *Can. Bar Rev.* 1–21 at 20 (arguing that if English law is ever to move away from *London Tramways* it ought to do so 'in the constitutional way').

[80] See Lawrence Collins, 'F. A. Mann (1907–1991)', in *Jurists Uprooted: German-speaking Émigré Lawyers in Twentieth-century Britain*, ed. J. Beatson and R. Zimmermann (Oxford: Oxford University Press, 2004), 381–440 at 382–5.

to caution against the Statement as a precedent in its own right, paving the way for further bold attempts by the courts to determine the extent and the nature of their own powers (such as Lord Denning's attempt to free the Court of Appeal from the chains of its own precedents). It is important to emphasize, nevertheless, that Mann was dissatisfied not with the intentions behind the Practice Statement, but with the manner in which those intentions had been given effect. Anyone with an eye to constitutionality might have been just as troubled, if indeed not more troubled, by what the House of Lords had done in 1898 as compared with what it did in 1966: Parliament, after all, cannot pass immutable legislation so as to restrict its future actions,[81] and so it might fairly be asked why the House of Lords was within its constitutional rights to have bound itself as it did in *London Tramways*.[82]

But this last argument is really nothing more than a diversionary tactic. Objections to the Practice Statement on constitutional grounds cannot be satisfactorily met by pointing out that there was nothing any less objectionable about the state of affairs that the Statement brought to an end. What really matters is whether there are convincing ways in which concerns about the constitutional propriety of the Statement might be addressed. Jurisprudence offers a variety of explanations as to why a court of last resort's decision to change the status of its precedents might be generally accepted, notwithstanding constitutional objections to the initiative. Perhaps the least interesting of these explanations is what might be termed the crude realist perspective. According to this perspective, a judge will adopt a strict approach to precedent only when it serves his or her purposes;[83] if following a precedent will produce an outcome that does not accord with those purposes, the precedent will not be applied. When the House of Lords issued its Practice Statement, therefore, it was simply relaxing its conventions on *stare decisis* so that

---

[81] See A. V. Dicey, *Introduction to the Study of the Law of the Constitution*, 8th edn (London: Macmillan, 1927), 65–8 n. 3.

[82] See Landau, 'Precedents in House of Lords', 233. One American commentator on *London Tramways* and the Practice Statement sees no constitutional difficulty in either instance because he assumes that the judicial branch of the House of Lords is Parliament, and even goes so far as to write about 'Parliament . . . ruling that it should not reverse itself' in *London Tramways*, and about how, in 1966, 'Parliament *reversed*' that ruling. See Peter Suber, *The Paradox of Self-Amendment: A Study of Logic, Law, Omnipotence, and Change* (New York: Lang, 1990), 202–3, 251 (emphasis in original).

[83] See K. N. Llewellyn, *The Bramble Bush: On Our Law and its Study* (New York: Oceana, 1930), 70–6.

they might reflect the reality of judicial law-making.[84] If this explanation is correct, why should the House of Lords ever have committed itself to a strict doctrine of *stare decisis* in the first place? One classic realist text offers an answer: 'men crave an undesirable and indeed unrealizable permanence and fixity in law' because they 'strive to find behind everyday experiences a Something resembling paternal control, a Something that can be relied upon to insure, somehow, against the apparent reality of the chanciness and disorder of events.'[85] The doctrine sustains, in other words, a child-like desire for certainty.[86] But this answer simply flips the question on its head: if the craving for certainty is so strong, why did the House of Lords then decide not to be bound by its own precedents?

One way to answer this last question – this is the answer that can be derived from historical jurisprudence – is that it is a mistake to think that the purposes of law, and the ways in which we value legal rules, remain stable. Law evolves: the House of Lords, by explicitly altering its position on precedent-following, was not so much doing something new as acknowledging a change which had been occurring over a long period of time. English forensic inquiry, Maine observed, 'assumes that no question is, or can be, raised which will call for the application of any principles but old ones, or of any distinctions but such as have long been allowed'.[87] Yet, he added, we readily recognize that the decisions of the superior courts add to the body of precedent: when such decisions are 'rendered and reported, we slide unconsciously or unavowedly into a new language and a new train of thought. We now admit that the new decision *has* modified the law'.[88] *London Tramways* constituted such a modification because, to quote Lord Halsbury, it established that a 'decision of [the House of Lords] once given upon a point of law is conclusive upon th[e] House afterwards'.[89] Even though it was historically inaccurate of Lord Halsbury to insist that this principle had 'been established now for some centuries',[90] it had certainly been evolving in the case law, as we have already noted, throughout the second half of the nineteenth century. Judicial opinion had reached a point, we might say,

---

[84] See R. B. Stevens, 'The Role of a Final Appeal Court in a Democracy: The House of Lords Today' (1965) 28 *MLR* 509–39 at 235–6.
[85] Jerome Frank, *Law and the Modern Mind* (Gloucester, Mass.: Smith, 1970 [1930]), 11, 18.
[86] *Ibid.*, 19. Hence, when Frank eventually discusses the doctrine, the relevant chapter is entitled 'Illusory Precedents'. See *ibid.*, 159–71.
[87] Henry Maine, *Ancient Law*, 15th edn (London: Murray, 1894), 31. [88] *Ibid.*, 31–2.
[89] *London Tramways* v. *London County Council* [1898] AC 375, 381. [90] *Ibid.*, 379.

where there was a need for crystallization, and this is precisely what *London Tramways* achieved.

The evolutionary-jurisprudential perspective accounts better for *London Tramways* than it does for the Practice Statement. In *London Tramways*, the House of Lords did indeed reach a judgment which crystallized a principle that had been evolving in the case law for some time. The Practice Statement, however, though it came as no surprise, was not the climax of a series of cases throughout which the House of Lords had been grappling towards a new principle but a reversal of the established principle in one fell swoop.[91] A more promising explanation of the Practice Statement's validity, notwithstanding its apparent lack of constitutional authority, can be found in Hart's *The Concept of Law*. Hart's book appeared before the Practice Statement, and so obviously cannot be read as attempting to explain what the House of Lords did. It does, nevertheless, offer two compelling explanations of radical judicial action.

Hart's first explanation is perhaps best summarized by the words of a Law Lord. '[S]ince the announcement was made by Lord Gardiner L.C. it must be taken to have had general executive approval', Lord Simon observed apropos of the Practice Statement in 1973; 'nor was any objection raised elsewhere in Parliament. The new practice ... must therefore ... be considered to be one of those conventions which are so significant a feature of the British Constitution.'[92] The proof of constitutionality, in other words, is in the pudding: the validity of the Practice Statement is evident from the fact that it has been accepted as such by judges sitting in the House of Lords and by the rest of the judiciary and the legal profession, and from the fact that there has been no substantial body of opinion suggesting that it is invalid.[93] In Hart's words, not

---

[91] See Stevens, 'The Role of a Final Appeal Court in a Democracy', 534; A. L. G[oodhart] (1966) 82 *LQR* 441–4 at 441; Anon., '*Stare Decisis*' (1967) 101 *Irish Law Times* 61–2 at 61 ('[F]or many years it had been rumoured that such a step would ultimately be taken'). There were, certainly before 1966, occasional hints that a new attitude to judicial precedent was emerging: see, e.g., *Midland Silicones Ltd* v. *Scruttons Ltd* [1962] AC 446, 476–7, HL, *per* Lord Reid ('I would certainly not lightly disregard or depart from any *ratio decidendi* of this House. But there are at least three classes of case where I think we are entitled to question or limit it: first, where it is obscure, secondly, where the decision itself is out of line with other authorities or established principles, and thirdly, where it is much wider than was necessary for the decision so that it becomes a question of how far it is proper to distinguish the earlier decision').

[92] *R* v. *Knuller (Publishing etc.) Ltd* [1973] AC 435, 485. For a similar line of argument see Cross, 'The House of Lords and the Rules of Precedent', 157–8.

[93] Cf. Carl Schmitt's proposition that a judicial decision will be correct if it can be assumed that another judge (meaning not every single judge but an average, legally learned

'every step taken by a court is covered by some general rule conferring in advance the authority to take it', and so 'when courts settle previously unenvisaged questions concerning the most fundamental constitutional rules, they *get* their authority to decide them accepted after the questions have arisen and the decision has been given. Here all that succeeds is success.'[94] When, in 1991, the House of Lords determined that it is possible for a husband to rape his own wife, it rejected not only the traditional position of the English common law but also the then statutory definition of unlawful sexual intercourse as intercourse outside marriage.[95] Blatant judicial law-making this may well have been, but the success of the initiative is evident from the fact that Parliament subsequently revised the statutory position so that it fell in line with – though it also had to clarify the law in light of – the decision of the House of Lords.[96] Time will tell whether it is right to consider as a similarly successful initiative the decision of the Privy Council in 2005 not to apply a much-criticized House of Lords precedent on provocation: the Court of Appeal has already, on two occasions, explicitly followed the Privy Council's decision in preference to that of the House of Lords.[97] Hart himself cites in support of his argument the decision of the Court of Criminal Appeal in *R* v. *Taylor*, where the Court declared that it was its 'bounden duty' to reconsider its own precedents wherever there is

judge) would, in light of the norms of 'the entire judicial practice', have reached the same decision; in other words, a judge's decision not to treat a prior decision as absolutely binding will be correct if it can be assumed that this is what another judge working according to the same rules of practice would have done. Carl Schmitt, *Gesetz und Urteil. Eine Untersuchung zum Problem der Rechtspraxis* (Munich: Beck, 1969 [1912]), 71 ('Eine richterliche Entscheidung ist heute dann richtig, wenn anzunehmen ist daß ein anderer Richter ebenso entschieden hätte'), 78–9. The relevant passages are excerpted and translated as Carl Schmitt, 'Statute and Judgment', in *Weimar: A Jurisprudence of Crisis*, ed. A. Jacobson & B. Schlink, trans. B. Cooper (Berkeley: University of California Press, 2000), 63–5.

[94] *CL*, 153. Emphasis in original.
[95] *R* v. *R* [1991] All ER 481. For the traditional common law position, see Sir Matthew Hale, *The History of the Pleas of the Crown*, 2 vols. (London: Gyles, 1736), I, 629; John Frederick Archbold, *A Summary of the Law Relative to Pleading and Evidence in Criminal Cases* (London: Pheney, Sweet & Millikin, 1822), 259 ('A husband ... cannot be guilty of a rape upon his wife'); *R* v. *Clarence* (1889) LR 22 QBD 23; *R* v. *Miller* [1954] 2 QB 282. For the then statutory definition, see Sexual Offences (Amendment) Act 1976, s. 1(1)(a).
[96] The Criminal Justice and Public Order Act 1994, s. 142 made it an offence for a husband to rape his wife, thereby repealing s. 1(1) of the 1976 Act.
[97] See *Attorney General for Jersey* v. *Holley* [2005] UKPC 23, PC (Jer.), refusing to follow *R* v. *Smith (Morgan)* [2001] 1 AC 146, HL. The decision in *Holley* is followed by the Court of Appeal, in preference to the decision in *Smith*, in *James and Karimi* [2006] EWCA Crim 14, and *Moses* [2006] EWCA Crim 1721.

evidence that an earlier decision led to the imprisonment of an accused person owing to a misapplication of the law.[98] Sometimes, instances where judges might, strictly speaking, be said to be overstepping the mark are 'calmly "swallowed"' not simply because there can be a reaction to the initiative only after it has been taken, but, more importantly, because by the time that the opportunity for reaction arises, the success or correctness of the initiative has become obvious.[99]

Hart's second explanation was to re-emerge in due course as part of Joseph Raz's argument that the normal, though not the only, way to justify political authority is to show that a citizen is better able to comply with reasons applying to him when he accepts the authority's directives as binding instead of trying to work out those reasons for himself and follow them directly.[100] The normal justification of authority, in other words, involves the assumption that the authoritative body will be in a better position than the citizen to track the demands of reason. The likelihood that we will make this assumption depends on our assessment of the authoritative body as an authority. Just as the normal reason for accepting advice is that it is probably sound advice, the normal reason for accepting an authority as legitimate authority is that we trust it: 'trust in an authority is trust that the authority is likely to discharge its duties properly'.[101] Our trust in the authority of courts, according to Hart, explains why a supreme court might alter its own practice on precedent-following and meet with little objection; for if it is generally accepted that the court takes its duties seriously, the prevalent assumption will be that it would never take such an action without good reason. The 'very surprising piece of judicial law-making', as Hart puts it, is usually accepted because of 'the prestige gathered by courts from their unquestionably rule-governed operations over the vast, central areas of the law'.[102] The fact that courts are generally guided by rules explains why they are not completely guided by rules: within a particular jurisdiction, courts may accrue something akin to credit for their longstanding conformity with standards of correct judicial decision, so that the occasional act of extreme boldness, such as the Practice Statement, acquires

---

[98] *R v. Taylor* [1950] 2 KB 368, 371, *per* Lord Goddard, C. J.   [99] *CL*, 153–4.
[100] See Joseph Raz, *The Morality of Freedom* (Oxford: Clarendon Press, 1986), 53; *Ethics in the Public Domain: Essays in the Morality of Law and Politics* (Oxford: Clarendon Press, 1994), 212–15.
[101] Joseph Raz, 'Authority and Justification' (1985), in *Authority*, ed. J. Raz (Oxford: Blackwell, 1990), 115–41 at 131.
[102] *CL*, 154.

authority not simply because it is successful but also because the track record of a particular court suggests that such action would never be undertaken lightly. Legitimate authority does not have to be constitutionally supported.

The point of presenting these various jurisprudential perspectives is not to claim that they somehow justify the House of Lords' decision to issue the Practice Statement, but to show how they might help us to understand why the Statement was accepted despite its apparent constitutional impropriety. Jurisprudence, in this context, can be seen to have a constructive explanatory function. Recall, however, that academic criticism of the Practice Statement has tended to run along two lines. Some jurisprudential perspectives do indeed assist those who want to make light of the claim that the Practice Statement cannot be justified constitutionally. But there is one perspective which has it that the Statement cannot be justified at all. Having seen how jurisprudence might be enlisted to the role of saviour by those who wish to defend the Practice Statement, let us conclude this chapter by considering the peculiar way in which it became the aggressor.

b. 'Believe me, I always lie'

Precedent in the House of Lords is a subject which ought to appeal to anyone who likes to tie things up in knots. After all, consider what we have discovered so far. In 1898, the House of Lords undertook an act almost tantamount to self-enslavement, declaring itself normally bound by its own precedents. The binding force of this declaration seemed questionable because it appeared to be the source of its own authority. In 1966, the House purported to loosen the chains by stating that it could now overrule its precedents whenever it seemed right to do so. This, again, seemed like an exercise in boot-strapping. If the declaration of 1898 was truly self-binding, should it not have been irrevocable apart from by legislative intervention? If it was not truly self-binding, must the same not be said about the Practice Statement? And if neither was binding, does it really matter what the House of Lords has said about precedent-following?

Presenting the actions of the House of Lords in this way probably strikes many common lawyers as a flight from common sense. The status of these declarations hardly matters, they will say: even before 1966, the House of Lords employed a variety of techniques for eluding those of its precedents that it disliked, and so the Practice Statement might be said simply to have articulated what the House was doing anyway.[103] Why obsess over what the House of Lords says about its own precedents when all that really matters is how it treats its own precedents? This is a fair question. But the fact is that some jurists did rather obsess over what the House of Lords had said.

Many an incongruous article has been published in the United States law school reviews, but few can be more incongruous than one entitled 'The Compleat Wrangler', which appeared in the 1966 volume of the *Minnesota Law Review*.[104] The article, sitting alongside more predictable fare on topics such as Minnesota antitrust law and the Uniform Commercial Code, offers a logical analysis of the doctrine of precedent, and particularly the doctrine as it then operated in the House of Lords. Its author, one Roy L. Stone-de Montpensier, is identified in the opening note of the article as 'Barrister-at-Law, Lincoln's Inn, Cambridge, England'. The geography might leave something to be desired, but the identity is not entirely inapt. Owing to blindness caused by diabetes, Stone was forced to abandon a career as a Chancery barrister and spend the last thirteen or so years of his life as a freelance supervisor at Cambridge. Apparently he delivered lectures from time to time in the Moral Sciences and Law Faculties and had ambitions to become a full-time academic, but he was never appointed to a university lectureship or a college fellowship. He was, indeed, a barrister who ended up in Cambridge.[105] Yet, despite being on the margins of academia, he was,

---

[103] This appears to be how most Law Lords regarded the Practice Statement in 1966: see Paterson, *The Law Lords*, 143–6; also Gerald Dworkin, '*Stare Decisis* in the House of Lords' (1962) 25 *MLR* 163–78 at 174–5.

[104] Roy L. Stone-de Montpensier, 'The Compleat Wrangler' (1966) 50 *Minnesota L. Rev.* 1001–25. Hereafter 'Wrangler'. The article appeared in the *Minnesota Law Review* at the behest of George Christie, who served on the law faculty at Minnesota from 1962 to 1966. Christie was a Fulbright Scholar at Cambridge (1961–2); he and Stone attended weekly meetings with the philosopher, John Wisdom (whose work is a clear influence on Stone), and the two men became close friends. The first edition of Christie's *Jurisprudence: Text and Readings on the Philosophy of Law* is dedicated to the memory of Stone. Christie reports that Stone added 'de Montpensier' to his name partly to foster an air of mystery about himself – Stone apparently also liked to tell people that he had been at Eton (he in fact received his secondary education in his home town of Cardiff) – but also to distinguish himself from Julius Stone, of whose work he had a decidedly low opinion. George C. Christie, email to author, 31 August 2005. Roy Stone's low estimation of Julius Stone is evident from the former's review of the latter's *Legal System and Lawyers' Reasonings* (1968) 78 *Ethics* 322–3 in which Roy criticises Julius for not sharing his conception of precedent, and for 'that maddening habit of adding one noun to another, as in "fact-value complex" and "result orientation"' (*ibid.*, at 322).

[105] For brief biographies of Stone, see Anon. [C. G. Hall], 'Roy Leon Stone de Montpensier' (1971) 2 *Cambrian L. Rev.* 11–12; and George Christie's 'Biographical and Introductory

unlike nearly all law teachers of his type, intellectually engaged and very prolific – more of a jurist than were most of his juristic contemporaries. During the 1960s, he published in a diverse range of journals, mainly on matters of law and logic,[106] and one can only wonder how he might have developed intellectually had he lived beyond the age of forty-seven.[107]

What is obvious from those papers that he did publish is that, like many jurists of his era, he was a jurisprudential grumbler – the 'compleat wrangler' indeed. Stone never seemed more comfortable than when professing bewilderment at the shortcomings – which, for him, usually meant the illogicality – of the initiatives undertaken by the not-so-peripheral. Wesley Newcomb Hohfeld got a B-minus or thereabouts.[108] Whatever Maitland's qualities as an historian, he was no philosopher (by which Stone invariably meant logician).[109] Dicey, Austin and Bentham propounded the same spurious doctrine of sovereignty as did Blackstone, who in turn misunderstood Coke.[110] English jurisprudence may have been undergoing a major

---

Note', in *Jurisprudence: Text and Readings on the Philosophy of Law*, ed. G. C. Christie (St. Paul, Minn.: West, 1973), 1024.

[106] See, e.g., Roy L. Stone, 'Logical Translations in the Law' (1965) 49 *Minnesota L. Rev.* 447–77; 'Metaphysics and Law' [1969] *Duke L.J.* 897–929; 'Philosophical Investigations and the Englishry of English Law: A Commentary on Cases, Calculi and Concepts' (1970) 1 *Cambrian L. Rev.* 45–56; 'The Logic of Ethical Statements' (1972) 32 *Philosophy & Phenomenological Research* 297–321. The last article appeared posthumously. Virtually all of Stone's published work appeared in the 1960s, the main exception being a defence of enlightened conservatism which he wrote in his mid-twenties: see Roy L. Stone, 'Conservatism To-day' (1948) 130 *National Review* 109–15.

[107] For a sympathetic assessment of Stone's jurisprudence, see T. B. Hadden, 'Law and Philosophy: The Contribution of Mr. Roy Stone' (1968) 26 *Cambridge L.J.* 131–40. In a telephone conversation (30 August 2005), Hadden recalled that he wrote the article partly in the hope that it would secure Stone a permanent post at Cambridge. Stone was still seeking such an appointment when he died in June 1970.

[108] Roy L. Stone, 'An Analysis of Hohfeld' (1963) 48 *Minnesota L. Rev.* 313–37.

[109] Roy Stone de Montpensier, 'Maitland and the Interpretation of History' (1966) 10 *American J. Legal History* 259–81. He was yet more dismissive of H.E. Bell's study of Maitland: see Roy Stone, Book Review (1965) 87 *Cambridge Rev.* 150–1 at 150 ('one wonders not that it was published but that it was written'). See also Stone's quibbling, co-authored review of John Kelly's magisterial book on Roman litigation ('The Oppressor's Wrong, the Proud Man's Contumely?' (1967) n.s. 17 *Classical Review* 83–6) and his logic-based critique of Gaius's account of *actiones in personam* ('Gaius noster and "Res nostra"' (1966) 83 *Zeitschrift der Savigny-Stiftung für Rechtsgeschichte. Romanistische Abteilung* 357–65). Perhaps not surprisingly, he tended to be far more positive about works by and concerning logicians: see, e.g., Roy Stone, 'Verbalism, Veracity and Validity' (1964) 85 *Cambridge Rev.* 443–9; Book Review (1966) 88 *Cambridge Rev.* 15–16; Book Review (1965) 82 *Cambridge Rev.* 318–21.

[110] Roy Stone de Montpensier, 'The British Doctrine of Parliamentary Sovereignty: A Critical Inquiry' (1966) 26 *Louisiana L. Rev.* 753–87.

revival in the 1960s, but it was largely a missed opportunity.[111] One legal matter seemed to make Stone despair more than all others – it was the matter which occupied him in 'The Compleat Wrangler', and to which he would return in later essays: the status of precedent in the House of Lords.

'The Compleat Wrangler' was published in May 1966 and it offers what Stone calls 'a new theory of law', the theory that 'the law is a calculus having a logic of its own'.[112] The logic of the law, according to Stone, is the logic of 'paraduction' or case-by-case procedure. In the previous year, in an essay in *Mind*, Stone explained that 'the judicial process ... contains well known and analysable functions such as *following* and *not following, applying, reconciling, distinguishing, overruling, doubting* and *criticising*'.[113] The technique of the lawyer is not identical to that of the mathematician, the logician or the scientist, for their logic is the logic of rationalization; 'legal decisions', by contrast, 'consist of non-necessary truths which are obtained by reflection: reflection upon the likenesses and dissimilarities of particular instances either actual or hypothetical'.[114] These reflections 'are unlike deductions because they are resolved not by those adamantine processes of logic or mathematics but by analogy, because the terms of the argument remain riddles'.[115] Law, in other words, invokes the logic of what Stone called ratiocination as opposed to rationalization.

In essence, Stone's argument appears to be that law is logical because it develops on a case-by-case basis, and because lawyers use their own peculiar logical methods – different from those of mathematicians and logicians, but logical nonetheless – when they compare and distinguish

---

[111] Roy Stone, 'Affinities and Antinomies in Jurisprudence' [1964] *Cambridge L.J.* 266–85; 'Is There an Empirical Approach to Jurisprudence?' (1965) 87 *Cambridge Rev.* 401–10, 447–53; 'Bacon as Lawyer and Jurist' (1968) 54 *Archiv für Rechts- und Sozialphilosophie* 449–83 at 466. For Hart's *The Concept of Law* he made something of an exception – see R. L. Stone, Book Review (1963) 6 *Northwest Rev.* 115–19 at 115 ('At last we have a book ... which jurisprudents, philosophers and lawyers should welcome ... [a] book ... marred only by its stylistic shortcomings').

[112] 'Wrangler', 1002.

[113] Roy Stone, 'Ratiocination not Rationalisation' (1965) 74 *Mind* 463–82 at 465. Hereafter 'Ratiocination'.

[114] 'Ratiocination', 481. The reasoning is remarkably similar to Wisdom's: see John Wisdom, *Philosophy and Psycho-analysis* (Oxford: Blackwell, 1953), 158; also Scott Brewer, 'Exemplary Reasoning: Semantics, Pragmatics, and the Rational Force of Legal Argument by Analogy' (1996) 109 *Harvard L. Rev.* 923–1028 at 952.

[115] 'Ratiocination', 482. In a similar vein, see Roy Stone de Montpensier, 'A Re-appraisal of Cicero's Jurisprudence' (1968) 54 *Archiv für Rechts- und Sozialphilosophie* 43–68 at 49.

cases. The fundamental problem with this argument is that it assumes rather than demonstrates that lawyers somehow act logically when they identify a likeness or a difference between case *A* and case *B*. There is no reason to think that common law cannot develop *illogically* on a case-by-case basis. The notion of treating like cases alike and different cases differently is, as has been extensively argued, incomplete or empty until supplemented by criteria of likeness or difference.[116] Where a precedent is being followed or distinguished it is not inconceivable, even though it is not often likely, that the choice of such criteria will defy logical explanation. Stone himself raised the possibility that rules of precedent-following might themselves be illogical. If self-referring laws are logically objectionable, for example, can we not readily find fault with the boot-strapping that had taken place in *London Tramways*?[117] Stone seems not to have liked the decision,[118] and he conceded that it might be an exercise in boot-strapping, but he did not consider it to be illogical.[119] The decision was logical, he argued, because it 'carries with it a principle of consistency . . . [T]he law is consistent and the law must be consistent, just as, and in the same way as, and for the same reason as mathematics and logic must be consistent . . . [T]he product of rational argument must always be consistent'.[120]

One of the principal reasons for the House of Lords' resolution to turn its back on *London Tramways* was that it recognized justice in inconsistency in those instances where an earlier House of Lords decision on identical facts can no longer be supported. Overrating consistency was not, however, the main difficulty with Stone's argument. The main difficulty with it was that, within two months of its having appeared in print, the House of Lords seemed to have made a mockery of it. There was Stone, defending *London Tramways* on the basis of consistency, and all of a sudden there was the House of Lords, ending the era of *London Tramways* and making a case for

---

[116] See, e.g., Hart, *CL*, 157–67; Winston, 'On Treating Like Cases Alike', *passim*; Peter Westen, 'The Empty Idea of Equality' (1982) 95 *Harvard L. Rev.* 537–96.

[117] For the argument that self-referring laws are objectionable on grounds of logic, see Alf Ross, 'On Self-reference and a Puzzle in Constitutional Law' (1969) 78 *Mind* 1–24. For the argument that they do not have to be, see H. L. A. Hart, *Essays in Jurisprudence and Philosophy* (Oxford: Clarendon Press, 1983), 170–8.

[118] See R. L. Stone, 'Symposium and Suit' (1962) 5 *Northwest Rev.* 10–24 at 14 (on English law and 'its too rigid adherence to precedence and precedents').

[119] 'Wrangler', 1014.   [120] 'Wrangler', 1015.

some degree of inconsistency. '[T]he Practice Statement', Stone wrote in 1967, 'has struck at the roots of the law, and its logic'.[121]

The illogicality of the Practice Statement can be demonstrated, he argued, by drawing an analogy to the Cretan Liar paradox.[122] 'All Cretans are Liars', said Epimenides, who was himself a Cretan, which means that his statement must have been false. 'Our decisions don't necessarily bind us', says the House of Lords, which is known to consider itself bound by its own decisions. But what does this mean? That the House of Lords is bound by its decision not to be bound by its own decisions? Stone did not see it that way. 'If the Practice Statement asserts that the precedents of the House of Lords are not binding on the House, and if the Practice Statement is itself a precedent of the House ... then the assertions in the Practice Statement are not binding ... Thus this announcement [i.e., the Practice Statement] is nugatory.'[123] If the Practice Statement is considered binding there is still illogicality because, so long as it is operative, there is at least one decision of the House of Lords which cannot be departed from – namely, the decision of the House, stipulated in the Practice Statement, that it will not be absolutely bound by its own decisions. 'The Statement seems to contain self-contradictions,' Stone concluded, 'and if not self-contradictions, then inconsistencies.'[124]

The comparison of the Practice Statement and the Cretan Liar is unsound. Recall the wording of the Practice Statement: '[t]heir Lordships ... propose ... to modify their present practice and, while treating former decisions of this House as normally binding, to depart from a previous decision when it appears right to do so'. The Cretan Liar makes a statement which admits of no exceptions, and Stone seems mistakenly to assume that any legal pronouncement, if it is to be binding, must have the same quality. He failed to appreciate that rules containing conditional clauses are still rules.[125] What especially exasperated Stone, indeed what distracted him, was the appearance of the word 'right' in the Practice Statement. In using this word, he asked, '[w]as the Lord Chancellor speaking English or law? ... No indication is given of the use and so of the meaning of the word'.[126] He seemed to be making a problem out of nothing. 'Right', in this context, simply means correct or

---

[121] Roy L. Stone-de Montpensier, 'Logic and Law: The Precedence of Precedents' (1967) 51 *Minnesota L. Rev.* 655–74 at 673. Hereafter 'Logic'.
[122] 'Logic', 661–2.
[123] Roy Stone, 'The Precedence of Precedents' (1968) 26 *Cambridge L.J.* 35–8 at 37.
[124] 'Logic', 674.
[125] See *CL*, 139 ('A rule that ends with the word "unless ..." is still a rule').
[126] 'Logic', 672–3.

appropriate in the eyes of the court. Writing around the same time as Stone, W. Barton Leach commended 'the simplicity and crispness' of the Practice Statement, the absence, as he put it, of 'a thirty page "speech" ... by the Lord Chancellor and then seriatim concurrences by each of the attending Law Lords'.[127] Stone seemed to be of the opinion that the Lord Chancellor should have delivered that speech. Quibbles about the word 'right' could not detract from the weakness of Stone's argument, a weakness which he at least implicitly conceded when he used the phrase '*if* the Practice Statement is itself a precedent of the House'. The Practice Statement was itself not a precedent, but a statement concerning how the House of Lords should act with regard to its precedents. Even if the Practice Statement were classified as a precedent, it would clearly be of a type qualitatively different from other precedents – a precedent about precedents – and so invoking the Cretan Liar paradox would still be a mistake. If the paradox were to apply to the Practice Statement, the House of Lords would have had to say nothing more than that it was establishing a binding precedent that its precedents do not bind.[128] But this is not what the House of Lords did.

The Cretan Liar, however, had caught the juristic imagination. In 1971, J.C. Hicks revived Stone's argument:

> [b]y their Practice Statement of 26 July 1966 the House of Lords announced their intention no longer to regard their own prior decisions as invariably binding. Is this announcement itself authoritative? If not, surely *London Street Tramways* v. *London County Council* is still good law, and the House of Lords is still bound by its own decisions. But if the Practice Statement is authoritative, then does it not contradict itself, in that there is one decision of the House (the Statement itself) which is ineluctably binding?[129]

The authority of the Practice Statement does not necessitate its being inescapably binding. The Statement is authoritative even though the change of practice that it sets out is itself capable of revision. Certainly,

---

[127] W. Barton Leach, 'Revisionism in the House of Lords: The Bastion of Rigid *Stare Decisis* Falls' (1967) 80 *Harvard L. Rev.* 797–803 at 798–9. He was not the only American lawyer who appreciated the brevity of the Practice Statement: see also Harold F. Birnbaum, '*Stare Decisis* vs. Judicial Activism: Nothing Succeeds Like Success' (1968) 54 *Am. Bar Assoc. Jnl* 482–8 at 486 ('[T]he Practice Statement is judicial activism at its clearest').

[128] See Cross, 'The House of Lords and the Rules of Precedent', 155. Cf. also J. C. Hicks, 'The Liar Paradox in Legal Reasoning' (1971) 29 *Cambridge L.J.* 275–91 at 288 where the argument is posed rhetorically.

[129] Hicks, 'Liar Paradox', 277.

revision is unlikely: further alteration to the House of Lords' approach to its own precedents would require that sufficiently strong reasons for the House discontinuing to abide by the Practice Statement present themselves. But it is not wholly inconceivable that such reasons could present themselves, and so the binding force of the Practice Statement cannot be accurately characterized as ineluctable. Whether, in fact, Hicks considered the Practice Statement to lack authority – and, if he did, why he considered it to lack authority – is not clear. If his thinking was that it could not be authoritative because it was the source of its own authority, then *London Tramways* – which, according to Hicks, was another exercise in boot-strapping[130] – would not be good law either, and so it would be wrong to conclude that the House of Lords is still bound by its own decisions. We would have to conclude instead that the doctrine of precedent in the House of Lords was still in its pre-1898 state of vagueness. What Hicks is sure of is that the Practice Statement was a judicial decision of the House of Lords. It has already been argued here that this is wrong. To find contradiction in the Practice Statement by summarizing it as 'the decision of the House of Lords not to be bound by its own decisions' is to fail to see that the words 'decision' and 'decisions' have different meanings here: 'decision' refers to the fact that the House of Lords decided that it would be free in some instances to overrule *rationes decidendi* which it has established in earlier cases. But the Practice Statement is not in itself the *ratio decidendi* of a case (though this is not to say that it could not be used as one).[131] Furthermore, it is worth reiterating that the House of Lords declared its intention to treat its former decisions as 'normally binding'; the Practice Statement does not amount to the claim that the House is never bound by its own decisions or any other Cretan-style declaration. Finally, it seems strange, to say the least, that Hicks should have placed no store in the fact that the House of Lords did consider the Practice Statement to be authoritative and did not take the view that *London Tramways* is still 'good law'. Like Stone, he appeared to assume that if one can demonstrate some illogicality in the Practice Statement – something that neither Hicks nor Stone succeed in doing – one has done enough to invalidate it, rather

---

[130] 'Liar Paradox', 284.
[131] Cf. Laurence Goldstein, 'Four Alleged Paradoxes in Legal Reasoning' (1979) 38 *Cambridge L.J.* 373–91 at 388–9, who regards this line of argument as an attempt to define *ratio decidendi* to suit the purposes of the claim. This is wrong. The Practice Statement, taken on its own, cannot be defined as a *ratio decidendi*.

as *Julius* Stone seemed to think that he had exposed the lack of authority behind the Practice Statement by pointing out that the Lord Chancellor did not act in his normal judicial capacity when he issued it. The retort of any judge or barrister would most likely be that down the path of either Stone only futility lies, for all that we need to know regarding the authority of the Practice Statement is that it is treated as authoritative.

For many academic commentators on the Practice Statement, however, this last assertion simply would not do. The problem still remains, Laurence Goldstein argued, of whence this authority derives.[132] Perhaps the simplest response to this problem is that the Practice Statement was treated as authoritative because not to treat it thus would maintain a *status quo* that nobody wanted: the persistence, that is, of a court of last resort which could not overrule itself and which either had to keep finding ingenious ways around some of its precedents or wait for Parliament to remedy its errors.[133] Jim Evans formulated a more sophisticated response: that the common law has always conceded to courts a freedom if not a duty to overrule their precedents and change their practices where reason or the common good requires this.[134] If this claim resolved the matter, it would be a mystery why the Practice Statement was ever necessary, for the House of Lords would always have been able to overrule its own precedents by pleading the requirements of reason. But in so far as Evans's claim met with objection it was not because he made the case for reason over precedents, but because he purported to have solved the Cretan Liar paradox. Evans argued that the Practice Statement applies, as indeed *London Tramways* applies, only to future cases, so that the problem of self-reference cannot arise.[135] Working from the premise that '[Roy] Stone's reasoning is sound',[136] Goldstein rejected Evans's argument:

> Let us imagine that, in 1986, the House of Lords decides that it wishes to revert to the old doctrine of binding itself rigidly to its previous decisions.

---

[132] Goldstein, 'Four Alleged Paradoxes', 389.
[133] See Lord Radcliffe, 'The Lawyer and His Times' (1967), in *Not In Feather Beds: Some Collected Papers* (London: Hamilton, 1968), 273 ('The House of Lords, as final court of appeal, has demonstratively cast aside the shackles that it probably need never have worn'). One of the reasons for allowing the House to cast aside these shackles is that it would be naïve to think that its errors will quickly, or indeed always, be remedied by Parliament: see *Davis* v. *Johnson* [1979] AC 264, 336, HL, *per* Viscount Dilhorne.
[134] P. J. Evans, 'The Status of Rules of Precedent' (1982) 41 *Cambridge L.J.* 162–79 at 175–9.
[135] *Ibid.*, 174.
[136] Laurence Goldstein, 'Some Problems about Precedent' (1984) 43 *Cambridge L.J.* 88–107 at 93.

It is a consequence of Evans's view that the pronouncement in which this declaration is made would not apply to itself; so what would apply to it is the rule laid down in 1966. Thus, contrary to intention, the 1986 decision would not be ineluctably binding.[137]

Evans himself refers to the relevant pronouncement applying *de futuro* (in the future). If he had stated instead that the relevant pronouncement should apply 'from now onwards', this would have reintroduced the issue of self-reference. The logical conundrum is obvious. But again, the conundrum is only troubling so long as one assumes – as Stone, Hicks, Goldstein and even Evans all assume – that when the House of Lords announces a change in its rules of precedent it is reaching a legal decision which is indistinguishable from the other legal decisions that it reaches, and therefore using rules of precedent to change the rules of precedent themselves. Not only is this assumption wrong, but it seems to have no purpose other than to stimulate debate about whether self-referential propositions can be grounded in logic. Francis Mann, we have seen, was concerned about the constitutionality of the Practice Statement; however, concerns about its illogicality cut no ice with him. Much of the academic commentary on the Statement, he asserted, is 'legalistic pedantry' which 'does not appear . . . to be of much practical value'.[138] He had a point. Roy Stone and those who followed in his footsteps were basically playing a game with the Practice Statement. Quite how this game was supposed to conclude nobody ever fully spelled out; the train of thought behind it seems to be that the Practice Statement is self-referential and therefore illogical and therefore invalid. But it is more or less beyond the realms of belief to imagine a barrister arguing, or a judge accepting, that the Practice Statement lacks authority because it suffers from illogicality. 'A professor of logic would find in even famous judgments some sad howlers', Lord Radcliffe once remarked, but it is unlikely that this would trouble many lawyers, most of whom 'more or less unconsciously accept that their formal process is not their real one'.[139] While the illogicality of a law might sometimes undercut its

---

[137] *Ibid.*, 95. Evans replied briefly to Goldstein – Jim Evans, 'The Status of Rules of Precedent: A Brief Reply' (1984) 43 *Cambridge L.J.* 108-10 – though the reply does not address the point dealt with here.
[138] Mann, 'Reflections on English Civil Justice and the Rule of Law', 331.
[139] Radcliffe, 'How a Lawyer Thinks', in *Not in Feather Beds*, 67–82 at 73–4. See also *Smith v. Harris* [1939] 3 All ER 960, 967, CA, *per* du Parcq L.J. ('The common law of this country has been built up, not by the writings of logicians or learned jurists, but by the summings-up of judges of experience to juries consisting of plain men, not usually

validity – because, for example, that law is impossible to follow (though even a law which is impossible to follow does not have to be invalid)[140] – it would be a mistake to think that a law cannot be valid because the reasons for its having been accepted cannot be explained logically: look for clear evidence of this fact, Frederick Pollock remarked, to the doctrine of mutual promises.[141] The logic-based assessments of the Practice Statement, whatever objectives might have been behind them, seemed to be of no help to anybody.

It would be a strange study of judicial precedent which was silent on the subjects of distinguishing and overruling. Addressing these topics, nevertheless, has required something of a detour, for the basic objective of most of this book so far has been to understand the phenomenon of precedent-following, whereas distinguishing and overruling are essentially methods by which we justify not following a precedent. It is important now that we return to our original course, and examine the reasons for following precedents. Some of these reasons have been considered in this book already; but the basic question of why we should ever want to follow precedents has not been addressed systematically, and considerable work still needs to be done in support of the contention, formulated at the outset of this study, that there is no single, overarching, satisfactory explanation of precedential authority.

---

students of logic, not accustomed to subtle reasoning, but endowed, so far as my experience goes, as a general rule, with great common sense, and if an argument has to be put in terms which only a school-man could understand, then I am always very doubtful whether it can possibly be expressing the common law').

[140] See Lon L. Fuller, *The Morality of Law*, rev. edn (New Haven: Yale University Press, 1969), 70–9; and cf. Matthew H. Kramer, *In Defense of Legal Positivism: Law without Trimmings* (Oxford: Oxford University Press, 1999), 46–8.

[141] 'Have you ever found any *logical* reason why mutual promises are sufficient consideration for one another (like the two lean horses of a Calcutta hack who can only just stand together)? I have not.' Frederick Pollock to O. W. Holmes, Jr., 16 October 1908, in *The Pollock-Holmes Letters: Correspondence of Sir Frederick Pollock and Mr Justice Holmes 1874–1932*, 2 vols., ed. M. DeWolfe Howe (Cambridge: Cambridge University Press, 1942), I, 146.

5

Why follow precedent?

There are many reasons for not following precedents. Unswerving adherence to precedents might be indicative of a judge's lack of courage, maturity, initiative, industry or sound judgment. 'The right course of decision is obvious to me', a judge will sometimes say, 'I need no case law to point me in the right direction'.[1] The primary objective of the court which produced the precedent was to decide a dispute, not issue an edict which later courts can readily identify and accept; and so, even when a precedent is followed, the judges who follow it know that they must do much of the working out of principle for themselves. In some areas of law, the implicit understanding might well be that decision-makers do not simply seek a precedent. This is classically understood to be the case in US constitutional law, where the Supreme Court takes a more relaxed approach to *stare decisis* than do American courts when dealing with most non-constitutional matters;[2] similarly, in US

---

[1] See, e.g., *Panama and South Pacific Telegraph Co.* v. *India Rubber, Gutta Percha & Telegraph Works Co.* (1875) LR 10 Ch. App. 515, 526–7 Div. Ct., *per* James L.J. ('If a man hired a *vetturino* to take him from one place to another, and found that the *vetturino*, after he had accepted the hiring, had conspired with his servant to rob him on the way, he would be entitled to get rid both of the *vetturino* and the servant. So, if a man sits down in a tavern or *osteria* to play at cards or dice with another man for a stake, and finds that his opponent has provided himself with cogged dice or marked cards, the man would be immediately entitled to leave the table, and would not be obliged to procure proper cards or honest dice. I am not aware, however, of any express decision on either of the cases I have suggested'). Sometimes, of course, a judge may be concerned that the case-law could point in the wrong direction: see, e.g., *Heap* v. *Ind Coope and Allsopp Ltd* [1940] 2 KB 476, 483 CA, *per* MacKinnon L. J. ('So far as I am concerned, I freely avow that, inasmuch as in common-sense and decency Mr. Heap ought to be able to recover against somebody, and in the circumstances of this case and having regard to the correspondence which has taken place in common-sense and decency he ought to recover against these defendants if the law allows it, my only concern is to see whether upon the cases the law does allow him so to recover').

[2] See John Paul Stevens, 'The Life Span of A Judge-Made Rule' (1983) 58 *New York Univ. L. Rev.* 1–21 at 3–4, though Stevens emphasizes that it would be wrong to think that *stare decisis* is of no consequence at all in US constitutional law.

administrative law it is broadly recognized that an administrative agency should be free to consider a problem in its fullness, as it were, without being constrained by its own or another agency's prior handling of the matter.[3] Sometimes it will be the case not only that precedents are not followed, but that there is no great expectation that they be followed.

But how are we to explain the many instances in which precedents are followed? The question permits of no single satisfactory answer. As one judge has observed, 'we do not have – and never can have – a comprehensive theory of precedent'.[4] The main objective of this chapter is to identify and analyze not the explanation, but the various explanations, for precedent-following. Some of these explanations have been considered in this book already. One argument, encountered early in this study, is that in certain contexts, such as the judicial context, precedent-following might be accepted by decision-makers and others as a common standard of correct adjudicative practice, deviation from which is likely to meet with criticism or censure. This argument is considerably more sophisticated and enlightening than anything advanced by classical legal positivists, who, instead of seeking to explain why judges follow precedents, were as much exasperated as bewildered by the fact that they do follow precedents, given that precedents are not handed down to later judges as coercive orders. In so far as decision-makers do internalize precedent-following as a norm, however, how are we to account for this fact? It was argued in chapter 2 that there is a stronger likelihood that decision-makers will follow precedents when the precedents themselves provide reasons for decisions on particular facts. When judges follow precedent, that is, they tend to do so on the basis of the reasons that were provided to justify the decision that was reached, and because of the applicability of those reasons to the facts of the case before them, rather than on the basis of any distinct legal proposition or rule that the precedent could be said to represent.[5]

To this last line of argument there attach at least three provisos. First, the authority of a precedent does not have to depend on the reasons (assuming there are reasons) supporting it. If you set a precedent banning dogs from your restaurant for the reason that it is unhygienic to allow dogs in an enclosed area where food is prepared and served,

---

[3] See Frederick Schauer, 'Precedent' (1987) 39 *Stanford L. Rev.* 571–605 at 604.
[4] Frank H. Easterbrook, 'Stability and Reliability in Judicial Decisions' (1988) 73 *Cornell L. Rev.* 422–33 at 423.
[5] See Stephen R. Perry, 'Judicial Obligation, Precedent and the Common Law' (1987) 7 *Oxf. Jnl Leg. Studs* 215–57 at 235–6.

I might rely on your precedent to ban cats from my restaurant, my reason being that cats are unhygienic, too. But you might have set a precedent that dogs are banned from your restaurant for the reason that you have a regular customer who is allergic to dog hair. I might still validly use your action as a precedent when I ban cats from my restaurant. But the force of the precedent lies not in the reason behind it – which, after all, specifically concerns dogs – but in the fact that it serves as an exemplary justification for the ruling that I want to make.[6] Secondly, it is possible that a judge could follow an earlier decision by approving its reasons but without accepting that it is a binding precedent. In *Osborn* v. *Bank of the United States*,[7] the Supreme Court determined that the state of Ohio had no right to tax the Bank of the United States. The tax, it was decided, was impermissible under the doctrine set out in *M'Culloch* v. *Maryland* determining the scope of congressional authority.[8] The Court in *Osborn* reviewed the reasoning in *M'Culloch* and reaffirmed it. But it reaffirmed on the basis that *M'Culloch* was soundly reasoned, not because there was a requirement of *stare decisis*. To treat *M'Culloch* as a binding precedent, Marshall C. J. contended, would be to make the mistake of treating it as law. 'Judicial power, as contradistinguished from the power of the laws, has no existence. Courts are the mere instruments of the law, and can will nothing'.[9] Finally, even if it is accepted that a precedent provides a reason for deciding a problem in a particular way, this does not mean that the reason must be considered conclusive or that the precedent must be followed. An appeal court might find the reasoning provided by a lower court persuasive, for example, but it will not be bound to follow the lower court's decision, and it might well depart from that decision if the lower court's reasoning is outweighed by other considerations.

None of these provisos should detract from the fact that precedents are vectors for reason, and are often followed because decision-makers believe that a problem can be satisfactorily resolved by reinvoking the reason for an earlier decision instead of working through the problem afresh. This idea of following a precedent to avoid reinventing the wheel is, we saw in chapter 3, a consequentialist explanation of precedential authority. By no means is it the only such explanation; in fact, most

---

[6] See Frederick Schauer, *Playing by the Rules: A Philosophical Examination of Rule-Based Decision-Making in Law and in Life* (Oxford: Clarendon Press, 1991), 25–6.
[7] *Osborn* v. *Bank of the United States*, 22 U.S. 738 (1824).
[8] *M'Culloch* v. *Maryland*, 17 U.S. (4 Wheat) 316 (1819).
[9] *Osborn* v. *Bank of the United States*, 22 U.S. 738, 866 (1824).

justifications of precedent-following are premised on the claim that the activity is a reliable means by which to achieve desired goals. These justifications require our attention – as, in due course, will two other arguments which are best described as deontological rather than consequentialist.

1. Consequentialist justifications

Consequentialist reasoning can never provide a complete justification of precedent-following. Such a justification would only be possible if one could weigh all the foreseeable consequences of making a decision by following precedent against all the foreseeable consequences of making the decision in any other possible way and then show that the decision by precedent is superior to any alternative approach to the problem. Even if we convince ourselves that by following a precedent we are likely to produce the best possible decision, this of course does not mean that others will be convinced. Whether others are convinced by our consequentialist justification for following a precedent will depend upon the value that they place on the end or ends that we have identified. If precedent-following is explained as a means to an end that is not highly valued, then the justification will seem weak. Consider, for example, the proposition that it makes sense to follow a precedent because departing from it can be costly. No doubt departures can be costly. '[J]udicial originality', one judge has recently observed, 'sometimes ... is actually disapproved on the grounds that it tends to destabilize law. Judges do not brag about the number of cases they have overruled'.[10] If a departure from precedent proves very unpopular, those judges to whom the initiative is attributed might be criticized, perhaps seriously, by lawyers, academics, journalists, politicians, interest groups, litigants and would-be litigants and even other judges. As was observed in the last chapter, furthermore, some public and private actors might act in ignorance of the new ruling or its implications, or might incur costs getting to grips with those implications, perhaps even litigating issues that would have been uncontroversial had the original precedent been left undisturbed. It is a rather weak argument, however, to say that decision-makers are justified in following precedents for the simple reason that departing from a precedent can prove troublesome. A decision-maker genuinely concerned with the costs of overruling may well think this way; but so too might the decision-maker who is essentially lazy, timid or unprincipled.

---

[10] Richard A. Posner, *The Little Book of Plagiarism* (New York: Pantheon, 2007), 22.

Favouring the path of least resistance is certainly a reason for following precedent, but it will very often be the wrong reason. It is on this instinct that the House of Lords eventually acted in 1966.

The fact that decision-makers tend to follow precedent with an eye to consequences suggests that precedent-following might be encouraged by ensuring consequences which decision-makers value. But it is often very difficult to ensure that following a precedent, just as it may be difficult to be sure that departing from a precedent, will have the consequences that decision-makers desire. Decision-makers may remain faithful to a precedent, for example, because they believe that the legal principle embodied in the precedent is a good one, and that following the precedent will therefore ensure that the best possible applicable principle is maintained. But following any precedent – even a precedent that has been generally welcomed – may generate sub-optimal law, for the specificity of the facts of the case may mean that the precedent is too narrowly conceived to do full justice to the principle at stake.[11] While the court which follows precedent in such an instance does not necessarily perpetuate bad law, it may fail to improve the law, or make less of an improvement than would have been made had it started with a clean slate; following the precedent might not ensure, just as departing from the precedent might not ensure, the application of the best possible principle.

Separate from the question of whether the consequence is guaranteed by the action is the question of whether the consequence is actually a good reason for the action. Some decision-makers might be less willing to depart from precedents, for example, if consistent precedent-following is more likely to lead to personal promotion. The difficulty with establishing this particular incentive in a judicial context is obvious: judges might compound error and injustice, following questionable precedents out of a concern for their careers. The argument is neither that judges do, nor that they should abide by *stare decisis* for this reason – one would generally expect their chances of promotion to be unaffected by their propensity to overrule.[12] The principal point, rather, is that the doctrine of precedent will be stronger or weaker within a judicial system depending upon what the consequences of not following precedent are. A lower court judge may feel bound to follow a higher court precedent because

---

[11] See Frederick Schauer, 'Do Cases Make Bad Law?' (2006) 73 *Univ. Chicago L. Rev.* 883–918.

[12] This is certainly the conclusion to be drawn from a study focusing mainly on the Eighth Circuit Court of Appeals in 1974: Richard S. Higgins and Paul H. Rubin, 'Judicial Discretion' (1980) 9 *Jnl Leg. Studs* 129–38.

he knows that any decision he might issue contradicting that precedent would be considered by later courts to lack authority, and by the litigants against whom he rules to be a firm ground for successful appeal.[13] He will also know that any such appeal will probably cost the litigants significantly, and that a refusal to follow the higher court precedent might lead others, including fellow judges, to question his responsibility. The judge who persistently refuses to follow earlier decisions will in all likelihood have a poor reputation, and for good reason. Not for nothing have many of the greatest common law judges been noticeably deferential towards precedent.[14] Such deference might suggest judicial weakness; but it will far more likely be indicative of humility in the face of earlier judicial labours, of a willingness to learn from the past and to treat other judges' achievements seriously. Precedent-following seems at least partly explicable by the fact that judges know their own culture and the requirements of the judicial process.

Such reasoning raises the question of whether precedent-following can be explained in terms of rational choice, as that term is commonly (narrowly) construed.[15] A judge might follow the precedents of other judges because doing so should increase the likelihood of these judges reciprocating when the opportunity arises, whereas overruling might

---

[13] See R. E. Megarry, 'Fair Wear and Tear and the Doctrine of Precedent' (1958) 74 *LQR* 33–8 at 37.

[14] See Richard A. Posner, *Overcoming Law* (Cambridge, Mass.: Harvard University Press, 1995), 142. Another version of the rational choice argument runs to the effect that judges, particularly fixed-term judges who periodically must seek reappointment to office, will sometimes follow precedent because they have an interest in responding to the wishes of groups outside the judiciary – voters, legislators, specific interest groups and the like – who believe that judicial discretion should be restrained and who may have a strong influence over whether particular judges are re-elected. See Caleb Nelson, '*Stare Decisis* and Demonstrably Erroneous Precedents' (2001) 87 *Virginia L. Rev.* 1–84 at 49.

[15] Rational choice construed as a technique, that is, for attaining and commensurating specific preferences and goals. The construal is narrow because it takes no account of the fact that rational human choice will sometimes be not a preference for a definite goal or goals but rather a commitment to an open-ended human good (the choice to marry would be an example) which resists proper explication in terms of cost-benefit analysis or any other such technique because it is only intelligibly valuable for its own sake. See John Finnis, 'Natural Law and Legal Reasoning', in *Natural Law and Legal Theory: Contemporary Essays*, ed. R. P. George (Oxford: Clarendon Press, 1992), 134–57 at 138–43. My objective in this chapter is not to offer an assessment of the different understandings of rational choice, but only to consider how the narrow, consequentialist conception of rational choice – what is commonly known as rational choice theory – might cast light on judicial precedent-following.

provoke retaliation when those judges, or their sympathizers, have a chance to evaluate his or her own precedents. The reason jurisdictions rarely create formal rules mandating *stare decisis*, according to this argument, is that rational self-interest tells judges that there is wisdom in respecting the precedents of their colleagues.[16] Cooperation over precedent results in some loss of judicial power, of course, because the cooperative judge will be constrained by decisions that a freer spirit would not follow; but this will probably be offset by the fact that the cooperative judge's own precedents will be more influential on successor courts than they would otherwise be.[17] The incentive to follow other judges' precedents can be expected to increase, furthermore, when interaction with those judges is regular and indefinite (i.e., the judges have life tenure), because a judge can use potential future benefits from cooperation over precedent – and the prospect of retaliation in the event of defection – to encourage cooperation in the present case.[18]

This consequentialist, rational-choice explanation models judicial activity, but it is not supposed to be a depiction of what real-life judges actually do. Even as a model it might, for at least two reasons, be considered objectionable. First of all, it might be argued that the model has limited explanatory power. A judge may adopt the precedent of another court

---

[16] Sometimes jurisdictions do create such rules – formal rules mandating precedent-following apply in many circumstances, for example, in the Michigan Court of Appeals – but such instances are rare. On Michigan, see Taylor Mattis, '*Stare Decisis* within Michigan's Court of Appeals: Precedential Effect of its Decisions on the Court Itself and on Michigan Trial Courts' (1991) 37 *Wayne L. Rev.* 265–311.

[17] See generally Lewis A. Kornhauser, 'Modeling Collegial Courts I: Path-Dependence' (1992) 12 *Int. Rev. L. & Econ.* 169–85; 'Modeling Collegial Courts II: Legal Doctrine' (1992) 8 *Jnl of Law, Econ. & Organization* 441–70; also William M. Landes and Richard A. Posner, 'Legal Precedent: A Theoretical and Empirical Analysis' (1976) 19 *Jnl of Law & Econ.* 249–307 at 273. Refusal to cooperate over precedent might make a judge more 'visible': a judge who declines to follow a precedent, and whose own decision in place of the precedent generates considerable litigation, will probably be cited frequently – see Posner, *Overcoming Law*, 113, n. 7 – though to be cited frequently is, obviously, not necessarily to be influential.

[18] See Erin O' Hara, 'Social Constraint or Implicit Collusion? Toward a Game Theoretic Analysis of *Stare Decisis*' (1993) 24 *Seton Hall L. Rev.* 736–78 at 751–3, 774–5; Eric Rasmusen, 'Judicial Legitimacy as a Repeated Game' (1994) 10 *Jnl of Law, Econ. & Organization* 63–83. Judges who refuse to follow precedents in retaliation against judges who did not follow theirs obviously are not reinforcing the norm of precedent-following, but they might justify their actions by claiming that the defector judges have provided them with a precedent for not following precedent, or by claiming that they are over-ruling in order to remedy the wrongs generated by the defectors' precedents: see Posner, *Overcoming Law*, 122.

whose members have little or no opportunity, incentive or inclination to repay the compliment; or he may follow a very old precedent, which could even have its origins in a different jurisdiction. In instances such as these, the rational choice perspective as outlined here does not explain why precedents are being followed. Secondly, the judge who plays tit-for-tat with precedent, rewarding cooperative colleagues by following their decisions and punishing defectors by ignoring or rejecting theirs, can be criticized for treating justice to litigants as a secondary consideration. Law is more than just precedent, we have seen, and when judges depart from precedent they tend to do so because they believe they are upholding rather than undermining the law. Judges who follow one another's precedents out of concern for their own standing and influence might be charged not only with vanity and insecurity but, more seriously, with losing sight of the bigger picture. Justice in decision-making tends to matter more to judges than mutual precedent-following, so the argument goes, and might do so even as a matter of self-interest, for judges who appear to place less value on justice than they do on cooperation over precedent are likely to be criticized and challenged by those who disapprove of such cooperation or consider it to have disadvantaged them or their clients.[19]

Though there is considerable force to both these objections, neither is completely convincing. First, there is no reason a judge should not do justice according to law while still following colleagues' precedents. The popular judicial principle that precedents should only be overruled if clearly wrong betrays a deeper truth: that judges generally expect precedents to be soundly reasoned, to be the products, as we have observed already, of hard-won judicial wisdom. Even if judges are unlikely to follow other judges' precedents simply because they hope this will lead other judges to follow their own, it is perfectly conceivable that judges might, having satisfied themselves that their colleagues' precedents are sound and will lead to a just outcome, resolve to follow those precedents in hope that their colleagues, exercising similar judiciousness, will reciprocate. Secondly, the argument that judges benefit by treating precedent-following as a cooperative strategy will seem more or less plausible depending upon the culture and the organization of the court system under consideration. Where a court is strongly collegial its judges will more likely be minded to respect the precedents established by their

---

[19] See Michael C. Dorf, 'Dicta and Article III' (1994) 142 *Univ. Pennsylvania L. Rev.* 1997–2069 at 2065–6.

colleagues, a point somewhat borne out by the fact that judges on such courts are sometimes reluctant to disturb particular precedents until their architects are no longer around.[20] Resistance to the idea that judges engage in mutual precedent-following is likely to be more prevalent where there is a greater expectation that judges will be lone rangers rather than collective decision-makers.[21] Evidence that rational choice theory offers a very limited explanation of precedent-following in particular judicial systems, however, does not sustain the conclusion that the theory must offer limited explanations in all judicial systems.

We saw in chapter 3 that the judge who follows a precedent not only decides efficiently, taking advantage of work done by predecessors, but will probably also be deciding strongly, because his judgment is congruous with the conclusions of other judges who have assessed the same problem, and so the judgment comes, as it were, with an implicit seal of approval. By following the precedent the judge shows himself to be a satisfied customer – perhaps *another* satisfied customer, if judges have relied on the precedent already – which means that the quality of the precedent is itself enhanced and that the judge who subsequently relies on it will be blessed with an even stronger seal of approval. Judges might therefore follow precedent in the knowledge this will most likely

---

[20] See, e.g., *Miliangos* v. *George Frank (Textiles) Ltd* [1976] AC 443, 460, HL, *per* Lord Wilberforce ('My Lords, even if I were inclined to question some of the arguments used in the speeches, I should find it inappropriate and unnecessary to say that, in the circumstances of the time and on the arguments and authorities presented, the decision was wrong or is open to distinction or explanation'); *Horton* v. *Sadler* [2006] UKHL 27 at [39], *per* Lord Hoffmann ('My Lords, it is with a reluctance verging on disbelief that one is driven to conclude that the deliberate opinions of Lord Wilberforce and Lord Diplock were quite wrong'); and cf. also *Gallie* v. *Lee* [1969] 2 Ch 17, 49, CA, *per* Salmon L. J. ('Surely today judicial comity would be amply satisfied if we were to adopt the same principle in relation to our decisions as the House of Lords has recently laid down for itself by a pronouncement of the whole House. It may be that one day we shall make a similar pronouncement. I can see no valid reasons why we should not do so and many why we should. But that day is not yet. It is, I think, only by a pronouncement of the whole court that we could effectively alter a practice which is so deeply rooted. In the meantime I find myself reluctantly obliged to accept the old authorities, however much I disagree with them'). William J. Brennan, one of his former law clerks recalls, was disinclined to overrule the opinions of colleagues who were still on the Supreme Court: see the comments of Robert O'Neil at www.law.virginia.edu/home2002/html/news/2006-spr/profs_clerks.htm (visited 3 July 2006).

[21] Perhaps we should not be surprised that rational choice conceptions of precedent-following are most frequently developed and sympathetically assessed by economists and lawyers in the United States, where collegiality has traditionally been a fundamental feature of the Supreme Court decision-making process.

contribute to the stability of the common law. Where problems have a tendency to recur, it makes sense to solve them by repeatedly using the same precedents, assuming the precedents are satisfactory and that the problems do not require significant reassessment in light of, say, changing social conditions. Judges who do this are not only relying on tested solutions and reinforcing common law doctrines but are also increasing the likelihood that litigants will regard certain issues as settled: precedent-following is a subtle method of signalling that an issue is *res judicata*. Of course, following precedents in order to generate doctrinal stability or legal closure will hardly be laudable where flexibility and openness are the qualities that serve litigants best. The point, however, is not that precedent-following is supportable because stability and closure are intrinsically good objectives, but that if judges consider these objectives desirable then precedent-following is one way by which they can pursue them.

It is tempting to merge the argument that precedent-following can be justified because it generates legal stability with another argument: that following precedent is likely to make the law more certain and predictable. Certainty and predictability are obviously distinguishable – even though a particular outcome may be more predictable than others it might still be far from certain[22] – though the arguments with which both concepts are commonly associated overlap considerably. It might be argued, first of all, that certainty and predictability combine as psychological desires: knowing when the news bulletins are broadcast on the radio each day, the times at which trains leave from Manchester to London and that teaching always starts in the final week of September gives me some sense of security in and control over my environment. To place a high psychological value on certainty and predictability is not, however, necessarily to place an overriding value on these ends. I do not know precisely how or when I will die, and I would prefer to keep it that way – knowing that I will die is certainty enough. Where precedent-following

[22] There is at least one other way in which the concepts might be distinguished for our purposes: it is conceivable that a court might be certain of the precedent to be applied in a particular case yet it might decline to follow the precedent because it confidently predicts that the precedent would be overruled on appeal. For evidence that lower courts, at least in the United States, sometimes do decide on the basis of prescience rather than precedent, see Evan H. Caminker, 'Precedent and Prediction: The Forward-Looking Aspects of Inferior Court Decisionmaking' (1994) 73 *Texas L. Rev.* 1–82. Certainty and predictability, furthermore, can be distinguished from stability: an unstable legal system might have many laws that are certain, and most legal outcomes in that system could be predictable.

is the norm we can, likewise, have too much certainty. Indeed, the claim that 'the most important reason for following precedent is that it gives us certainty in the law'[23] is rather too stark, for there would be no reason to rejoice over the fact that adherence to precedent has rendered the law certain if the law was certainly wrong and could only be put right by legislators – recognition of this fact was, again, one of the motivations behind the House of Lords' Practice Statement in 1966.[24] The notion that the doctrine of precedent yields certainty is in any event misleading because, as we have seen, the doctrine leaves judges with considerable room for manoeuvre; if it did not, then opportunities for the courts to develop common-law principles would be seriously limited. The fact that *stare decisis* is not absolute – that it gives us not certainty but only *some* certainty in the law – is its primary virtue.

To the extent that certainty is valued, furthermore, it is not so much an end as a step on the way towards an end facilitated by precedent-following. 'People want to know under what circumstances and how far they will run the risk of coming against what is so much stronger than themselves', Holmes famously observed, 'and hence it becomes a business to find out when this danger is to be feared'.[25] A court's commitment to precedent may provide us with a valuable degree of certainty: when acting and planning we want to be able to foresee the consequences of our actions, and so we may find it very useful to know that if problem X arises because of what we do then the court, given how it has consistently handled this problem in the past, will rule A. The certainty generated by the precedent is not itself the end, however, but that which is crucial to achieving an end: i.e., being in a position where

---

[23] A. L. Goodhart, 'Precedent in English and Continental Law' (1934) 50 *LQR* 40–65 at 58.

[24] In *Plessy* v. *Ferguson*, 163 U.S. 537 (1896), as is well known, the United States Supreme Court created a precedent to the effect that laws enabling the provision of 'separate but equal' public facilities, thus allowing racial segregation in the public sphere, were permissible under the equal protection clause of the Fourteenth Amendment of the US Constitution. As Hershovitz observes, '*Plessy* v. *Ferguson* allowed Southerners to plan their affairs in the certainty that the federal government would not interfere with state-created racial caste-systems. The value of the activities planned in reliance on *Plessy* was hardly sufficient to warrant continued adherence to the precedent ... [I]f one appeals to certainty to justify following precedents irrespective of merit, then one must be prepared to defend the value of the conduct planned in reliance on the rules entrenched.' Scott Hershovitz, 'Integrity and *Stare Decisis*', in *Exploring Law's Empire: The Jurisprudence of Ronald Dworkin*, ed. S. Hershovitz (Oxford: Oxford University Press, 2006), 103–18 at 111.

[25] Oliver Wendell Holmes, Jr., 'The Path of the Law' (1897) 10 *Harvard L. Rev.* 457–78 at 457.

we can confidently anticipate how courts will rule on matters important to us. The certainty generated by precedent, as has often been observed, enables citizens to obtain definite advice on how to order their affairs.[26]

The doctrine of precedent, precisely because of its capacity to generate a degree of legal certainty, is probably valued most in those areas of law where actors place a high premium on rules being consistent and predictable – contracts, for example, or indeed any field of law concerned primarily with regulating regular voluntary transactions between citizens.[27] Recognizing that precedent-following fosters legal certainty, Frederick Pollock argued, is the key to understanding the 'truly scientific character' of the common law: 'case-law has a scientific aim, namely, the prediction of events by means of past experience, and the possibility of such prediction rests, as in other sciences, on a fundamental assumption of uniformity'.[28] The fact that there is only a degree of uniformity, never absolute uniformity, between cases did not deter Pollock from pressing the point: 'our comparison is not the worse but the better for the confessedly approximate nature of legal predictions', because 'no general proposition of science is known to be more than approximately true, nor is any prediction known to be more than approximately accurate'.[29] There is a hint of desperation to Pollock's reasoning – the common law must be scientific because its courts, like scientists' experiments, produce the same outcomes, more or less, on the same facts – and

---

[26] See, e.g., James Ram, *The Science of Legal Judgment* (Philadephia: Littell, 1835; orig. English edn 1834), 66–70; *Davis* v. *Johnson* [1978] 2 WLR 182, 207, CA, *per* Goff L.J. ('[T]he necessity for preserving certainty in our law, which has great value in enabling persons to obtain definite advice on which they can order their affairs . . . '); Max Radin, 'Case Law and *Stare Decisis*: Concerning *Präjudizienrecht in Amerika*' (1933) 33 *Columbia L. Rev.* 199–212 at 199.

[27] See Perry, 'Judicial Obligation, Precedent and the Common Law', 249; *Blumenthal* [1983] 1 AC 854, 913, HL, *per* Lord Brandon ('[W]here, once such decision has been made, it must for the future be followed and acted upon without the risk of its later being held to have been wrong and departed from on that account. In this connection I would lay stress on what is generally accepted to be the special need for certainty, consistency and continuity in the field of commercial law'); *Practice Statement (Judicial Precedent)* [1966] 1 WLR 1234 (when considering whether to overrule one of its own precedents the House of Lords 'will bear in mind the danger of disturbing retrospectively the basis on which contracts, settlements of property and fiscal arrangements have been entered into and also the especial need for certainty as to the criminal law'); cf. also Raz, *AL*, 191; John Bell, 'Sources of Law', in *English Private Law*, 2 vols., ed. P. Birks (Oxford: Oxford University Press, 2000), I, 3–43 at 39, para. 1.91.

[28] Frederick Pollock, *Essays in Jurisprudence and Ethics* (London: Macmillan, 1882), 238, 246.

[29] *Ibid.*, 255.

it is difficult to imagine many contemporary legal thinkers being so much as interested in putting the common law on a par with the natural sciences, let alone constructing so shaky an argument to accomplish the objective.

About the connection between precedent and predictability, however, we ought not to be so dismissive. When courts decide consistently on the same facts they not only provide us with important information for the purposes of organizing our individual affairs but also make it more likely that citizens generally will negotiate the legal system with confidence: just as it is 'very much contrary to the public good' to have a body of common law 'so uncertain that no-one could ever know what the law was or where he stood',[30] consistency in decision-making to the degree that people can usually find out where they stand is a considerable public benefit. Furthermore such consistency, Cardozo observed, tends to complement legal stability. 'What has once been settled by a precedent will not be unsettled over night, for certainty and uniformity are gains not lightly to be sacrificed. Above all this is true when honest men have shaped their conduct upon the faith of the pronouncement'.[31] By following precedent, in other words, a court not only generates legal certainty and builds up citizens' trust, but also puts in their minds reasonable expectations as to how particular problems will be treated in the future; would-be litigants might sometimes justifiably rely on these expectations, and a court might feel uncomfortable about departing from a precedent if the consequence of doing so is that a party will suffer considerable reliance loss.[32] The predictability that comes from a court's consistently following a precedent, we might say, raises the possibility of a litigant arguing that the court ought to consider itself estopped from doing anything other than following that precedent in the case at hand.

---

[30] *Att. Gen. of St. Christopher, Nevis and Anguilla* v. *Reynolds* [1980] AC 63, 680, PC, *per* Lord Salmon.

[31] Benjamin N. Cardozo, *The Paradoxes of Legal Science* (New York: Columbia University Press, 1928), 29–30. See also *Quill Corp.* v. *North Dakota*, 504 U.S. 298, 317 (1992) (Stevens, J. [quoting *Runyon* v. *McCrary*, 427 U.S. 160, 190–1 (1976)]: 'The "interest in stability and orderly development of the law" ... counsels adherence to settled precedent').

[32] See Perry, 'Judicial Obligation, Precedent and the Common Law', 249; Søren J. Schønberg, *Legitimate Expectations in Administrative Law* (Oxford: Oxford University Press, 2000), 9–11. Schønberg notes that the issue might sometimes be framed in terms of frustrated expectations instead of detrimental reliance.

The main problem with justifying precedent-following on the grounds of certainty and predictability is that the activity does not guarantee either: *stare decisis*, as we know, allows judges considerable flexibility, and so would-be litigants and their lawyers cannot always be confident that a court will follow the precedent they want followed, or in the way that they want it followed. Precedential uncertainty is the mother of much litigation.[33] The order in which problems come before a court is normally a matter of chance, furthermore, and so even where precedent-following enables a considerable amount of planning on the part of citizens it might still be possible that the precedent would have yielded a different *ratio* and supported different reliance interests if the court had taken two or more cases in a different sequence.[34]

Particularly unconvincing, for at least two reasons, is the justification of precedent-following on the basis of estoppel. Even if a litigant has correctly understood the import of the precedent on which he has relied, first of all, courts are unlikely to resolve the question of whether the precedent should be followed purely by considering if the litigant would be harmed were the court not to follow it.[35] Judges will want to balance against the possibility of individual harm the possibility that following the precedent might not be in the broader public interest; in such instances, prospective overruling might be the wiser option.[36] Secondly, and more importantly, the argument assumes what needs to be proved: the litigant who claims to have suffered a detriment, having relied on a precedent which a court might reasonably be expected to have followed, supposes the

---

[33] While precedential certainty brings its own problems: rigid *stare decisis* would demand the repetition and toleration of some results which are either sub-optimal or even unequivocally unwelcome. See Schauer, 'Precedent', 597–8.

[34] For the argument that precedent-following leads to path-dependent decision-making (i.e., decisions the content of which is generated not only by the content of earlier decisions but also by the sequence in which the earlier decisions were rendered), see Maxwell L. Stearns, 'Standing Back from the Forest: Justiciability and Social Choice' (1995) 83 *California L. Rev.* 1309–1413; also Easterbrook, 'Stability and Reliability in Judicial Decisions', 425–6. More generally on the jurisprudential implications of path-dependence, see Mark J. Roe, 'Chaos and Evolution in Law and Economics' (1996) 109 *Harvard L. Rev.* 641–68.

[35] Of course, if the litigant's reliance on the precedent stems from a misunderstanding of it, the estoppel argument can have no bite whatsoever. See E. W. Thomas, *The Judicial Process: Realism, Pragmatism, Practical Reasoning and Principles* (Cambridge: Cambridge University Press, 2005), 149.

[36] See In re *Spectrum Plus Ltd* [2005] UKHL 41; Earl Maltz, 'The Nature of Precedent' (1988) 66 *N. Carolina L. Rev.* 367–93 at 368–9; and Richard H.S. Tur, 'Time and Law' (2002) 22 *Oxf. Jnl Leg. Studs* 463–88.

court to be already committed to the doctrine of precedent. Reliance does not justify precedent-following but rather emerges out of the fact that precedent-following is already the norm.[37] The argument from estoppel entails circularity.

Although the fact of reliance cannot explain the *initiation* of precedent-following, it may be cited as a good reason for *continuing* to follow a precedent that has already been followed. A prisoner, for example, might assume he will be eligible for home leave after serving a certain period of his sentence because prisoners with similar histories and sentences have been granted leave after that period; he might make plans on the basis of that expectation and his disappointment might be reasonable if the expectation is not legally satisfied.[38] But the prisoner, in making his case, is arguing not that the prison authority should commit itself to precedent-following but that the prison authority, given that it has already demonstrated this commitment in other instances, should honour it in his case also. This does not mean, of course, that every expectation deserves protection. An expectation could itself be unreasonable: the grandson in *Riggs* v. *Palmer*,[39] who murdered in anticipation of inheriting under his grandfather's will (something which the language of the relevant statute appeared to guarantee), no doubt suffered some frustration of expectation when he was denied the right to benefit by the New York Court of Appeals; but it would be implausible to characterize the denial of that right as unfair.[40] Still, where precedent-following is an established practice, there is some room for the argument from estoppel.

The argument also has limited explanatory force where a precedent takes the form of an unexplained exception in a context where precedent-following is already established. Courts will rarely provide this context – judges tend not to be in the business of creating exceptions without explaining them – but the abstract possibility of an unexplained exception generating an argument from estoppel deserves our attention if only because such an argument might occasionally supplant the more familiar argument that precedent-following is essentially about

---

[37] See Richard A. Wasserstrom, *The Judicial Decision: Toward a Theory of Legal Justification* (Stanford, Ca.: Stanford University Press, 1961), 68–9.
[38] See *R* v. *Home Secretary, ex p Hargreaves* [1997] 1 WLR 906, CA (Civ. Div.).
[39] *Riggs* v. *Palmer*, 115 NY 506; 22 N.E. 188 (1889).
[40] See David Lyons, 'Formal Justice and Judicial Precedent' (1985) 38 *Vanderbilt L. Rev.* 495–512 at 511; also 'Formal Justice, Moral Commitment, and Judicial Precedent' (1984) 81 *Jnl of Philosophy* 580–7 at 585.

consistency. Imagine that Janet has an evening out once every month and, on these occasions, pays Alex £20 to babysit. Recently, Alex attained good grades in his A-levels. When he next babysat for Janet, she gave him £25. Although the extra money was given to mark Alex's achievement, Janet never explained the bonus thus, and, when she thought about the matter afterwards, she realized she could not be sure that Alex would have inferred that the extra money was given as a way of congratulating his success. When Alex next babysat for Janet, she paid him £25. Having not articulated a reason for the increased amount on the previous occasion, she now thinks that Alex will have assumed she simply raised his rate of pay. The standard £20 babysitting service is now being treated as if it were no different from the exceptional instance – different cases are being treated alike – and Janet considers herself estopped from restoring the old rate of payment. It is not on grounds of consistency that she feels she should now pay £25 – she recognizes that to return to paying £20 would look inconsistent, but she does not think that by doing this she would *be* inconsistent. Rather, she believes that Alex has a reasonable expectation that £25 will be the standard rate of payment from now onwards, because she did not explain her first £25 payment to be exceptional. She unintentionally created a new precedent, which she now feels obliged to follow.

The argument from certainty is primarily a justification of precedent-following from the litigant's perspective. Judges will value precedent-following for its capacity to generate certainty, of course, but whereas the litigant, or his lawyer, is likely to exaggerate the importance of following a precedent – because following the precedent guarantees the desired outcome – the judge must constantly keep an eye, as Cardozo put it, on 'the equilibrium between precedent and justice'.[41] A stronger justification for precedent-following from a judicial perspective is that if judges were not expected to treat precedents as binding, the capacity of the common law to curb arbitrary judicial discretion would be significantly diminished. Precedent, particularly accumulated precedent, can place a significant justificatory burden on those minded to decide differently on the same facts. '[T]he precept that like decisions be given in like cases', Rawls elaborates:

> significantly limits the discretion of judges and others in authority. The precept forces them to justify the distinctions that they make between

---

[41] Cardozo, *The Paradoxes of Legal Science*, 30.

persons by reference to the relevant legal rules and principles ... [A]s the number of cases increases, plausible justifications for biased judgments become more difficult to construct.[42]

Precedent provides a default position, we might say, and decision-makers will sometimes be unwilling to abandon that position because they lack the justifications for doing so. The argument that precedent-following serves the end of judicial restraint was, we saw in the last chapter, set out memorably by Hamilton in *Federalist 78*.[43] That judges should agree to a system which restrains them thus is by no means irrational. Submitting to constraint by precedent will sometimes be a case of bolstering one's authority by limiting it, because citizens will more readily trust and accept the directives of a decision-maker who does not insist on exercising unfettered power.[44] When precedents do not constrain, moreover, one's own precedents do not constrain: all judges would be free to ignore the decisions of others, and so there would be no reason to expect any decision to have authority beyond the immediate case. Judges who submit to a system of precedent-following are more likely to be judges with power and influence – judges whose decisions will sometimes be treated as precedents to be followed.

It is not inconceivable that some judges adhering to this system will regard it essentially as a public relations exercise: seeing prudential value in appearing to decide in a constrained fashion, they might know how they want to decide a case and so find another judge's precedent to

---

[42] John Rawls, *A Theory of Justice* (Oxford: Oxford University Press, 1972), 237.

[43] Another version of this argument is that precedent-following 'tends to correct the biases that might otherwise lead judges to discount the likelihood or importance of reliance on prior decisions'. Emily Sherwin, 'A Defense of Analogical Reasoning in Law' (1999) 66 *Univ. Chicago L. Rev.* 1179–97 at 1186. The justification of precedent-following on grounds of bias correction is flawed. Where the judge who established the original precedent decided according to his or her own biases, judges who follow his or her precedent perpetuate the biases of the precedent-setting judge (even though, in doing so, they might not be deciding according to their own biases). To resort to the *status quo* is not necessarily to adopt a neutral position. See Cass R. Sunstein, *The Partial Constitution* (Cambridge, Mass.: Harvard University Press, 1993), 4–6; Wasserstrom, *The Judicial Decision*, 78–9.

[44] As Hamilton well recognized: see *Federalist 18, 28*, in Alexander Hamilton, James Madison and John Jay, *The Federalist* (New York: Barnes & Noble, 2006 [1787–88]), 93–5, 151–2. For a similar argument, based on the notion that relying on a precedent to declare a matter *res judicata* may enable the United States Supreme Court to stay its hand on constitutional issues which it does not yet feel ready to tackle afresh, see Henry Paul Monaghan, 'Stare Decisis and Constitutional Adjudication' (1988) 88 *Columbia L. Rev.* 723–73 at 750–1.

support their decision – confident that when their own precedents are followed by other judges, much the same trick is being played. The disingenuousness of this exercise does not alter the fact that a precedent is being followed. Nevertheless, the judge who follows the precedent in this instance is not actually constrained by it. The public relations conception of precedent, as we might term it, reveals that following a precedent and being constrained by a precedent are not necessarily the same things.

Hamilton, it will be recalled, emphasized that it is specifically arbitrary discretion that precedent-following curbs. The court that sets a precedent might be the highest court in the land, composed of the most eminent judges, and the court which is expected to follow the precedent may be unwilling to say it is doing anything other than just that. But precedents are decisions of first impression, and the later court, though an inferior court, could be in a better position to determine the legal principle at stake, and may see ways of improving upon what the precedent-setting court established. The later court might not want to make the improvements it identifies, particularly if it fears that its initiative might be interpreted as an effort to overrule the decision of a higher court. If it does try to improve upon what the precedent-setting court achieved, it will have to exercise its discretion, most likely by distinguishing the case at hand from the precedent. This will be discretion exercised not without constraint, however, but in light of what a prior decision, or a series of prior decisions, has established. A desirable end of precedent-following, we have observed, is that it creates some certainty, but not complete certainty, in judicial decision-making. The activity can be commended, likewise, because it eradicates only some judicial discretion; for were it to eradicate all judicial discretion, the doctrine of *stare decisis* would be inappropriate to the common law.

2. Deontological arguments

It may be possible to add to, and one could certainly formulate differently, the various consequentialist justifications for precedent-following set out in this book. The aim, however, has been not to produce a definitive list of consequentialist justifications, but to show that such justifications raise presumptions in favour of following precedents – presumptions which will be weaker or stronger depending on decision-makers' objectives. Composing a list of deontological justifications for precedent-following can only result, it might be thought, in a list of one:

a deontological argument supposes that precedent-following is inherently valuable rather than valuable because of the ends that it serves, and so there is really only one deontological justification requiring our attention – the claim that precedents ought to be followed because precedent-following is somehow intrinsically good.

But it is possible to formulate at least two distinct versions of the deontological justification for precedent-following. First, there is the argument 'that precedents ought to be followed simply because they are precedents'.[45] At first glance there seems to be no argument whatsoever here: the statement is about as vacuous as saying that cherries ought to be picked because they are cherries, or mountains climbed because they are mountains. Even if we interpret the argument charitably it seems simplistic, for we may recognize that the problem we are about to decide has already been adjudicated by somebody else – we may even approve of their prior adjudication – yet still be unwilling to treat their decision as having the status of a precedent which should be followed: an example of this would be the judge who is willing to treat a foreign court's decisions as informative and its reasoning as persuasive but who considers it a serious error to accord those decisions the status of binding precedents within his or her own jurisdiction.[46] For one jurist, nevertheless, this first deontological argument provides us with the only genuine explanation of why judicial precedents are followed:

> If a court follows a previous decision, because a revered master has uttered it, because it is the right decision, because it is logical, because it is just, because it accords with the weight of authority, because it has been generally accepted and acted on, because it secures a beneficial result to the community, that is not an application of *stare decisis*. To make the act such an application, the previous decision must be followed because it is a previous decision and for no other reason ...[47]

A defence of this argument is offered by Anthony Kronman. The argument, as he conceives it, is not deontological (a term which Kronman resists)[48] but traditionalist and existentialist. According to Kronman, 'the

---

[45] Dorf, 'Dicta and Article III', 2059 n. 227.
[46] See, e.g., Richard A. Posner, 'No Thanks, We Already Have Our Own Laws' [2004] *Legal Affairs* 40, at www.legalaffairs.org/issues/July-August2004/feature_posner_julaug04.msp (visited 10 July 2006); also Sir Matthew Hale, *The History of the Common Law of England*, ed. C. M. Gray (Chicago: University of Chicago Press, 1971 [1713]), 19–20.
[47] Radin, 'Case Law and *Stare Decisis*', 200.
[48] Anthony T. Kronman, 'Precedent and Tradition' (1990) 99 *Yale L.J.* 1029–68 at 1066.

past deserves to be respected merely because it is the past – not, of course, uncritically or unconditionally, but for its own sake nonetheless'.[49] This way of thinking – what Kronman terms 'traditionalism' – 'is today in disrepute'; yet 'for most of the time that human beings have lived together in organized communities, every aspect of their communal lives – social, religious, political, and economic as well as legal – has to a large degree been organized on the assumption that the past has an inherent authority of just this kind, a sanctity that obligates us to respect the patterns it prescribes'.[50] This duty to respect the past is attributable, Kronman believes, to our sense of cultural trusteeship:

> [t]he world of culture that we inherit from those who went before is a gift, the gift that makes us who we are, and we show thanks for this ... by taking up the work of conservation on which the existence of that world depends. In doing so we express our indebtedness to the past, and our conviction that we are bound, within limits, to respect it for its own sake, just as we are obligated to respect our parents for a reason that is anterior to all considerations of utility or rights.[51]

That we respect the past for its own sake is evident, Kronman continues, from the fact that we often continue the projects of our ancestors 'despite their inability to compel our collaboration'; and it is only because we recognize our own insistence on honouring the past that we 'have any grounds for believing that the future will honor what we do'.[52] Our valuing precedents purely because they are precedents is evident from '[t]he partnership among the generations'.[53]

There are two basic difficulties with Kronman's position. First, the partnership among the generations is by no means conclusive proof that we value the past for its own sake. If anything, it seems more likely that we will only persevere with those of our ancestors' projects which we expect will enable us to attain desired ends. Secondly, even if it is conceded that we do, in large measure, respect the past for its own sake, respecting the past has to be distinguished from following precedent. A predilection for respecting the past, wherever it exists, may well cause us to be mindful of precedents – to be willing to take account of them along with whatever else we find accumulated in the storehouse of human wisdom – but it does not compel us to follow them. We may respect and admire the accomplishments of our ancestors – indeed, to use Kronman's somewhat stronger image, we may feel obligated to

---

[49] Ibid., 1039. [50] Ibid., 1044. [51] Ibid., 1066. [52] Ibid., 1068. [53] Ibid.

respect our parents – without feeling any obligation to follow in their footsteps. The argument that we respect the past for its own sake cannot support the conclusion that precedents ought to be followed because they are precedents.

The second version of the deontological justification of precedent-following is somewhat more compelling and obvious. As a matter of equality or formal justice,[54] so this argument goes, essentially similar cases should be treated in the same way, just as essentially different cases should be treated differently.[55] 'Precedent means simply that like cases should be treated alike',[56] and there is inherent value in treating like cases thus 'because equal treatment of those similarly situated with respect to the issue before the court is a deep implicit expectation of the legal order'.[57] Note that the argument is not that there may be strong

---

[54] On equality as formal justice, see Aristotle, *Nicomachean Ethics*, 1131^a ('If . . . the unjust is unequal, the just is equal, as all men suppose it to be, even apart from argument').

[55] Although the focus here is on like cases and their like treatment, we should pause to consider the last part of this sentence, which is often assumed to be a logical correlate of the immediately preceding part: see, e.g., Neil MacCormick, 'Why Cases Have *Rationes* and What These Are', in *Precedent in Law*, ed. L. Goldstein (Oxford: Clarendon Press, 1987), 155–82 at 160 ('It is a matter of formal justice, in the sense in which it calls for like decisions in like cases – and unlike ones in unlike cases'). Often, we will indeed be faced with cases of a certain type which are different in enough relevant ways to require their being treated differently. But it is possible also:

(1) that two cases of a certain type, although different, are none the less alike in enough relevant ways to require their being treated similarly; and
(2) that two cases of a certain type, although different, are none the less alike in enough relevant ways to permit but not require their being treated similarly.

The idea that treating different cases differently is always a requirement stems from the confused belief that whenever discrimination is permissible it is mandatory. A rule stating that women are allowed to join a club implies that men are entitled to join it as of right. It does not follow that men must be treated differently from women and so not allowed to join. The club's rule may differentiate between men and women, but the club might still, for example, want to secure a good mixture of male and female members. Because of the rule, male applicants and female applicants to the club cannot demand to be treated as if they are alike. But the rule leaves it open to the club to treat them thus if it so wishes. See Tony Honoré, *Making Law Bind: Essays Legal and Philosophical* (Oxford: Clarendon Press, 1987), 201.

[56] Ruggero J. Aldisert, 'Precedent: What It Is and What It Isn't; When Do We Kiss It and When Do We Kill It?' (1990) 17 *Pepperdine L. Rev.* 605–36 at 608.

[57] Edmond N. Cahn, *The Sense of Injustice: An Anthropocentric View of Law* (New York: New York University Press, 1949), 14. Peters has suggested that Dworkin's notion of law as integrity provides a third deontological justification for precedent-following. See Christopher J. Peters, 'Foolish Consistency: On Equality, Integrity, and Justice in *Stare Decisis*' (1996) 105 *Yale L.J.* 2031–115 at 2038–9, 2073–7. Since around 1986, Peters

prudential reasons for following precedent, but that, absent circumstances which might permit carrying out an injustice, failure to follow precedent is positively wrong.[58]

Before considering this particular justification, it is worth very briefly reiterating an argument which was developed in chapter 2. The belief that treating like cases alike is a good in its own right does not necessitate the conclusion that *stare decisis* is likewise intrinsically good: a legal system, we have seen, does not have to be committed to a doctrine of precedent in order to respect the principle of formal justice. What is required now is an assessment of this principle independent of *stare decisis*.

The first and simplest question to ask about the principle of formal justice is whether we do in fact believe that like cases should always be treated alike. Even when we do believe as much, we do not necessarily think that one case should be treated as a precedent in a later case concerning materially identical facts. For one reason or another, a court may have reservations about simply following the earlier case. The case might have been decided a very long time ago, or in a different jurisdiction, and the court might conclude that although the case seems

---

claims, Dworkin has argued that 'following precedent ... ensures that government, through its courts, will "speak with one voice" in applying principles to its citizens – the essence of "integrity."' *Ibid.*, 2077, quoting Ronald Dworkin, *Law's Empire* (London: Fontana, 1986), 165. What is immediately notable about Peters' claim is that it is framed in consequentialist rather than deontological terms: precedent-following is a means of ensuring integrity. Peters proceeds to criticize the implications of Dworkin's argument as a deontological position. There is no need to take issue with those criticisms here. But it ought to be questioned whether Dworkin is indeed striving to create the distinctive deontological argument for precedent-following that Peters attributes to him. For Dworkin, integrity is not reducible to adjudicative consistency (see, e.g., *Law's Empire*, 165–6, 219–20), and so a judge who decides with integrity will not necessarily treat like cases alike. Integrity will on occasions be the reason for 'separating the fact of precedent from its previously announced theoretical basis' – an example of this would be where a court determines that the *ratio* yielded by an earlier decision is in fact different from the one it had previously been thought to yield – or even for departing from precedent, for 'large-scale changes when the declared theories of the past are themselves identified as mistakes, as in the case, for example, of the precedents of the *Lochner* era'. Ronald Dworkin, *Justice in Robes* (Cambridge, Mass.: Belknap Press, 2006), 70. The Dworkinian deontological justification of precedent-following seems to have been constructed (not by Dworkin) purely for the purpose of being critiqued.

[58] There are, of course, consequentialist arguments for treating like cases alike. Since decision-makers who do so are dispensing the same justice to everyone, for example, they help secure and maintain basic rule of law values such as consistency and impartiality in adjudication. The objective here, however, is to assess formal justice purely as a deontological justification for precedent-following.

soundly decided and on all fours with the case at hand it nevertheless belongs to a different legal culture and so ought to be treated only as reasoning in support of today's decision rather than as a precedent for it. Far more significantly, there are some strong reasons for thinking that we do not always believe that like cases should be treated alike. If I put a pound in the box of the charity collector I pass at the top of the high street I doubt I will donate anything to the person further down the street who is collecting for an equally deserving charity. Even if I were to put fifty pence in this second collector's box, I would still have failed to treat like cases alike. Does this mean my behaviour is morally wrong? If it is not, the explanation might be that I was under no obligation to either collector in the first place, whereas judges and other adjudicators are normally fulfilling a duty to assess the claims of others.[59] When I fulfil such a duty, however, I do not necessarily take the view that like cases ought to be treated alike, even if I judge them to be alike: consistency in judgment does not compel consistency in action.[60] Editors of academic journals make this distinction quite often, deciding to reject articles not on grounds of quality but because they have recently published material on the same topic, perhaps by the same author. Indeed, it is not uncommon for many categories of decision-maker to take the view that treating like cases alike may mean ignoring some broader picture. Strict equality of treatment is equality now and forever. Nobody could seriously expect such treatment; to do so would be to insist that eligibility criteria remain constant. The decision-procedures of some organizations – immigration authorities, for example – sometimes have built into them the explicit right not to have to treat materially identical cases in the same way, part of the reason for this being, one assumes, that yesterday's applicant, though materially identical to today's, belonged to a different world. Often, however, there is no need for such organizations to be explicit. We know that the world changes, and that this often justifies or even necessitates differential treatment.

It might be thought that the problem of incommensurability in decision-making provides a further reason to be wary of the principle of formal justice. Imagine that in case X a court had to choose between P^1 (protecting the environment) and P^2 (protecting particular economic rights), and that

---

[59] For another version of this argument, expressed in terms of the protection of rights (rather than the assessment of claims) by judges, see Norman C. Gillespie, 'On Treating Like Cases Differently' (1975) 25 *Philosophical Quarterly* 151–8 at 154.
[60] See *ibid.*, 157.

there exists no metric which makes it possible for the court to say that P^1 or P^2 is more valuable than the other, or even that they have the same value. In X, the court opted for P^2. A court now has to decide Y, and, owing to *stare decisis* and the fact that Y is similar to X in all relevant respects, might be expected to treat X as a binding precedent. But would the court in Y be justified in departing from precedent on the basis that X was not – because it could not be – supported by reasons demonstrating that the protection of P^2 is preferable to the protection of P^1? Marmor answers in the affirmative:

> [a]s long as the relevant judicial decisions are morally and otherwise within the bounds of permissibility ... , courts should be allowed, at least in certain cases, to reach different preferences amongst otherwise incommensurable values. The uniformity of decisions that is dictated by the principle of treating like cases alike seriously undermines the courts' ability to respond to the needs of diversity and pluralism.[61]

It seems, however, that if a court is 'to respond to the needs of diversity and pluralism' in the type of situation that Marmor envisages, all it can do is chop and change between the protection of incommensurable values. The court which decides Y might opt to protect P^1 instead of P^2, believing this choice to be 'justified by the need to cater to different populations with divergent needs and preferences'.[62] But then the court which decides materially similar case Z might consider P^2 to be the better option after all, and of course there might be further reversals when similar cases come before later courts. Incommensurability dictates that the decision of the court in Y can be shown to be neither better nor worse than the decision of the court in X, and so, because it cannot be said to be an improvement on X, later courts will probably feel unconstrained in returning to a preference for P^2. 'All this, I admit, is very inconclusive', Marmor concludes,[63] and, to be fair, his point is not that courts recognize incommensurable options and then swing between them, but that in instances when courts do recognize the incommensurability of options they ought not to be afraid of questioning if 'the value of predictability in judicial decisions ought to prevail'.[64] The problem, however, is that sacrificing predictability for the reasons he has in mind – because the options are incommensurable and because a

---

[61] Andrei Marmor, 'Should Like Cases be Treated Alike?' (2005) 11 *Legal Theory* 27–38 at 35.
[62] Ibid.   [63] Ibid., 38.   [64] Ibid., 35.

court which switches between them is being responsive to the needs of diversity and pluralism – means both that future courts have to choose between conflicting precedents and that individual decisions are vulnerable to appeal. Rather than veering back and forth between options, courts do better to make a choice and try to stick with it. The general judicial disinclination to overrule precedents, remarked upon in the last chapter, suggests that judges by and large think this way.

Defending the principle of formal justice against the arguments set out above requires more than a critique of the argument from incommensurability. What more might be said? Those who would defend the principle of formal justice might contend that those instances in which we seem disinclined to treat like cases alike are in fact instances where we consider the cases unalike. In the case of the second charity collector, the materially different fact was that I had made a donation to another collector; in the case of the article submission, the editor regards as a material difference the fact that the journal now contains material on this topic; an immigration department might refuse an applicant a visa the type of which he has been granted before because of heightened concerns about security. No two cases, as we know, will be identical, and so all can be distinguished at one level or another; if they could not, they would not be *different* cases. Since this is so, the crucial question for anyone defending the principle of formal justice is that of what it means to speak of *like* cases being treated alike.

The basic difficulty with the principle of formal justice, it is often argued, is that it lacks substance.[65] To assert that like cases should be treated alike and different cases differently is unhelpful unless the assertion is supplemented with criteria of likeness and difference.

> [A]ny set of human beings will resemble each other in some respects and differ from each other in others and, until it is established what resemblance and differences are relevant, 'Treat like cases alike' must remain an empty form. To fill it we must know when, for the purposes in hand, cases are to be regarded as alike and what differences are relevant. Without this further supplement we cannot proceed to criticize laws or other social arrangements as unjust. It is not unjust for the law when it forbids homicide to treat the red-haired murderers in the same way as others;

---

[65] See Isaiah Berlin, 'Equality', in his *Concepts and Categories: Philosophical Essays* (London: Pimlico, 1999), 81–102 at 82–3. Berlin's essay was originally published at (1955–6) 56 *Proc. Aristotelian Soc.* 301–26.

indeed it would be as unjust if it treated them differently, as it would be if it refused to treat differently the sane and the insane.[66]

Note that the principle of formal justice has to be supplemented not merely with criteria of likeness and difference, but with criteria of *relevant* likeness and difference. Treating cases as alike or different requires a reason or principle for the treatment; there is no substantive justice in determining, for example, that all white people should be treated alike because they are white.[67] Demonstrating the likeness of cases means settling on a principle to govern their treatment: for example, if we decide that anyone who satisfies a particular definition of poverty deserves special welfare entitlements, then A and B, claimants in different cases but both fitting the definition of poverty, should be entitled to the same treatment.

Applying the same principle to different people presupposes not only that those people are roughly equal according to the principle being applied but also that their other personal and circumstantial features are irrelevant to its application. Identifying like cases and ensuring their like treatment is, therefore, essentially an exercise in managing relevance. If the principle applied to a particular case describes it incompletely, there will be no guarantee that decision-makers 'will take account of all the features of the case relevant to determining the fairness of the application'.[68] This is perhaps not the most serious drawback to the exercise. 'Like cases' are those cases which we have decided, according to our definition, should be treated alike. 'To say that one person is morally or legally "like" another in respect to some treatment is to say that, despite the nearly infinite differences between them, the features they share are made relevant by the particular moral or legal rule at hand'.[69] The rule of relevance, besides being contingent and subject to change, is evidently tautological. 'To say that a rule should be applied "equally" or

---

[66] Hart, *CL*, 159–60. In the same vein, see D. N. MacCormick, 'Formal Justice and the Form of Legal Arguments' (1976) 6 *Études de logique juridique* 103–18 at 114–15; and, more generally, Amartya Sen, 'Equality of What?', in *The Tanner Lectures on Human Values: Volume 1*, ed. S. McMurrin (Salt Lake City: University of Utah Press, 1980), 197–220.

[67] See Bernard Williams, *In the Beginning Was the Deed: Realism and Moralism in Political Argument*, ed. G. Hawthorn (Princeton, NJ: Princeton University Press, 2005), 97–114.

[68] See Kenneth I. Winston, 'On Treating Like Cases Alike' (1974) 62 *California L. Rev.* 1–39 at 17.

[69] Peter Westen, 'The Empty Idea of Equality' (1982) 95 *Harvard L. Rev.* 537–96 at 583.

"consistently" or "uniformly" means simply that the rule should be applied to the cases to which it applies'.[70]

This last argument has met with various objections,[71] the principal of which is that it contradicts what we know about the concept of equality. The principle of formal justice often comes into play before standards of treatment have been settled: our sense, that is, that two or more persons do not differ in any relevant respect often precedes any consideration of what treatment they should receive.[72] When one person has already been accorded particular treatment, moreover, the principle of formal justice can be a *reason* for giving her peers the same treatment. Acting on this reason might even mean repeating a decision which should not have been reached in the first place.[73] If I provide one student with information about the content of a forthcoming exam I will probably feel compelled to provide the same information to the rest of the class. I may now regret providing any student with information about the exam – ideally, nobody should have received this benefit. But since that ideal has been frustrated, I am likely to reason that it is better that the benefit be extended to all of the class than that only one receives it.

Perhaps the most obvious difficulty with the principle of formal justice is not its emptiness but the fact that '[r]egarding the principle that like cases should be treated alike implies moral grounds for respecting

---

[70] Ibid., 551. Cf. Benjamin N. Cardozo, *The Nature of the Judicial Process* (New Haven: Yale University Press, 1921), 64 ('We see that to determine to be loyal to precedents and to the principles at the back of precedents does not carry us far upon the road. Principles are complex bundles. It is well enough to say that we shall be consistent, but consistent with what?').

[71] See, e.g., Erwin Chemerinsky, 'In Defense of Equality: A Reply to Professor Westen' (1983) 81 *Michigan L. Rev.* 575–99; Anthony D'Amato, 'Is Equality a Totally Empty Idea?' (1983) 81 *Michigan L. Rev.* 600–3; and cf. Peter Westen, 'The Meaning of Equality in Law, Science, Math, and Morals: A Reply' (1983) 81 *Michigan L. Rev.* 604–63; Christopher J. Peters, 'Equality Revisited' (1997) 110 *Harvard L. Rev.* 1210–64 at 1218–20; Kent Greenawalt, '"Prescriptive Equality": Two Steps Forward' (1997) 110 *Harvard L. Rev.* 1265–90.

[72] See Kent Greenawalt, 'How Empty is the Idea of Equality?' (1983) 83 *Columbia L. Rev.* 1167–85 at 1170–1.

[73] See Joseph Raz, 'Professor Dworkin's Theory of Rights' (1978) 26 *Political Studies* 123–37 at 135. More generally, on the capacity of a past decision which we consider incorrect to turn a present decision which would otherwise be incorrect into a correct one, see Larry Alexander, 'Constrained by Precedent' (1989) 63 *Southern California L. Rev.* 1–64 at 5–17.

flawed precedents'.[74] Lyons has argued that this need not be so, that we can alter our moral commitments without being inconsistent.

> That is because we are free to change our moral opinions honestly. The constraint of consistency does not mean that we are prohibited from modifying, qualifying, refining, or otherwise revising our moral judgments, including the standards we apply. We are free to reject judgments that we made in the past, if they can no longer be supported by standards we now accept; indeed, we are bound by the constraint of consistency to do so ... I cannot be convicted of inconsistency just because I change my understanding of some aspect of the observable world about me or its microstructure.[75]

Lyons' argument does not seem quite right. It will often be reasonable for us to revise our moral judgments; not to do so, indeed, may be unreasonable. That we are being reasonable, however, does not mean we are consistent. In the types of instance to which Lyons adverts, we are being inconsistent, but reasonably so.[76] Rather than strain to find consistency where it is absent, we do better to acknowledge that consistency can be overvalued. The most significant drawbacks to consistency have been considered already in this study. Determining relevant likenesses and dissimilarities between cases can be very difficult, because all cases are similar in some respects and differ in others.[77] The consistent decision-maker may be consistently following bad decisions: it is difficult to imagine that anybody who says that like cases should be treated alike is doing anything other than abbreviating their true sentiment – that like

---

[74] Lyons, 'Formal Justice and Judicial Precedent', 498. See also Peters, 'Foolish Consistency', 2111–12.

[75] Lyons, 'Formal Justice and Judicial Precedent', 508.

[76] Technically correct though it may be to say that we are inconsistent in such instances, it is less pejorative to say that cases are being treated differently rather than inconsistently. On the distinction between difference and inconsistency, see John E. Coons, 'Consistency' (1987) 75 *California L. Rev.* 59–113 at 66–72.

[77] See Theodore M. Benditt, 'The Rule of Precedent', in *Precedent in Law*, 89–106 at 89–90; Michael S. Moore, 'Precedent, Induction, and Ethical Generalization', *ibid.*, 183–216 at 186–7; Schauer, 'Precedent', 595–7; Maltz, 'The Nature of Precedent', 369–70; and, more generally, Amos Tversky, 'Features of Similarity' (1977) 84 *Psychological Rev.* 327–52. One might think the point to be so obvious as to be not worth making. Now and again legal philosophers do, however, skim over the difficulties: see, e.g., Raphael A. Akanmidu, 'The Morality of Precedent in Law' (2001) 14 *Ratio Juris* 244–51 at 249 ('Precedent, as it functions in law, provides a basis for reference to past decisions in law. This reference amounts to a search for what has been the case in the previous decision. This reference also makes for the search for objectivity. Objectivity, in this sense, represents an important platform for comparison of cases').

cases should be treated alike except where doing so repeats an injustice.[78] Absolute consistency in adjudication leaves no room for flexibility. The fact that discretion – 'that puzzling activity of decisionmakers who simultaneously are bound by a rule, yet free to exercise judgment'[79] – is not only tolerated but often clearly built into the rules which judges apply indicates that we expect and indeed value some inconsistency of treatment in the courtroom.[80] Decisions consistent with precedent may neglect the ways in which the world and our information about it have altered.[81] Indeed, the meaning of a precedent might itself alter over time: the life of *Brown* v. *Board of Education* in the United States – a controversial decision in 1954, but one which would better be described as iconic today – is an extreme example of how a precedent might now stand for something very different from what it stood for when it was decided.[82] The general difficulty – that finding a likeness between the precedent and the case in hand is to risk ignoring the danger of the shifting sand – is well remarked upon by Lord Radcliffe:

> A judge might commend himself to the most rigid principle of adherence to precedent, might close his day's work every evening in the conviction that he had said nothing and decided nothing that was not in accordance with what his predecessors had said or decided before him; yet, even so, their words, when he repeats them, mean something materially different in his mouth, just because twentieth-century man has not the power to speak with the tone or accent of the man of the seventeenth or the eighteenth or the nineteenth century. The context is different; the range of reference is different; and, whatever his intention, the hallowed words

---

[78] See Honoré, *Making Law Bind*, 200. [79] Coons, 'Consistency', 72.
[80] See *ibid.*, 97–8 ('Legislating for ... a multiplex moral environment may well induce the rulemaker to shelter in an ambiguity where diverse outcomes can be charged to the institutions that apply his commands. Rules allowing inconsistency of treatment can be instruments to such a purpose ... [I]n the area of race relations, a rulemaker may be equally content with either a world of pure racial neutrality or one of affirmative action. He can arm those who must apply the rule with what may seem to them instruments of moral contradiction').
[81] See Lewis A. Kornhauser, 'An Economic Perspective on *Stare Decisis*' (1989) 65 *Chicago-Kent L. Rev.* 63–92 at 68–73.
[82] *Brown* v. *Board of Education*, 347 U.S. 483 (1954). Even today, the meaning of the decision is highly contested: conservatives often see it as standing for colour-blindness, for example, whereas liberals tend to regard it as a rejection of racial inequality. On the capacity of precedents to mean something different today from what they meant yesterday, see Barbara Baum Levenbook, 'The Meaning of a Precedent' (2000) 6 *Legal Theory* 185–240 at 211; Schauer, 'Precedent', 574.

of authority themselves are a fresh coinage newly minted in his speech. In that limited sense time uses us all as the instrument of innovation.[83]

Finally as regards over-valuation of consistency, there is the relatively minor but by no means inconsequential matter of path-dependence. To say that two cases are materially alike but decided differently implies that at least one of them was decided wrongly. It does not actually imply that the second, rather than the first, must be wrong; however, the practice of precedent-following privileges the first decision.[84] Sequence does not in itself generate fairness. Imagine a very simple scenario, not involving precedent-following, whereby in X v. X a court decided that on the facts the defendant should be fined £100 while a few years later, in the case of Y v. Y, the same court decided that another defendant on materially identical facts should be fined £50. If the defendant in X v. X learns of the subsequent decision in Y v. Y he might complain that he would have received much better treatment were he the second rather than the first to the courthouse door. This does not necessarily mean that the second decision was the right decision. The court might take the view that the decision in X v. X was the fair one and that it is regrettable that it cannot now double the fine imposed on the defendant in Y v. Y. The defendant in X v. X might desire that, too; but it is far more likely that he would like to see his own fine halved rather than the other defendant's doubled. What he wants is not to see like cases treated alike because he values such treatment as a good in itself; rather, he wants to see like cases treated alike so that he gets as good a deal as someone else got – or, failing that, so that someone else gets the deal that he got. Selfishness or resentment may sometimes lie behind the desire for adjudicative consistency.[85]

It should be clear by now that the notion that there is intrinsic value in treating like cases alike is vulnerable to numerous objections. The last point to be made before concluding is that it is possible to over-emphasize these objections. Judges of course do supplement the principle of formal justice with their own understandings of likeness and difference.[86] And by virtue of the fact that there is a doctrine of precedent these

---

[83] Lord Radcliffe, 'The Lawyer and His Times' (1967), in his *Not in Feather Beds: Some Collected Papers* (London: Hamilton, 1968), 265–77 at 271.
[84] See Benditt, 'The Rule of Precedent', 90–1.   [85] See Coons, 'Consistency', 102, 105–6.
[86] It seems reasonable to speculate, furthermore, that the pull of adjudicative consistency will usually be stronger in an official context such as judicial decision-making as compared with instances in which discretion to determine the entitlements of others is exercised in a private capacity. See Gillespie, 'On Treating Like Cases Differently', 154–5; also Lionel Smith, 'The Rationality of Tradition' in *Properties of Law: Essays in*

understandings tend to become shared or common, or are improved upon, over time. Do not underestimate, Hume implored, that 'kind of capricious analogy' that characterizes 'many of the reasonings of lawyers'.[87] One precedent might be opposed by another precedent, and all precedents are at the mercy of judicial whim.[88] But when a precedent prevails, when it 'becomes a sufficient reason for a new decision',[89] it does so because it appeals to lawyers' imaginations.

> Sometimes the interests of society may require a rule of justice in a particular case; but may not determine any particular rule, among several, which are all equally beneficial. In that case, the slightest *analogies* are laid hold of, in order to prevent that indifference and ambiguity, which would be the source of perpetual dissension ... Many of the reasonings of lawyers are of this analogical nature, and depend on very slight connections of the imagination.[90]

The capacity of the legal imagination to discover 'slight' albeit sound analogies to past precedents in hard cases of the type that Hume envisages, Postema has remarked, 'resembles the capacity to formulate novel sentences which a community of speakers of the language can recognize as appropriate'.[91] Those operating according to a system of case law, like those who share a language, have the ability to discriminate between plausible and implausible assertions of analogy. Such conventionalism – we treat like cases alike and different cases differently because this simply is our practice or habit of mind – might seem a little too straightforward. There may be widespread disagreement among those involved in a particular practice – such as judicial decision-making – regarding whether certain analogies are plausible or implausible. We may all be in

---

Honour of Jim Harris, ed. T. Endicott, J. Getzler and E. Peel (Oxford: Oxford University Press, 2006), 297–313 at 303–4.

[87] David Hume, *Enquiries Concerning Human Understanding and Concerning the Principles of Morals*, ed. L. A. Selby-Bigge, 3rd edn, rev. P. H. Nidditch (Oxford: Clarendon Press, 1975 [1777]), 210.

[88] See *ibid.*, 308–9 ('If one pleader bring the case under any former law or precedent, by a refined analogy or comparison; the opposite pleader is not at a loss to find an opposite analogy or comparison: and the preference given by the judge is often founded more on taste and imagination than on any solid argument').

[89] *Ibid.*, 308.   [90] *Ibid.*, 195–6.

[91] Gerald J. Postema, 'Some Roots of Our Notion of Precedent', in *Precedent in Law*, 9–33 at 30. See also Steven J. Burton, *An Introduction to Law and Legal Reasoning* (Boston: Little, Brown & Co., 1985), 90–9, who develops a similar argument to the effect that lawyers will often be able to discern 'family-style relations among cases', even though they might not be able to demonstrate that those cases are alike on their facts.

this together, but we may differ quite radically in our understandings of what *this* is.[92] Much if not most of the time in the process of decision-making, none the less, judges do have similar instincts about and basically agree on what is and is not similar. Such consensus might not withstand close philosophical or even forensic scrutiny – it is often the lawyer's task to persuade a court that two sets of facts which look materially identical in fact are not – but it is sufficiently robust to facilitate the practice of judicial precedent-following in general.

Decision-makers invariably know that their determinations of similarity and difference have far-reaching consequences. *Stare decisis* will be less strict, and distinguishing more commonplace, when judges are disposed to assuming that more or less any difference between cases could be a significant difference, whereas we might expect more precedent-following when judges are in the habit of treating similar facts as essentially the same facts.[93] For those subject to the decisions, the consequences can be especially serious. Within the British university system, for example, different faculties have different examining and marking conventions. The convention within one law school might be that a student answers three examination components, each of which is marked out of 100, and receives an overall percentage grade. The exam regulations of this school might stipulate that an overall mark of, say, 57.9, or even 57.6, be rounded up to 58 per cent, while a mark of 58.3 be rounded down to the same. Anyone who is used to grading by a more finely calibrated system might consider this an instance of treating different cases alike, whereas those who would justify this system will argue that the differences are not sufficiently large to warrant making a distinction. However one sees the matter is beside the point. All that needs to be emphasized is that the determination of what constitutes a material difference has an impact on outcomes. Sometimes, decision-makers might recognize an essential difference between two cases yet believe that it is important in the interests of justice to treat them as if they were alike: a statute allowing government departments to withhold evidence the production of which would harm the public interest might not formally extend to particular groups, for instance, but a court might decide to treat an interest group like a government department and accord it the protection of the statute if it believes that failing to do so would be every bit as harmful as would denying statutory protection to a

---

[92] See Moore, 'Precedent, Induction, and Ethical Generalization', 200.
[93] See Schauer, 'Precedent', 596.

body formally entitled to it.[94] Common-law growth is often attributable to analogical argument – to courts determining 'that if a certain reason is good enough to justify one rule then it is equally good to justify another which similarly follows from it'.[95] The exercise is not always to be commended – one might have all sorts of motives for insisting that there are crucial similarities between what are in many ways different cases – but there is no doubt that lawyers and judges often undertake it.[96]

3. Conclusion

Precedents not only guide our efforts to deal with current problems, but also play a crucial role in enabling us to understand what sorts of problems we are confronting; not only do they steer us towards certain answers to the questions that we address, that is, but in addition they frequently help us to understand what the questions are. The capacity of previous decisions to guide and enlighten in the present instance cannot be fully explained by an overarching theory but has to be attributed to a variety of reasons. No case for precedent-following, consequentialist or deontological, is water-tight; there can be no all-encompassing explanation of why precedents have a hold on our attention. We know, nevertheless, that precedents very often do have a hold on our attention – that our awareness of a precedent can lead us, to some greater or lesser degree, to act differently than we otherwise would have done. We know also that weak fibres can intertwine to make strong ropes. Judicial precedents, taken alone, often look like rather fragile entities; taken together, however, they are one of the most compelling reasons for the authority of the common law.

It has been asked of late if the common law itself is really law.[97] During the course of this book it should have become clear why the question is at least understandable: if the common law is precedent, and if judges are not legally bound to follow precedents, how can the common law be law? But it should also have become clear that common law is more than just precedent, and that, in any case, to conclude that precedents are not laws if specific sanctions do not apply to judges in the event of their departure from them is to subscribe to a distorted legal

---

[94] See *D* v. *NSPCC* [1977] 1 All ER 589, HL.   [95] Raz, *AL*, 204.
[96] See generally Lloyd L. Weinreb, *Legal Reason: The Use of Analogy in Legal Argument* (Cambridge: Cambridge University Press, 2005).
[97] Frederick Schauer, 'Is the Common Law Law?' (1989) 77 *California L. Rev.* 455–71.

philosophy. The value of the doctrine of precedent rests not in its capacity to commit decision-makers to a course of action but in its capacity simultaneously to create constraint and allow a degree of discretion. A theory capable of demonstrating that judges can never justifiably refuse to follow precedent would support a doctrine of *stare decisis* ill-suited to the common law. For the common law requires not an unassailable but a strong rebuttable presumption that earlier decisions be followed. It requires that past events be respected as guides for present action, but not to the extent that judges must maintain outdated attitudes and a commitment to repeating their predecessors' mistakes.

INDEX

absolute discretion as basis for decisions 66
accessibility of precedents 5–7
age of precedent as measure of value 63–4
analogy
    basis for precedent, as 47–57
    reason by 2
Austin, John
    on judge-made law 18, 38–40
authority of precedent 24–5 *see also* binding aspect of precedent; *stare decisis* doctrine; value of precedents
    bases for 12–13, 15–16
    enactment force 60
    level of court, influence of 62
    limits to 16–17
    shown when not followed, as 111–13
    statutes, compared with 58–9
    weakening of, because of lack of full facts 3
availability heuristics, precedents as 94–9

Bentham, Jeremy
    on judge-made law 17, 43–4
bias correction as reason for following precedent 166
binding aspect of precedent 12–22, 23–4, 96, 99–108 *see also* authority of precedent
    historical development 17–18
    House of Lords' power to overrule *see under* House of Lords
    limits to 111
    London Tramways v *LCC* 125–6

Canada, Supreme Court of
    overruling of own precedents 124
cascading of precedents, negative effects of 98–9
case law
    distinguishing *see* distinguishing
    interpretation of, compared with statutes 59
    like treatment of *see* like cases, treatment of
    overruling *see* overruling
    unreported cases, use of 6
    whether Practice Statement restricted to future 147–8
certainty, precedents as source of 80, 159–63
certainty test for determining *stare decisis* (Goodhart) 91
classical positivism *see* positivist jurisprudence in relation to precedent
clean slate
    improvement of law compared to following precedent 154
    inefficiency compared to following precedent 97
coercive theory of law 14
commands, precedents as 45–7, 100–2
common law
    relation of precedent to 182–3
Compleat Wrangler, The (Stone-de Montpensier)
    binding force of Practice Statement, on 145

Concept of Law (Hart)
  constitutional basis of radical judicial action, on 136–9
  theory of precedent in 19–22
consensus in decision-making 179–81
consequentialist justifications for following precedent 97, 153–67
consistency 159–63
  need for 177–9
  R. Stone's 'new theory of law' as to 143–4
constraint, precedent as 4–5, 10, 59–62, 165–7
costs of overruling
  concern for, as reason for following precedent 153
creative aspect of precedent 10–12
Cretan Liar paradox in relation to Practice Statement 144–5
current decisions as basis for precedent 4
customary aspect of precedent 8–9

decision-making
  contribution of precedent according to availability heuristics approach 94–9
  economy of, enabling by precedent 97
  future as constraint on 4–5, 10
decisions
  absolute discretion as basis for 66
  House of Lords, discerning *ratio decidendi* in 70–2
  judicial restraint by precedent, and 165–7
  meaning of, as distinct from 'decision' in Practice Statement 146
  'piggybacking' 93–4
  rules as guide for 20
  status as precedents in USA 6
  value as precedents 95–6
  whether *ratio decidendi* necessary for 77–8
declaratory theory of law 39–45
deontological arguments
  following precedent, for 167–82
  treatment of like cases, for 170–82
dependence on precedent 31

dissenting opinions
  authority of 62
distinguishing 67–76, 113–15
  compared with overruling 27
  lower courts, by 167
doctrine of precedent, development of 31–57
  historical development
    eighteenth century 17–18, 35
    medieval period 32–3, 52
    nineteenth century 18, 37–48
    reasons for 35–57
    seventeenth century 34–5, 48–51
    Tudor period 25, 33–4, 52
  reasons for
    benefits of following precedent 35–7
    positivist jurisprudence, growth of 37–48
Dworkin, Ronald
  on precedential constraint 59–62, 170–1

economy of decision-making
  enabling by precedent 97
efficiency of decision-making
  clean slate versus following precedent for 97
  enabling by precedent 97–9
enactment force of precedents 60
equality within like cases 176
erroneous decisions 40–1, 61
  precedent as means of reducing 95–6
estoppel
  as justification for following precedent 163–5
exclusionary aspect of precedent 100–8
exclusionary reasons 105–6
exemplary aspect of precedent 7
experience as basis for precedent 2–3

factual basis of precedent 3–4
fairness
  in relation to justice 60–1
first-order reasons 105–6
following precedent, reasons for 150–3
  bias-correction 166
  consequentialist justifications 97, 153–67
  costs of overruling, concern for 153

following precedent (cont.)
  deontological explanations 167–82
  estoppel 163–5
  judges' motives *see under* judges
  traditionalism, according to 168–70
  value of precedent 157
formal justice *see* like cases, treatment of
formulary system 52
future as constraint on decision making 4–5, 10

Goodhart, Arthur
  certainty test for determining *ratio decidendi* 80
  reasoning as source of *ratio decidendi*, on 80–7
gravitational force of precedents 60–2

Hart, H.L.A. *The Concept of Law*
  constitutional basis of Practice Statement, and 136–9
  theory of precedent in 19–22
hierarchical system of appellate courts
  influence of level of court on authority of precedent 62
  influence on growth of *stare decisis* 56
  level of court influencing authority of precedent 62
Hobbes, Thomas, *Leviathan*
  theory of precedents as commands in 47–8, 100–2
House of Lords
  judgments, discerning *ratio decidendi* in 70–2
  London Tramways case, decision on binding precedent in 125–6
  overruling own precedents 27–8, 40–2, 58, 104, 122–8
    reasons 135–6
    usage and constraints 127–8
  Practice Statement *see* Practice Statement, House of Lords
  precedents in 103
hypothetical instances
  as basis for precedents 3

ignoring precedent 15–16 *see also* overruling
improvement of law
  clean slate compared to following precedent 154
inferior courts *see* lower courts
information management, importance of *ratio decidendi* for 90
internal point of view 20–2
inversion test for determining *ratio decidendi* 76–7

joint opinions 79
judges *see also* judiciary law
  comity as reason for following precedent 155–6, 157–8
  concern for justice as reason for overruling 157
  decision-making
    consensus in 179–81
    restraint by precedent on 165–7
  independent judgment by
    precedents as pre-empting 100–8
    scope for 27
  judiciary law *see* judiciary law
  legislative role *see* judiciary law
  motives for following precedent 29
    career and promotion prospects 154
    confidence in value of precedents 157
    reputation, concern for 154–5, 166–7
  regard for precedent 15–16, 24, 155
  seventeenth century 34
  when not following 111–13
reputation
  concern for, as reason for following precedent *see* motives for following precedent *above*
  contribution of precedents to 95
  measure of value of precedent, as 62
use of precedents as shortcuts 26–7, 92–9
use of social rules as guide for decisions 20
judicandum est legibus non exemplis 34

INDEX

Judicature Acts 1873–75
  influence on growth of
    stare decisis 56
judiciary law 38–40
  judges' decisions as basis for 22
  judges' scope for making 27–8
jurisprudence on precedent
  historical development 14–22
jurists
  role of 23
justice
  fairness, in relation to 60–1
  over precedent 157

Kelsen, Hans
  Pure Theory of Law 14
Kronman, Anthony
  traditionalist argument for
    following precedent 168–70

law making by judges *see* judiciary law
law reporting, development of 53–6
legal training
  importance of *ratio decidendi* for 90
like cases, treatment of 29, 60–1
  different cases as like, treating 170
  equality, interaction with 176
  incommensurability, problem of 172–4
  like cases alike, treating,
    deontological arguments for 170–82
  likeness and difference, criteria for 174–5
  material differences, importance of decisions on 181–2
  moral considerations 176–7
  reasons for not treating alike 171–2
  relevance as to 175–6
logic, basis of law in
  Roy Stone and 142–3
London Tramways v *LCC*
  House of Lords' decision on binding precedent in 125–6
lower courts
  distinguishing by 167
  precedent-following by 40–1
  overruling by 130–1

mistaken decisions *see* erroneous decisions
Montrose, J. L.
  notational system for identifying *ratio decidendi* 87–9
motives for following precedent
  see following precedent, reasons for

New Zealand Court of Appeal
  overruling of own precedents 124
notational system for identifying
  ratio decidendi (J. L. Montrose) 87–9

obiter dicta
  ratio decidendi, distinguished from 26, 67–73, 76–90
objections to following precedent 98–9
opinions
  joint 79
  relative importance within a decision 57
  single 62–3
overruling 27–9, 104–5
  anticipation of, as reason for not following precedent 159
  costs of, concern for 153
  distinguishing, compared with 27
  ignoring precedent 15–16
  justice, concern for, as reason for 157
  lower courts, by 130–1
  own precedents 122–8
    House of Lords, by *see under* House of Lords
    New Zealand Court of Appeal, by 124
    Supreme Court of Canada, by 124
  reason as basis for 147
  US Supreme Court, practice in 118

past actions as basis for precedent 9
past events as basis for precedent 1–2
'piggybacking' decisions 93–4
political decisions, effect on precedent of 12

positivist jurisprudence in relation to precedent 14–22
  declaratory theory of precedent 39–45
  historical development 37–48
  influence on judicial thinking 43–5
  precedents as commands 45–7
  reason as basis for precedent 47–57
post-verdict arguments 25, 52, 53, 56–7
Practice Statement, House of Lords 123, 126–49
  constitutional basis of 131–9
  Cretan Liar paradox, analogy with 144–5
  decision, as 146
  'decision' and 'decisions', difference in meaning between 146
  extent to which binding 139–49
  future cases, whether restricted to 147–8
  logical basis for validity 148–9
  logical consistency of 144–5
  ratio decidendi, as 146
  source of authority of 145–7
  whether a precedent 145
precedential constraint, Ronald Dworkin on 59–62
predictability
  precedent as source of 159–63
protected reasons 105–6
Pure Theory of Law (Kelsen) 14

Queen's Bench Division, overruling own precedents by 124–5

ratio decidendi 67–92
  as basis for precedents 25–6
  basis for *stare decisis* 91
  certainty test for determining 80
  decisions, necessity for 77–8
  definition 75–90
  House of Lords decisions, discerning in 70–2
  importance of earlier 91–2
  information management, importance for 90
  inversion test for determining 76–7
  joint opinions, and 79
  legal training, importance for 90
  multiple *rationes* 73–4
  necessity test for determining 77–8
  notational system for identifying 87–9
  obiter dicta, distinguished from 26, 67–73, 76–90
  point at which created 74–5
  Practice Statement as 146
  reasoning, distinguished from 67–8
  reasoning as source of 80–7
  reasons for determining 90–2
ratiocination
  distinguished from rationalisation 142
rational choice
  following precedent as 155–8
Raz, Joseph
  precedents as exclusionary reasons 102–8
reason as basis for precedents 47–57 *see also ratio decidendi*; reasons, precedents as
  by analogy 2
  'artificial' and natural reason distinguished 49–50
  by experience 2–3
  overruling on basis of reason 147
  precedents as reasons *see* reasons, precedents as
  relative importance of opinions within a decision 25–6, 57
reasoning
  measure of value of precedent, as 65–6
  non-unanimous 62
  ratio decidendi, distinguished from 67–8
  source of *ratio decidendi*, as 80–7
reasons *see also ratio decidendi*, shortcuts
  disregarding precedent, for 111–13
  exclusionary 99–108
  precedents as 57, 58–110
  protected (first-order) 105–6
  second-order exclusionary reasons 105–6
  use of earlier 93–9

reasons for following precedent *see*
　　following precedent, reasons for
relevant likeness and difference 175–6
reliance on following precedent 163–4
restraint, Ronald Dworkin on
　　precedent as 165–7
rules
　　formation of 23
　　as guide to judicial decisions 20
　　jurists' role in clarifying 23

second-order (exclusionary) reasons
　　105–6
self-overruling 122–8
shortcuts
　　use of precedents as 26–7, 92–9
single-opinion judgments as
　　precedents 62–3
social rules
　　as guide to judicial decisions 20
sources of law
　　effectiveness of precedents as 92–3
stability
　　contribution of precedents to
　　　　96, 158–9
stare decisis, doctrine of 12–13, 14–19,
　　27–8
　　appellate court system, development
　　　　of, influence on growth of 62
　　basis in *ratio decidendi* 91
　　erroneous decisions 40
　　historical development 34–5, 42
　　　　Judicature Acts, influence of 56
　　　　law reporting, influence of
　　　　　　development of 53–6
　　　　post-verdict arguments,
　　　　　　development of 25
statutes
　　authority of precedents compared
　　　　with 58–9
　　interpretation of case law compared
　　　　with 59

Stone, Julius
　　constitutional basis of Practice
　　　　Statement, on 131–2
Stone-de Montpensier, Roy L.
　　The Compleat Wrangler
　　　　binding force of Practice Statement,
　　　　　　on 145
surprise precedents 5–7

traditionalist argument for following
　　precedent (Kronman) 168–70

unanimity of decision as measure of
　　value 62
unexplained exceptions as precedents
　　164–5
unreported cases, use of 6
USA
　　decisions as precedents,
　　　　status of 6
　　overruling 118
　　prohibition on use of English
　　　　authorities 98

value of precedents 12, 95–6
　　age, based on 63–4
　　judges' reputation 62
　　legal reasoning, quality
　　　　of 65–6
　　reason for following, as 157
　　traditionalism argument, according
　　　　to 168–70
　　unanimous or majority
　　　　view 62
　　whether higher or lower
　　　　court 62

Wambaugh, Eugene
　　inversion test for determining *ratio
　　　　decidendi* 76–7
weakening of precedents
　　lack of full facts, because of 3